D0527245

The Day of the Hillsborough Disaster

A Narrative Account

The Day of the Hillsborough Disaster

A Narrative Account

compiled and edited by
Rogan Taylor, Andrew Ward and Tim Newburn

Joy,
With very best wishes,
Tim 26.4.95.

Liverpool University Press

First published 1995 by
LIVERPOOL UNIVERSITY PRESS
PO Box 147
Liverpool
L69 3BX

Copyright in this compilation © 1995 by
Rogan Taylor, Andrew Ward and Tim Newburn

Quotations from Lord Justice Taylor's interim report
on the Hillsborough Stadium Disaster are
Crown copyright © 1989

Quotations from Rob White's account of the disaster are
copyright © 1989 by Rob White

Attention is drawn to the rights of the copyright owners
as noted in the Authors' Acknowledgements in this book

All rights reserved. No part of this work may be reproduced,
stored in a retrieval system, or transmitted, in any form or
by any means, electronic, mechanical, photocopying,
recording, or otherwise without the prior written
permission of the publishers or the copyright holders
noted above.

British Library Cataloguing-in-Publication Data
A British Library CIP Record is available for this book
ISBN 0–85323–199–0

Set in Linotron 202 Meridien by
Wilmaset Limited, Birkenhead, Wirral

Printed and bound by
The Alden Press in the City of Oxford

In God's name, I pray that nobody shall ever have to describe a similar experience to this one again.

Rob White, *Hillsborough, 15th April, 1989: A Personal Account of the Tragedy*

To all who suffered,
especially those who continue to struggle
with the consequences of that dreadful day

CONTENTS

Authors' Acknowledgements

This book has its origins in research funded by the Joseph Rowntree Foundation and published as *Disaster and After*. A further small Rowntree grant enabled this project to begin and we are grateful to Janet Lewis of the Foundation for her support. We would also like to thank the staff at the Centre for Football Research at Leicester University, especially Ann Ketnor and Janet Tiernan who transcribed many of the interviews despite the emotional stress involved.

We have used considerable material from the Inquiry conducted by Lord Justice Taylor which is subject to Crown copyright. Crown copyright is reproduced with the permission of the Controller of HMSO. We are also most grateful to the *British Medical Journal* for permission to reproduce parts of an article by Dr Tom Heller, *Hillsborough Interlink* for permission to reproduce letters and interview material, and to *The Spectator* for permission to use extracts from an article by Steve Way. We have a special debt to Rob White for permission to use his account of the disaster, and to his family, his wife Linda and Dr Creer.

We could not (and would not) have attempted this project without the support of the Hillsborough Families' Group. We are deeply indebted to them, and their chairman, Trevor Hicks, for their initial support, and helpful advice during the final stages.

Finally, we would like to thank all those who contributed to this book. Inevitably, for many of them, it was an ordeal to recall in detail the unfolding of events at Hillsborough. It is difficult to describe adequately our sense of awe at their courage. We can only hope that we have done justice to their accounts.

Rogan Taylor, Liverpool
Andrew Ward, Oxford
Tim Newburn, London

January 1995

Introduction

What follows is an account of the whole day of the Hillsborough Disaster, on 15 April 1989. The disaster ultimately claimed 96 Liverpool fans as a result of crushing on the Leppings Lane terrace.

That day over 50,000 people attended Sheffield Wednesday's ground to watch the FA Cup semi-final between Liverpool and Nottingham Forest. They all have their own stories to tell, along with players, officials, relatives and many others who were drawn into the tragedy. We have tried to provide a range of accounts, a series of perspectives, occasionally punctuated by short passages from the Taylor Report or other written accounts, in the hope that a clearer picture of that terrible day will emerge.

Although our concern in this book is the day itself, we recognise that a comprehensive account of the Hillsborough Disaster requires discussion of a wider set of social and political issues. The disaster came at a time when football hooliganism was high on the political agenda and Liverpool people were still affected by the 1985 Heysel Disaster. On that May night, crowd disorders involving Liverpool fans led to 39 deaths at Heysel Stadium, Brussels, before the start of the Juventus–Liverpool European Cup Final. English clubs were later withdrawn from Europe, the Football Supporters' Association was formed, fanzines proliferated and administrators continued to search for remedies for hooliganism.

Violence was shifting from the grounds to the streets outside, but a proposal for a compulsory membership scheme for all football fans—unpopularly known as 'the ID card scheme'—gained pace after the 1988 European Championships in West Germany, when disorder amongst travelling English fans received widespread publicity. At the time of 'Hillsborough', the Football Spectators Act was poised to become law despite considerable opposition, and it would have come into force but for the Taylor Report. It was the latest Act of Parliament put forth by a Conservative government that was close to celebrating ten years in office. That government's aggressive policies against trade unionism included combatting the 1984–85 miners' dispute, the policing of which involved many of the South Yorkshire officers present at Hillsborough on 15 April 1989.

Football had experienced disasters before—Hillsborough itself had seen an incident on 4 February 1914, when a wall collapsed and 75 people were injured—and any wider analysis needs to consider three major tragedies: the 1946 Bolton Disaster, when 33 people died at an FA Cup match; the

1971 Ibrox Disaster, when 66 people died at the end of a Rangers–Celtic game; and the 1985 Bradford fire, when 55 people died at Valley Parade. But 'Hillsborough' should not be seen solely as part of a history of *football* disasters. In the late 1980s, an unprecedented series of disasters shocked the British public, including the Herald of Free Enterprise sinking near Zeebrugge (March 1987), the Hungerford massacre (August 1987), the Enniskillen bombing (November 1987); the King's Cross fire (November 1987), the Piper Alpha oil-rig explosion (July 1988), the Clapham rail crash (December 1988), the Lockerbie air crash (December 1988), the Kegworth air crash (January 1989), the Purley rail crash (March 1989) and the sinking of the Marchioness in the River Thames (August 1989).

Histories will undoubtedly view 'Hillsborough' as a significant watershed in football's history. The Taylor Report has redesigned the landscape of British football grounds and consequently, has changed the relationship between fans and their clubs. In the immediate aftermath of the disaster, when Liverpool FC players and staff coped with great dignity, the club itself underwent a transformation that is worthy of analysis. And there are many other facets to the larger story of 'Hillsborough': the tactics of certain sections of the media after the disaster, the consequences of post-traumatic stress, the response of the caring professions and emergency services, and so on. These are all important stories, but they are beyond the scope of *this* book, which is put forward as a permanent record of what really happened on 15 April 1989, the day of the Hillsborough Disaster.

Inevitably, there are passages in this book which are extremely distressing. Readers must be prepared for terse, uninhibited descriptions of death at close hand and of truly harrowing experiences suffered by those searching afterwards for loved ones. There will be many readers, not unlike ourselves, simply unable to comprehend or assimilate some of these events. Yet we owe it to those who were there to listen to, and *hear*, what they have to tell us.

Not even the accounts of survivors can, however, fully communicate what it was really like at the worst centres of the crush. We can try to imagine being trapped there and empathise with those who were but, unlike them, we cannot revisit the totality of their sensations: the relentlessly increasing pain, the helplessness, the sight, taste, touch, sound and, perhaps most of all, the hot *smell* of death that sunny afternoon.

But we believe the story should be told, indeed, *reclaimed* by those to whom it really belongs. Distortions, lies and legends abounded in the weeks following the tragedy and, even now, there are some who seek to re-write the disaster for their own personal, political or commercial ends. Those who suffered have a right to our best attempts to understand what took place and to use the strength of their accounts to help the healing process. As Rob White concluded, after writing his own account of the day: 'I do accept that only I will ever really know what happened to me, but by recording these details, and by talking about them, I shall gradually come to terms with them.'

Most of all, we hope that this book will make some contribution, however small, to that process.

On New Year's Day, 1989, Liverpool lost 3–1 to Manchester United at Old Trafford. Thereafter, for the next 103 days, Liverpool supporters were swept along with Aldridge, Barnes, Beardsley and company on a wave of success. Kenny Dalglish's team won 15 and drew two of the next 17 games with football close to perfection. They soared to the top of the League and reached the semi-final of the FA Cup. A second 'double' was in sight. And then, on 15 April, came Hillsborough.

Lord Justice Taylor, interim report, paragraph 21

On 20 March 1989, the Football Association (the FA) requested that their Cup semi-final between Liverpool and Nottingham Forest be held on 15 April at Hillsborough Football Stadium. The corresponding semi-final between the same two teams had been held there in April 1988. The arrangements had been successful in the view both of the police and of the host club. Sheffield Wednesday (the club) were therefore willing to accommodate the 1989 match. South Yorkshire Constabulary were prepared to police it but only if the ticketing arrangements were the same as those for 1988. Otherwise, the FA would have to look elsewhere. Those arrangements did not please Liverpool or its supporters either in 1988 or 1989. They thought the ticket allocation was unfair for reasons to be explained later. Reluctantly, however, the police requirement was accepted and the match was fixed for 15 April at Hillsborough.

Note: Lord Justice Taylor quotations in this book are taken from Home Office, *The Hillsborough Stadium Disaster, 15 April 1989: Inquiry by Rt Hon Lord Justice Taylor, interim report*, published by HMSO, August 1989. The interim report described the disaster, provided a brief summary of its causes and produced interim recommendations. The final report, Home Office, *The Hillsborough Stadium Disaster, 15 April 1989: Inquiry by Rt Hon Lord Justice Taylor, final report*, published by HMSO, January 1990, produced 76 final recommendations about crowd control and safety at sports events.

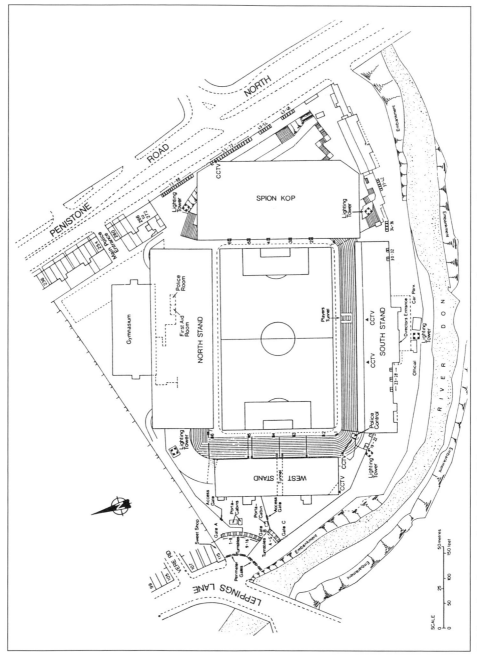

Sheffield Wednesday Football Club, Hillsborough Ground (Reproduced with permission. © Crown Copyright. All rights reserved)

THE DAY OF THE HILLSBOROUGH DISASTER

Ian Battey, charge nurse, Accident & Emergency, Northern General Hospital, Sheffield

I came into nursing in 1980 after being made redundant from the steel industry, where I worked as a computer operator for three years. I worked my way through my nurse training in a number of different staff-nurse posts, in surgery and medicine, before I decided to specialise in Accident & Emergency, which was something I had always wanted to do. The hands-on crisis management appealed to me. I was working in the A & E department at Northern General Hospital from the middle of 1984, as staff nurse and charge nurse, as I worked my way up through the hierarchical system within nursing. My wife is also a nurse, and at the time of Hillsborough our children were five and two. The 15th of April isn't a normal Saturday because it's my daughter Sarah's birthday. My daughter was five on that day, so she got me out of bed at about half-past five or quarter-to-six in the morning, to open her birthday presents. I distinctly remember her saying to me 'Do you have to go to work this afternoon, Dad?' because we were having a party. Even at five she knew what was going off and that I had to go to work, which wasn't a problem as far as she was concerned. So we had to open all the presents.

Woman Police Constable Jill Thomas, South Yorkshire Police

I'd got about 10 years' service in at the time. I'd only just returned from maternity leave after having my daughter. I'd been back at work a fortnight, since 1 April. A colleague of mine had put my name down to work the match while I was actually on maternity leave. I didn't know I was supposed to be going that day until about 10 days before. I remember getting up really early because my husband was going to look after our little baby all day. I got up about six-thirty. I remember getting up out of bed and wanting to do everything before I went to work. I'd actually given my daughter her breakfast, changed her, bathed her and put her back down to sleep before my colleague came to pick me up.

Detective Constable Dennis Cerrone, South Yorkshire Police

I'd been in the police force for 13 years at that point. I was actually in the CID but with this being a big match the manpower demands were such that they quite often had to draw on police from different departments who didn't normally work at football matches. Having said that, a lot of people who were in CID did work them regularly. I just worked semi-finals at that time—they were generally more interesting matches and I didn't like putting myself out for a normal everyday match. But I thought 'Well, I'll go down and watch that 'cause a semi-final's a bit more interesting, and Liverpool as well, you see some class players'.

From memory I think I reported at Woodseats Police Station around nine o'clock in the morning. Then I think we took a bus down to Hillsborough and got there about tennish. It was like a party really. It was a fine day and we were all like fans, all excited and bubbling over, because most of the people I work with are football fans. I wouldn't say it was a carnival atmosphere, but it was a happy atmosphere in some respects, an exciting atmosphere. You can feel the excitement, can't you, in a football ground when you walk in? It's there all the time, isn't it? I mean, you've got these professional problems which you might have to face up to, but it was really quite a good atmosphere and the police were glad to be there, particularly as most of them are football fans anyway and probably a lot of them would have worked it for nothing! There was none of that depressing 'We've gotta do this, we've gotta do that'. You can't see all the match and you can't take part in the match like you can if you're a fan, but you're there and you can watch it and a lot of them were pleased about that.

Lord Justice Taylor, interim report, paragraph 47

At the 1988 semi-final, policing had been under the control of Chief Superintendent Mole, then commander of F Division within whose area Hillsborough lies. He was still in post on 20 March 1989 when the FA broached the 1989 semi-final, but he was due to hand over command of F Division on 27 March to Superintendent Duckenfield on the latter's promotion to chief superintendent. Both were present at an initial meeting on 22 March, but on 27 March Mr Mole bowed out and Mr Duckenfield took over. Under him were sector commanders, all superintendents with much experience of policing football matches at Hillsborough and else-where. In particular, Superintendent Marshall was in charge of the area outside the Leppings Lane entrance and the approaches to it. Superintend-ent Greenwood was in command inside the ground, but this included the area between the turnstiles and the perimeter fence. They thereby swapped roles from the previous year. Under Mr Duckenfield's overall command were some 801 officers and men on duty at the ground plus traffic officers and others from D Division to deal with the influx of supporters into the city centre. In all, therefore, some 1,122 police were deployed for this match, amounting to about 38 per cent of the total South Yorkshire force. Included in the mounted section of 34 were officers from Liverpool and Nottingham to assist respectively in marshalling their home supporters. The total at the ground was divided into serials consisting usually of eight to ten constables plus a sergeant and an inspector. The serials were posted to duties at various stations in and around the ground in three phases: before, during and after the match. All of this was provided for in an Operational Order which followed closely the Order drawn up for the 1988 semi-final and took into account the force's 'Standing Instructions for the Policing of Football Grounds'. The Order described the duties of each serial at each phase. It was supplemented by oral briefings before and on the day of the match.

Dennis Cerrone

We were sat in the front of the stand for the briefing. I would think it was officers for the ground that were briefed there. There would be others on duty outside the ground. Most people had worked football matches, and had been at lots before, and you generally knew what was expected of you. One of the main things is to find out which serials, i.e. groups of police, you're on, and who your inspector is, and who you were working with and which part of the ground was going to be your responsibility. That was all clarified and sorted out. My duties were at the Leppings Lane end, in the turnstile area. There was an inspector in charge, and then there'd be a chief superintendent who had command of everything and various superintend-ents who had different responsibilities. I tell you what I do remember, which stuck in my mind for months after: the chap who gave the briefing, Chief Superintendent Duckenfield, said three or four times that the safety of the fans was paramount. It was ironic, that. He emphasised that the safety of the people in the ground was paramount. That briefing was about 10 or 11am, I can't remember exactly. Obviously there were no fans in the ground. We're there fairly early and you just wander round and familiarise yourself with where you're going to work.

Jill Thomas

The briefing was quite early, about 10 o'clock, and I think it was in the North Stand. I remember thinking 'We've got a lot of bobbies on duty today.' I remember the briefing quite clearly because there was a girl I knew from Barnsley and she sat behind me. Just as I sat down for the briefing I also saw my brother, who was a policeman, and I hadn't seen him for ages. I didn't really get a chance to speak to him then. I thought I would be able to see him after the match. I think it was Chief Superintendent Duckenfield doing the initial briefing. I can't remember any words that were spoken but I remember them saying that they hadn't received much intelligence [about travelling fans] from Liverpool. I thought about that afterwards.

Andy Williamson, assistant secretary of the Football League, Lytham St Anne's

I had received an invitation from the Football Association to attend either of the semi-finals. I chose to go to Hillsborough. I was accompanied by a pal of mine who, as it happens, is a Sheffield lad, a Sheffield Wednesday supporter for his sins, and we set off in good time to get to Hillsborough on the Saturday morning. We went by the M62 and came off at Huddersfield to come into Sheffield on the north side, close to Hillsborough. When we approached the main junction from the M1 down to Hillsborough, the traffic was such that we turned back and, because my pal was a Sheffield lad, he knew a route into the ground which avoided most of the traffic. It was probably about noon. Very early. We had intended trying to get to the stadium by twelve thirty or one o'clock and we did because we avoided most of the traffic.

I was attending the game as a guest, but I can tell you, from my personal experience of looking at Hillsborough as a possible venue, for perhaps a League Cup Final replay or a League Cup semi-final replay, for instance, the policy of the local constabulary was always to allocate the Kop end of the ground to clubs and supporters who travelled from the south. In my experience that had been the policy for a number of years. Clubs who were travelling from either the north or the west would be allocated the Leppings Lane end as routine, and I think I'm right in saying that the North Stand went with the Leppings Lane and the Main Stand was allocated with the

Kop. I'm sure it would be fair criticism that perhaps football authorities, and I would include the Football League in that, didn't make strong enough representation to the authorities to have that situation at least mitigated in some way. It still applies in certain areas. I mean, at Wembley, for instance, the ends allocated are very much determined by the direction of travel. At Wembley, of course, both ends are exactly the same size, apart from the players' tunnel, so it's a matter of a few hundred tickets and doesn't really make any difference. At Hillsborough, in terms of FA Cup semi-finals, for instance when Leeds played Coventry [in 1987], Leeds were allocated the Leppings Lane end and Coventry were on the Kop, so it had been the policy, despite the number of travelling supporters, for some years.

Tony Ensor, Liverpool FC director

The game was played at Sheffield Wednesday's ground. We'd been there the year before and we'd played the same opponents. Peter Robinson [Liverpool FC chief executive] had asked that we be accommodated at the other end. His requests on crowd control to the FA and UEFA over the years had rarely been complied with, and the results have been unfortunate to say the least.

John Williams, senior researcher at the Centre for Football Research, Leicester University, and Liverpool fan

Liverpool FC and their fans again complained about the ticket allocation which saw a club with twice the average attendance of opponents Nottingham Forest receiving 4,000 fewer tickets than their rivals. At major football matches these days it is the police who speak with the loudest voice. Liverpool fans, arriving from the north, took the smaller Leppings Lane end of the ground. Forest fans spread themselves on the giant Kop terrace.

Ray Lewis, Football League referee from Great Bookham

I started refereeing in November 1962. I went through the Surrey County FA and progressed to the Isthmian League referees' list in 1969, and was automatically appointed to the Football League linesman list in that year. In 1974 I was appointed to the referees' list of the Football League. Prior to 1989, I'd done one FA Cup semi-final, between Watford and Tottenham Hotspur, and one Milk Cup semi-final, between Liverpool and Burnley. I suppose I must have learned about the Forest–Liverpool game about three or four weeks prior to it. I'd had the nod that I had been appointed to a semi-final and automatically thought that I was going to have the other one and not what was, on paper, the number-one semi-final. It was very much an honour. I was thrilled to bits to receive the appointment and really looking forward to it. In fact, Jack Taylor said in his book that sometimes you get more thrill out of receiving the appointment than you do from doing the game.

I decided that it would be a good idea for us—myself, the two linesmen and the reserve official—to meet up the night before the game, because meeting up an hour and a half before the kick-off is not good preparation for a match of this importance. We made arrangements to meet up and stay overnight in Sheffield. We relaxed on the Friday evening and Saturday morning. There's an advantage of being together Saturday morning because you can quietly give your instructions for the game and then not have to worry about trying to get five or ten minutes' peace in the dressing-room (or wherever you're going to do it) at the ground. As far as I'm concerned the instructions are about match control for the day.

We had a car each so it was a peaceful journey up to the ground. There was plenty of support around and the supporters wearing their favours, and you could sense there was a semi-final atmosphere being created. It was an absolutely super day. It was ideal because it wasn't too hot but it was bright and sunny and the nerves were beginning to work. The tension begins to build up. And this is why we need that opportunity of not rushing things. We just need to take everything in in plenty of time, for the simple reason that the referee is the responsible member of the Football Association. He's the person who not only makes decisions on the field of play but sometimes has to handle things prior to the game.

Graham Kelly, chief executive of the Football Association, London

There was no particular reason why I chose to go to Hillsborough rather than Villa Park. If what happened had to happen, it was perhaps as well that I was there and not at Villa Park, both personally and professionally. You look at matches and you think 'I fancy that one more than that one', but that wasn't a major consideration in this particular case. A lot of it is connected with what other FA personnel are doing. On that particular day, the chairman of the FA Council, Bert Millichip, was attending the Villa Park match, so it fell naturally that I and other colleagues went to Hillsborough.

I was satisfied that the issues had been looked at very carefully by the appropriate people at the Football Association, with the benefit of police advice and all the other considerations which come into the choice of the semi-final, and, having attended the previous year, I had no qualms whatsoever. I drove up the M1 and arrived at the ground at about 12.30. The host club normally put on a small luncheon so I attended that luncheon.

Jenni Hicks, Liverpool supporter resident in Pinner, Middlesex, mother of Sarah Louise, aged 19, and Victoria Jane, aged 15

We [the Hicks family] were all allocated tickets because we were season-ticket holders. Unfortunately Trevor [her husband] and I were season-ticket holders in the Main Stand at Anfield, and although we thought we would both get seat tickets we didn't. We were allocated one seat ticket in the North Stand and one standing in the Leppings Lane, because of availability of space at Hillsborough. And the girls, who were season-ticket holders on the Kop, automatically got standing tickets. It was the same procedure as the year before. Trevor, Sarah and Victoria stood on the Leppings Lane terraces in 1988. And I was allocated a seat that year, too, in the seating above the Leppings Lane end. In 1989 I was in the North Stand.

Trevor Hicks, managing director of Perma Systems Ltd, Liverpool supporter and father of Sarah and Victoria

In fact we'd had a bit of a tiff because Jenni had got a seat for the previous semi-final, in 1988, and I had been standing then, and obviously that was the way it turned out yet again. The year before we had in fact been in what I now know to be Pens 3 and 4. I think it was Pen 4 and we were near the back and it was quite squashed, but we'd gone through one of the gates in the radial fences to Pens 5 and 6 and stood there. It was too hot, too stuffy and it was a classic big game.

For big games we always believed in getting in nice and early, particularly with the girls wanting to stand with all their friends. You had to get a good 'spec'. Hillsborough was the first away game we'd been to that season. We'd stopped going to away games because of various problems the previous year. We used to go to all the London games, for instance. Being season-ticket holders at Anfield, we could always get a ticket for away games with the Liverpool fans. So we used to make our way to a fair number of grounds in the country, particularly the ones south of Birmingham, but we'd had all sorts of problems with the girls getting hassled and things. At big games at Anfield, Victoria would usually go in my seat with Jenni, and I'd go in the

Kop with Sarah. I was a lot taller. It's very unusual to have a houseful of ardent football supporters where the ranking order starts with the females and ends up with the men. I mean, they were more passionate than I by a long way, but the facilities for women are appalling. They're bad enough for the guys. You all need wellingtons to go to the toilet and this type of thing, and it was always the away fans who were treated the worst. It was becoming less attractive to tolerate those conditions and the law of diminishing returns—enjoyment to discomfort—was going the wrong way so I think that's why we had stopped going to away matches, although it wasn't a conscious decision.

Jenni Hicks

We had a long journey and we travelled up to Sheffield on the M1. We joined at the Watford section. There were no problems really on the journey up. The motorway wasn't particularly busy. We stopped at the service station before Sheffield to use the toilets. There were quite a few Forest fans, but there were no problems on the motorway. Not as many as we thought there might have been.

Trevor Hicks

One of the things that always makes me laugh about the segregation policy is that we were Liverpool supporters travelling up with all the Notts Forest supporters. We travelled north up the M1 so, as we approached Nottingham particularly, we started picking up all the Notts Forest fans, and there was the usual banter on the motorway, everybody flying their colours, waving to each other, making rude signs, but mainly it was the general carnival atmosphere you see, even on the motorways, when you are approaching a big game.

   We parked in that little car-park in the corner, what I believe to be Hillsborough Park, so we could come across the little bridge over the River Don and into the ground that way. Whenever we travelled, Jenni liked good quality food, particularly for the girls, so we had our sandwich lunch in with Notts Forest fans, all having a laugh and a joke, all doing the same thing. But we knew that we only had a five or ten minute walk to the ground from where we were, so we had plenty of time.

Ian Battey

I was on a late shift that day, which meant I started work at 12.30. The hospitals in Sheffield have a peculiar opening system as far as casualty services are concerned, which means that one of the major hospitals is open 24 hours a day some days of the week and the other one [the Royal Hallamshire] is open 24 hours a day other days of the week. Saturday was the Northern General Hospital's night to be open, which meant that on a normal Saturday it would have been a 12.30 till 9 o'clock shift. There was really no difference that morning apart from it being Sarah's birthday, so it was coming to work, getting into work, having a cup of coffee, waiting for the rest of the members of staff to come in, and then going round and accepting reports, the ins and outs of the morning, what was expected of the afternoon at 12.30 and letting the morning staff and those on 'half days'— because we used to have half days at that point—off home to enjoy the rest of their Saturday.

I was expecting a normal day, dealing with the normal run-of-the-mill Saturday stuff. In some respects I was regretting having to be at work because it was a beautiful day outside. People were talking about going home and doing their shopping or enjoying the day in the garden or whatever, and we were stuck there until nine o'clock that night expecting the normal run-of-the-mill Saturday casualties. A number of sports injuries are normally expected on Saturday afternoons, after the morning football matches or the amateur matches during the day, and the kind of family stuff that people wouldn't want to go and bother their GP for because they shut on Saturday lunchtime. I remember we had about an hour's wait when I took over, people sitting in the waiting-room waiting to be seen, maybe 18 or 19 people.

Having worked in A & E for a number of years, and being quite an avid Sheffield Wednesday supporter, I knew Hillsborough reasonably well, and I knew that, apart from one or two fixtures in a year where we had trouble outside the ground, we wouldn't normally expect anything different for a semi-final than for a normal run-of-the-mill Saturday. The behaviour of fans at Hillsborough had never caused us any problems in the past, and we weren't expecting any that day. We'd have the odd one or two casualties. You'd get the odd glassing or somebody falling down, or being pushed down the stairs or whatever, and I think we accept that as being fairly routine. We used to get casualties from some fixtures, like Leeds, and I vividly remember problems from visits from Chelsea fans or Millwall fans, but it tended to be problems outside the ground rather than inside the ground. As a routine, nothing would cause us any concern, nothing that we'd consider bringing in extra staff for, or anything of that nature.

Alan Hansen, Liverpool central defender and captain

I didn't want to play, because it was my first game back for nine months, which was a long, long time, and this was the semi-final of the Cup, and I knew about semi-finals of the Cup. The semi-final of the FA Cup is the most harrowing game you will ever play in, because of what's at stake and the enormity of getting beaten and missing out on the Cup Final, which is probably the biggest game in the football calendar. It's a one-off occasion. You're better winning the Championship or the European Cup, but playing the FA Cup Final is probably the ultimate. Of course, we'd been beaten by Wimbledon the year before, going for the double.

About nine o'clock the previous evening Ian Rush had come in my room, sent there by Roy Evans because Barry Venison had a virus. Rushie's saying to me 'You might be playing', and I'm saying 'You've got to be joking. I'm not playing. I'm refusing to play.' We get up in the morning, have some breakfast, then go for lunch, go for a walk and at one o'clock, I turned to Rushie and said 'There's no way I'm going to be playing because they would have sent for me.' And, just then, Roy Evans knocks on the door: 'The manager wants to see you and Rushie.' So we go in the little room, and there's Ronnie Moran, Roy Evans and Kenny Dalglish. Kenny says 'The two of you will have to be involved.' I said 'What does that mean, we'll have to be involved?' He said 'Well, you'll have to play and Rushie'll have to be on the bench.' I said 'I can't play here, there's no way I can play, it's my first game for nine months.' He said 'Well, we've heard the reports of the [reserve team] game on Tuesday. You looked all right on Tuesday. You've trained well. You've got to play for us.' I said 'But this is the semi-final of the Cup. I've had one game in nine months. I'm going to be struggling.' He said 'Well, you've got to play.'

Peter Jackson, Liverpool solicitor, chair of the Merseyside branch of the Football Supporters' Association

The day out started at about half-nine because I'd been up early with my eldest son. There was only Daniel at the time; Moira was six months pregnant. I'd been out on my bike round Calderstones Park early and I was champing at the bit, the old story. It was a big game, you're excited, you're nervous and Moira kicked me out about half-past nine. I wasn't picking up Rogan Taylor until ten o'clock. I remember sitting in Rogan's kitchen at a quarter to ten and he'd only just got out of bed. Anyway, we left at ten o'clockish and picked up Pete Garrett. Then we picked up my brother-in-law, Larry, at Widnes, which suited us because we were going the back way to Sheffield, which we thought would be the better way, on to the M56 through Manchester and over the top of the Snake Pass, as an alternative to going on the M62 and M1. We'd been there a few times and we thought that that would be the better way. The M56 was no problem. We got to Bredbury on the ring-road round Manchester—there's motorway now—but there were roadworks there, and delays and all sorts of hassle. We'd left early so it didn't make any difference to us. We knew we were going for a beer when we got there anyway. Rogan had to meet John Williams at about two o'clock to get a ticket so there was a number of reasons why we wanted to be there early, but it was a good job we had left early because of that delay. We would have been there by about twelve o'clock if we'd had the normal run, and I seem to remember us getting to our usual pub, which is about a five minute walk from where we'd park, at about quarter past or twenty past one. We didn't stop en route so you're talking about an hour's delay, purely due to traffic congestion or roadworks or whatever.

Steve Hanley, Nottingham Forest supporter
I had been excited all week and couldn't wait for Saturday morning—the red shirt freshly laundered following the excesses of last Sunday's League Cup win [when Nottingham Forest beat Luton Town 3–1 in the Final]. Saturday started as a beautiful day and the journey north was accompanied by many Forest fans. I was due to meet some friends at a pub to the north of Sheffield—the pub was shut and as I hung around outside some Scouse lads asked if they were on the right road. When I said I was going too, and they saw the tree on my shirt, they grinned and said 'Oh, you're one of them.' 'No, you are', I replied. And this was typical of the feelings close to the ground. No animosity. Everybody really looking forward to the match—we *had* to win this one.

Pat Nicol, school welfare assistant, single parent, mother of three children, including 14-year-old Lee
My eldest son's a Liverpool supporter. He'd never missed an away match or a home match. But Lee, being only 14, had never been to an away match before. Lee wasn't very mature really. But his school friends were going to the match and the week before he'd asked me if he could he go. I said 'No'. But then he was upset. He was moody all week and he said to me 'If I get a ticket, can I go?' I said 'If you get a ticket you can go.' My elder son said there

was no chance of him getting a ticket. But he got one. So Andrew said he would go with him to the match and told me not to worry, but Andrew's a chef in the Park Hotel and he had to work because there was a late booking or something and he couldn't get the day off, and Lee couldn't go in Andrew's car. Lee was still adamant he was going. His friends were all going with different relatives and there was no room for Lee in their cars. I thought 'He can't go anyway, that's fate.' And then right at the last minute, on Friday, his friends said they wouldn't go in the cars and coaches, they would all go by train so they would all be together. Four of them went. There was Austin Grimmond, who was exactly the same age as Lee but a bigger lad, a foot taller, and Austin's cousin, Alan Trees, who was sixteen, and I don't know who the other lad was.

Lee was a milkboy, so he used to go out at quarter to five in the morning, do his milkround and come back about half past eight. He got changed into all his red gear, and got his sandwiches and that. I wasn't very happy. I was worried over him being in a strange place, but Andrew assured me that the police are waiting for you when you get to the station and you're shifted along to the ground and you're put in there and you're escorted out when the match is finished. I was more worried over louts on the train and all that. I mean, Sheffield don't like us, Manchester don't like us and I thought that's where trouble would start. So I said 'If you have any problems, Lee, just get in a taxi and come home. Do you understand? Get a taxi and come home. I'll pay when you get here.' He said 'From Sheffield, Mum?' He knew he could just pick up the phone. He knew I'd be here all day. But Andrew said to me 'Mum, he'll be all right, he's been going to the Kop for that long, he'll get looked after. The police look after them on the train. Now, don't worry about him.' So he went off at ten o'clock in the morning with his sandwiches. There's an opening at the top of the street there and for some reason he turned and came back and said 'I know you're worried about me, Mum, but don't.' I still had my dressing-gown on because that's my washing day, and he said 'Go and get dressed and you can come with me and you can go to the market and to the shops while I go to the match and I'll meet you after the match.' So I said 'Just go and enjoy yourself, Lee.' He said 'You know what, Mum, this is the happiest day of my life.' Because he had the independence, he felt then he was a true fan, he was going to the away matches. This was the start of it all. And that was the last time I saw him alive.

Eddie Spearritt, taxi-driver, Liverpool supporter resident in Runcorn, father of 14-year-old Adam

It was a lovely day, obviously, full of great expectations. Adam and myself wanted Everton and Liverpool to get through that day, simply because it would be an all-Mersey derby [in the FA Cup Final]. Adam had the attitude that if Liverpool didn't win then Everton should. He didn't go to matches as regular as he would have liked because of the problem of getting to the ground and coming home from the ground. He'd once asked me if he could go to the match and I said 'Which parents are going?' and he said there were no parents going, just friends, so I said he couldn't go. (He was thirteen then so it was more or less a year before.) And then a couple of days after that, he asked me if he could go down to town, meaning Liverpool town, and again I asked the same question, as parents do, and again I got the same answer 'No, it's just friends', so again I gave him the same answer—'No'. And a couple of days later I was thinking to myself 'I used to go to a match on my own when I was eight, and do all the things he's asking to do.'

I took him to football matches from when he was a couple of years of age. I love football, so consequently when he was born I wanted him to play for Liverpool and things like that, as most Dads do. Adam just loved it. He lived up here [Runcorn] and he loved the house and he loved the school and all that. He was born in Liverpool Maternity Hospital and always considered himself a Scouser, and he loved that type of programme where they get the old Liverpool humour out. We'd gone to Wembley when Liverpool had played West Ham in the Milk Cup [1981]. We'd had a good day then even though it was only a draw, but we won the replay anyway.

That week of Hillsborough we had an awful lot of problems getting tickets. I couldn't get any. He used to think that I could just go to Liverpool and get tickets and it suddenly dawned on him, about the Wednesday, that I hadn't got any tickets, so he phoned me up at work to say there was a boy at school who had a voucher and didn't want it. He said 'Can you come and get this voucher and get my ticket?' It meant me travelling all the way home and then all the way back and I had my school-run and things like that. I said 'Oh, OK', but I actually got the [taxi-firm] operator to phone him back and tell him to leave the voucher where I could see it so I could just run in and get it. So when I pulled up, he'd actually left it on the front door, sellotaped to the glass, and I thought to myself 'You silly little bugger, anyone could have took that.' When I got to the door I found he'd actually left it on the inside—he wasn't that daft! I got back from there and I went to the operator and I asked her if she had anything to go to Anfield or into town and she gave me a town job, so I had four passengers in the car going to town, I had his voucher in my pocket, and I got as far as Upper Parliament Street and the car broke down. I was driving a Sierra diesel and it's got five fan-belts, not just one, and one of the fan-belts had gone and that controlled the brakes and the heating-system so obviously there was nothing I could do. I went over to a garage and I asked them if they had a fan-belt. They didn't have one so after all the school runs were done my mate came and picked me up and we got the car to Hope Street police station, left it there overnight. I said to me mate 'What the hell am I going to do about our Adam's ticket?', so he said 'I'll run you up and get it.' So that's what we did. I came home and as soon as I got home he said 'Did you get the ticket?' I said 'No, I broke down and I couldn't get there.' I sat here for about ten minutes and I said to Jan [his wife] 'I'm going to have to get rid of all this rubbish in my pocket.' I was saying 'Oh, I'll have to save that' and 'I need that receipt' and 'I don't need that' and then I came to the ticket and I threw that on the floor saying 'I don't need that.' Adam was sitting on the settee, and he dived on it. And the next day I got one for the Notts Forest end. I said 'You can go in the Liverpool end and I'll go in the Forest end', obviously thinking that if there was going to be any trouble he was safer in the Liverpool end. Then, on the Friday, I actually got a ticket for the Leppings Lane end as well, so I gave the Forest-end ticket to a lad I was working with. So it was 'all systems go'. We both had tickets for the same place.

The only time I'd actually been to Hillsborough was in the sixties when Liverpool played Leicester in the semi-final and that was obviously totally different. I mean, I didn't know anything about the area. I didn't know that you were penned in, or anything like that. All I knew was what commentators on the TV had said, and what was in the press, that it was one of our great stadiums. That was it.

Lord Justice Taylor, interim report, paragraph 58
At about 12 noon Chief Inspector Creaser asked Superintendent Murray whether the pens on the West Terrace were to be filled one by one successively, but was told that they should all be available from the start and the fans should find their own level.

Dennis Cerrone
I think—again from memory—it was perhaps about twelvish when the first people started arriving and it may have been as early as that when they

started going into the ground. At the Leppings Lane end, the road curves round over the bridge and coaches pull up just before the turnstiles, and then they all get out and go in the ground. I remember them coming down and queueing. Coaches were bringing them up and then dropping them off. There were a lot of police there from Liverpool on the mounted section at that end and we were talking to them. I think there were at least two I saw who were from Liverpool. I don't think I saw any of our own people on the horses.

It was still that nice atmosphere, people from Liverpool coming up and saying 'Hello, love, nice day for it.' They were drinking pop, having ice-creams and it was great.

Jill Thomas

I was on Penistone Road before the match, at one of the turnstiles, with the same colleague who had picked me up from home that morning. The families came early. They were coming through and there was a lot of banter, a lot of good spirit. Where we were standing, it was beautiful, a glorious day. I'd got my mac on and it was boiling. The atmosphere was lovely. I remember having my picture taken. Somebody wanted to have their picture taken with the two police officers, and somebody else said 'That made a lovely picture, I'll take one.' And we were all stood with our arms round each other, smiling, with the North Stand behind us, having our pictures taken. It was great. It really, really was.

Mike Lewis, editor of 'Sport on Two' on BBC Radio 2

On the face of it, when we all came in on the Saturday morning, it was going to be a great day. It was in the days when both FA Cup semi-finals were held on a Saturday. It was also the opening day of the cricket season—MCC against Worcestershire at Lord's. There was some good horse-racing around, and some rugby, but the two centrepieces were Liverpool–Forest and Everton–Norwich. There was also Rangers–St Johnstone in the Scottish Cup semi-final, so it was a terrific day, one of the best days of the season, and we were all looking forward to it.

I was editing the programme, Pat Thornton was the producer and John Inverdale was the presenter. The programme had been set up during the week, and there was a feeling of anticipation in the sports room on the Saturday morning, because the FA Cup semi-finals were potentially great games. The major decision to be made was which game to go to at half-time.

We expected to be at Hillsborough, because that was where Peter Jones had gone, with Alan Green. If it was nil-nil in both games we would have gone to Hillsborough. If Liverpool had been two-up, or Forest had been two-up, then we may well have gone to Villa Park, where Mike Ingham and Bryon Butler were the commentators. In the early moments of Cup games, the commentators always try to outdo each other. After 30 seconds one's saying 'What a great game we've got here.' Then you go to the other one and he's saying 'You think you've got a great game there, we've got an even better game here.' So we were expecting a bit of that.

Ray Lewis, match referee

I don't necessarily think I have got things that I would classify as super-stitions. I always lay my kit out on the bed before I pack it, to make sure I've got everything, because to fall into an embarrassment of not taking a pair of shorts or something could be slightly wild when you're there. When I get to the ground I like putting my kit on a hook again to make sure that everything is there. I don't normally get boots out until I've inspected the pitch to see what stud I'd be wearing. I know that some people go through things like having a shower before the game but by and large I've never felt myself to be superstitious. Lying things on the bed to make sure everything is there could be classified as superstition; I just think it's planning for the occasion. I think it is important that you take out two whistles and two watches and you check that you've got them. But to actually put them into the pockets in the same order every Saturday, no.

It would have been more or less the same routine: go down to the tunnel, have a look and make sure everything's all right. I probably bumped into the groundsman there and passed the time of day with him: 'Any problems?', 'No', 'Fine'. Had a word with Graham Mackrell, the secretary: 'Any problems?', 'No', 'Fine'. And then probably went in and had a cup of tea and a sandwich in one of the reception rooms. On that occasion we did the normal routine thing.

Dennis Cerrone

I was standing, in uniform, in the turnstile area. Certain other bobbies were there too. I don't remember anything in particular, nothing that made me think 'That's wrong, that shouldn't have happened.' There was one inci-dent. I think somebody went on one of Liverpool coaches and there was some beer on a coach, and it's not allowed, is it? I didn't know that—I thought you could have it on the coach as long as you didn't bring it in. I don't know what happened over that, but I know there was something on this coach and I'm not sure whether it was an official coach or not. That's something that just stands in my memory.

It started to get busier. People were coming in quickly around oneish.

Jenni Hicks

We arrived in Sheffield at about 12.30 or 12.45. We found suitable parking. We were actually parked in a mixed car-park with Forest and Liverpool supporters. It was predominantly Forest supporters, but there was a very jovial atmosphere amongst the Forest and Liverpool supporters who were there—'We are going to win today' sort of thing—and no animosity. It was a glorious day, we had taken a packed lunch, and the atmosphere was tremendous in the car-park. We were all out of our cars having our picnics. No problem.

We had the picnic and proceeded to walk to the ground. I would say we were only ten minutes' walk from the ground. The intention was that Trevor and the girls would stand together. In fact, I would have preferred to have stood with the girls. I knew Trevor didn't particularly like standing. I didn't mind. I had stood with the girls on several occasions and it didn't worry me too much. And I would have preferred that to being on my own in the seats. At quarter to two on that afternoon, we stood outside the Leppings Lane gate and discussed exactly that. And it was the girls who said 'Oh, come on, Mum, you are only little, you are not going to see. There is going to be a big crowd today, you won't see a thing. Go in the seats, you will be better.' Trevor was quite dubious; I think he would have quite happily taken the seat. Because he was always saying 'Oh, come on, you are always saying "women and equality" and one thing and another. I don't mind.' I think it was the girls really who insisted. Sarah was quite practical about it. She was the eldest. She said 'No, no, she will be better off there. You'll be much better off in the seats today, Mum.' When it was decided that I was definitely going to sit, it was decided for me not to meet them at the Leppings Lane gate but to stand in this little newsagent's doorway. The girls said to me 'Don't stand here, Mum, because when they come out there will be a lot of people. Stand in this little tobacconist's shop.' I can remember trudging off to the North Stand feeling quite disappointed that I wasn't going to be with them. I think Vicki picked this up and as I walked away to the North Stand, I heard this voice shout 'Mum', and she ran after me and she gave me a big hug and an extra kiss before she went in. Yes, and that was the last time I saw her alive.

Trevor Hicks

It would be between quarter to one and one o'clock when we made our journey from the car to the ground. The area was open, it was light density and no queuing. There was perhaps half a dozen policemen. I don't remember any of the police horses being in position at that time. Basically we had plenty of time, plenty of space, and one of the reasons we went in early was so that we avoided it all. I suppose some people would say we went in too early but we wanted to be part of the build-up to the big occasion. We arranged a rendezvous point, at that little tobacconist just outside the Leppings Lane terrace entrance, and, even at the gates as we were entering the turnstiles to go in the ground, Jenni was on the point of swapping her ticket with me. If she'd have stood with the girls she would probably have been killed because she's only little. Not that size matters. Some of the guys who died were quite big. So it was agreed that Jenni would take the seat in the North Stand and the girls and myself went in.

One of the chaps who used to work for me in the factory in the Midlands had a son who was a real Liverpool fan. He couldn't go to many games and I'd promised to bring him a programme back. And obviously I wanted a programme for myself. So I stopped on the entrance to the tunnel. As you came through the turnstiles it looked as if the only way to the standing was to go down through the tunnel with the big sign above it that said 'STANDING'. I don't remember that much detail from '88 but I'm sure we'd gone in that way. Anyway, I'd stopped to buy my programmes and to be honest I was looking for a cup of coffee. We'd brought soft drinks with us, to have with our sandwiches, but we hadn't brought any coffee, so I fancied a cup of coffee. While I was busy getting my programmes, I had my last clear recognition of the girls alive. They were just entering the tunnel and were obviously using it as a chance to scarper, so Dad would be out of sight, they would be with their mates and 'Big Brother' wouldn't be watching. Otherwise I would have stood probably twenty, thirty feet away from them, something like that, so that we were together but separate. I looked around for coffee and all I could see for refreshments was to my right. Twenty, thirty yards away was this small coffee-kiosk. It was underneath the steps going into the Leppings Lane seated area (which was above the standing). I actually went along there to buy a coffee and by doing that I saw a tiny sign on the concrete pillar at the end of that Leppings Lane stand, and that let you into Pens 1 and 2, the ones on the corner, and that's how I ended up being exactly next to the police box on roughly the same level. It was banked up fairly steeply in that corner. My head would be about two feet below the floor of the police box. We now know from the video evidence that the girls were in Pen 3. Fairly early on it was quite densely populated, if I could use that phrase. Where I was there was hardly anybody. I mean, I literally could have sat anywhere I wanted.

Brian Barwick, editor of BBC's 'Match of the Day'

It was my first year as editor of 'Match of the Day' and the major contract we had in those days was the FA Cup, because ITV had the Football League. We invented 'Match of the Day—the Road to Wembley' and that particular season we had had a spectacularly good 'Road to Wembley' and we'd managed to be at Sutton when they beat Coventry. We were left with two semi-finals—Liverpool and Nottingham Forest, and Everton and Norwich City—which looked as though they would produce a very good Cup Final. On that particular afternoon Desmond Lynam, the presenter, and Jimmy Hill, the expert, went to Hillsborough to see the game first-hand before coming back down the motorway to present the programme. I watched 'Football Focus' [between 12.20 and 1 pm] and then went in to the Television Centre in London to prepare to watch both games coming in with a view to shaping the programme once we had seen the action and heard the interviews.

We are often joined by people who either can't get to see their favourite team because they are playing up the other end of the country or because they want to spend the day with us on 'Match of the Day', and on that particular afternoon we were joined by Sir Brian Wolfson, the chairman and chief executive of Wembley, and Jarvis Astaire, who is also part of the Wembley set-up. They came in because Sir Brian Wolfson's a Liverpudlian.

Steve McMahon, Liverpool footballer

The players were assembled in the changing rooms waiting for our manager Kenny Dalglish to announce the team, as it was the custom of the manager to keep even his players guessing until this late hour for the final line-up. As it happened, when Kenny announced the side there was a major surprise in his selection. Alan Hansen, who had not played for several weeks, was chosen out of the blue at centre-half. I have never seen Alan Hansen looking so nervous before a game. He is normally so cool, calm and collected, nothing ruffles him, but on this occasion he seemed completely 'gone'.

Alan Hansen

So there's fear and trepidation going to the ground because normally you're going to be a nervous wreck before the semi-final of the FA Cup, but that day I am gone completely. Of course I get in the dressing-room and the lads who had been injured, Gary Gillespie and Kevin MacDonald, have come in the dressing-room and come to me and started laughing because they knew what I was going to be like. They knew I was going to be a nervous wreck. They were saying 'You'll be all right, you'll be all right.'

Trevor Hicks

I'd taken my little radio with the earpiece. If you remember, the big debate that morning was whether Hansen was going to play or not, so I was probably tuned into Radio Sheffield or something like that. I was sitting on the steps. It was a beautiful day and it was a real carnival atmosphere. Everyone was really happy and I think everybody thought we were going to win. So we were there to cheer them on to Wembley and that was what it was all about. I'll be honest, I don't think safety really came into my mind, especially in the couple of hours in the run-up. We were all sitting there, it was a beautiful day, I'd got my coffee, I had my programme, I'd got a good position to stand but I was sitting on the terrace at the time and we were having a general chat with the guys around. I'd heard the announcement that Hansen was going to play. I thought 'Good, that'll tighten up the back.'

Dr Tom Heller, Sheffield general practitioner

I was on call for a practice adjacent to the Hillsborough ground for the weekend of Saturday 15 April. On Saturdays when there is a home match at the stadium I avoid passing the ground when crowds are coming and going. My home is one side of the ground and the practice is on the other. On the 15th the atmosphere was special for the semi-final; people were parking their cars miles away from the stadium and walking to the ground many hours earlier than the crowds usually do for home games. I remember being especially cheerful (despite being on duty) and proud that Sheffield was the centre of the sporting world that day. The snooker world championship was on just down the road, and at Hillsborough the semi-final that many people thought should have been the Final of the FA Cup was being held.

Outside every public house and on every verge on my way home there were relaxed groups of young men chatting and joking in their 'uniforms' of tight faded jeans, off-colour teeshirts, and something red and white. Both sets of supporters wear red and white; I wonder who was who on those verges and which of them now live to tell their tale of the day when such a terrible tragedy happened out of a relaxed and gentle sunny moment?

Ray Lewis

About quarter to two we actually walked the pitch, just in case the penalty spot hadn't been put there or something. That has been experienced at top-level grounds! We checked the flags and everything. Because the game was being televised, and the highlights were being shown in the evening, the commentator or the producer would want to know the Christian names of the linesmen, etc. You have to get the donkeywork out of the way when you have the time to spend two or three minutes with these types of people; otherwise you find it becomes too much of a rush and you get yourself in the wrong frame of mind for that occasion. The ground was then beginning to fill up, the atmosphere was being created. Difficult to say how many. I think that there were more people at the Nottingham Forest end than there were at the end Liverpool were going to use. But I wouldn't have thought there was anything unusual as far as that was concerned. Team sheets, if I remember rightly, were presented at quarter past two. The FA Cup is slightly different to League matches—team sheets don't have to be in till thirty minutes before an FA Cup game—but clubs get into a habit and the team sheets were in at a quarter past two. And I think at that stage there was no concern whatsoever of problems that were to come later. A senior police officer came in, as is normal, to give instructions of the possibility of evacuations or whatever, and things like that, and that is normal routine. It doesn't have to be a game of that importance. It happens on grounds when you only have 1,500 or 2,000 people.

Lord Justice Taylor, interim report, paragraph 59

By 2 pm it was apparent to those inside the ground and those monitoring events in the police and club control rooms that the number of Nottingham fans in their places greatly outnumbered those from Liverpool. The Kop and the South Stand were filling up steadily, but the North and West Stands were half empty. It was noted about that time that the turnstile figures showed only 12,000 had entered as against 20,000 at the same time the previous year. On the West Terraces, although Pens 3 and 4 were filling, the wing Pens 1,2,6 and 7 were nearly empty. At 2.15 pm a Tannoy message asked fans in Pens 3 and 4 to move forward and make room for others.

Eddie Spearritt

I'd arranged for two friends to pick me up outside a local pub around about twelve o'clock so we actually left the house about five to twelve and walked round to the pub. My two friends had been working that Saturday morning so we actually went into the pub and Adam had a coke, I had a glass of shandy and my two mates had a glass of lager. Adam knew the two lads— the four of us had played golf together—so we had a great laugh. At one stage Adam was actually crying with laughter.

Even though we were held up in traffic, we weren't really concentrating on that. Because we had our tickets there was no real problem. We were getting near Glossop and we were stuck in traffic. One of the lads said 'I'll jump out and get a paper', so he goes and we start moving on and he comes running out of the shop and he tries to get in the car as it's moving. We're not travelling at any speed or anything, but Adam was crying with laughter. And that's the way it was. We went over the Woodhead Pass and he'd never been over there. There was bits of snow on the top. I was pointing that out to him, saying how lovely it looked. And our journey was great. We really had a good time. We weren't just sitting there saying 'Isn't this traffic awful?' The four of us were laughing and joking. We got there just after two. Around ten past two we came down the dual carriageway towards the roundabout by Hillsborough. There was a bus station on the left, you turn left at the roundabout, and my mate said 'We'll get in here', and we pulled up, and as we did a coachload of Notts Forest fans came up and there was all good banter and no aggravation there. A policeman told us we couldn't park where we'd stopped so we had to go back up the dual carriageway and start to come back down and we found a place in one of the side roads. We walked down from there. We actually got to the ground round about half two.

Andy Williamson

I got to the ground about one o'clock. I was even privileged enough to have a car-parking space right next to the Main Stand. The car-park was already very full. I may have got the last space, even at that time. We were taken by the number of people that were around outside the ground, even as early as that, although obviously recognised that there were still a lot of people behind us, judging from the traffic that we'd met earlier. A lot of people were not anxious to get into the stadium. That was one of my recollections. They seemed to have other things to do in preference to getting into the ground early, like enjoying the sun and the nearby river. After going into the stadium shortly after one o'clock, we did take our seats in the stand quite early, probably about twenty-five to three, and even then one of the things that was very evident was the number of people that were in the central section of the Leppings Lane terrace, compared to the wing terraces. We both remarked about the overcrowding even as early as that. Because there was enough space in some areas of the wing stands for us to actually see the terrace. It was as empty as that. The very extremes. And obviously people were concentrated in the central section. That was apparent, as I say, almost half an hour before the game. It was so blatant, to be perfectly honest, that it was something that I think you kept looking at. Your attention was constantly drawn towards it.

Bruce Grobbelaar, Liverpool goalkeeper

The sun shone on us the year before. This day it was brilliant and we had this opportunity to go out there and perform in front of millions of people in the semi-final, and for some strange reason, during the kick-in, the centre part of the stand was getting full and there was nothing on either side. That was about half past two.

Dr Colin Flenley, a West Midlands general practitioner and Liverpool fan

We went up from Birmingham, met some friends from Liverpool in a pub just north of Sheffield and drove down to the match. In '88 everything seemed very organised. We were in the Leppings Lane end, just round the side of the goal. There was a police cordon before you actually got to the turnstile and we were searched and got into orderly queues and then went in through the turnstile with no problem at all. Some of my friends had seat tickets and they said to me 'You want to go round the side because it can get a bit crowded in the centre if you go down through the tunnel.' So I went round the side with one of my mates and had a fantastic day.

In 1989, tickets seemed to be very sparse and in fact I didn't get a ticket until about eleven o'clock on the Friday evening. I've got friends who have season tickets for Liverpool and one of my friends phoned me up and said he'd got a cancellation, someone couldn't go, so he'd got a ticket for me. So, as the year before, I travelled up with a friend from Birmingham and we met our friends from Liverpool in the same pub, and everything was very relaxed. We got to the pub about quarter to two. The pub that year wasn't as crowded as it was the year before. We had two pints and then drove down to about half a mile from the ground. There were five of us in the party. Four of them had seat tickets and I was the only one with a ticket for the Leppings Lane end. As they said last year, they said to me this year 'Just go round the side because it can get a bit crowded in the middle.'

Rob White, Liverpool fan, former Nottingham University student

[This] FA Cup semi-final was my third visit to Hillsborough in 12 months. The other two visits were for the Sheffield Wednesday v Liverpool League match in January 1989 and, perhaps more importantly, the 1988 FA Cup semi-final between the same two teams as the ill-fated match on 15 April. At the previous semi-final I had stood in the centre section of the Leppings Lane terrace, and for the League match I had sat in the West Stand, which is also reached via the turnstiles at the Leppings Lane end. On 15 April this year [1989], my ticket was again for the standing area of the Leppings Lane terrace.

I had intended to arrive at the ground at about 2pm, as I did at last year's semi-final, but a series of traffic hold-ups along the M62 motorway had meant that the journey from Liverpool had taken longer than anticipated. I was travelling with a colleague from work, and he suggested a number of diversions along the way which enabled us to avoid some of the congestion.

When we eventually reached Sheffield, there were still many other people parking their cars and many coaches just arriving at the same time as us, so I was not too concerned that we had arrived later than I had hoped. I believe that the time that we parked was about 2pm.

For some reason, the recommended route to Hillsborough this year, as detailed by South Yorkshire police before the match, was different to the route recommended by the RAC last year. This may have been due to the fact that after last year's match the direct route from Sheffield to Manchester (along the A616 and the A628) had been so congested that the traffic was moving literally at walking pace for miles and miles. I therefore thought that I would follow the different route that had been recommended to familiarise myself with it, particularly for the purpose of avoiding a repeat of the congestion I had experienced the previous year on the return journey. I had not anticipated such delays on the way to Sheffield, though. Furthermore, the different route meant that I had to park in an unfamiliar area compared with previous visits, so I was not sure how far away the ground was when I got out of the car. I didn't think that it could be far, though, because there were a number of traffic policemen around showing people where to park.

My colleague stopped off for a couple of minutes to buy himself lunch, but even so we thought that we still had plenty of time. After all, the ticket itself recommended taking up a position 15 minutes before kick-off, and I thought that we would certainly arrive before then. Even with this brief stop, I suppose we reached the ground between about 2.20pm and 2.30pm, which should have been ample time, albeit later than we had hoped. However, we had not anticipated the confusion that greeted us as we approached the turnstiles. I searched in my pocket for my ticket to see which of the two entrances (that led from the street to the actual turnstiles) we needed to use, and realised that even though we were several yards from the outer blue gates which lead up to the turnstiles, we in fact needed to move over to our right slightly in order to approach our allocated turnstiles through Entrance B. There were so many people approaching the ground that it was difficult to make even this slight change of direction. Other people to the right had, likewise, realised that they too were approaching the wrong entrance to the turnstiles, and the result was that many people were colliding with each other in the road as they tried to get to the correct place.

I'm sure that at last year's semi-final there were police and stewards directing people in the road on the approach to the turnstiles, and so this problem did not arise then. Furthermore, this marshalling last year meant that orderly queues had been formed up at the turnstiles and, as is the case at most grounds I have visited, these queues were kept apart last year by policemen, some of them mounted, moving between them and so avoiding the problem of the queues merging into a solid mass of people outside the ground.

Peter Jackson

The mood in the pub was identical to every big semi-final or final. It was boisterous and loud and noisy. It was Scouse. There was no trouble and no hassle. I remember there were people dancing on the table, singing 'We'll win the double, we'll win the double again', to the tune of 'Roll out the barrel'. There was no problem. There were Forest fans around but as usual, as in 1988, there was no antagonism between the two. We stayed in the pub for two pints. The sun was shining and we sat outside by the river. I remember speaking to some Spanish gentleman who tried to convince us that he had played for Atlético Madrid.

We must have left the pub about two o'clock. We walked up the hill from the little village of Hillsborough, the shopping centre, over the top and down the other side, and it was only when we got to the bottom of the hill that you could actually see the ground and you could see the mass of people outside. That was the Leppings Lane end that we were actually going into. Pete Garrett, Larry and I were all going into the West Stand at the Leppings Lane end, so you go in through the turnstiles at the Leppings Lane end of the ground. My initial reaction was not to bother, to be honest, to sit on the side and wait and see what happened, because I just didn't fancy it. There was no fear of what might happen. It wasn't a premonition or anything like that. I just saw it and I thought 'I don't really fancy this, I'd rather sit here. It's a lovely day, the crowd will get in, at five to three it will have gone and I'll walk in. I've got a seat, I know what I'm doing, I've done it before, this is easy.'

It was a total mess outside. There was no queue outside, there was no organisation, you couldn't see police officers, you couldn't see stewards. Despite my desire to stay outside, we went in. Pete Garrett said 'Oh, come on, we'll manage this', and we joined the back of the throng, if you want to call it that. This was about quarter past two. Within ten minutes we were going nowhere. It wasn't like other crowds with a common purpose, intending to go somewhere—forwards, backwards, sideways, whatever. It just seemed that the throng was getting bigger. It was getting more compact and we weren't going forward. There was no discomfort initially but there was within ten or twenty minutes.

Eddie Spearritt

Derek and my mate had two stand tickets. Adam and I made an arrangement with them that if we were getting beat two-nil with a quarter of an hour to go, we'd get out handy. You know, 'See you at quarter to.' When we were coming down by the roundabout, my mates went in a little corner shop, and then Adam and I just walked up. From when we left the car I didn't see anything that I hadn't already seen at thousands of football matches that I'd been to. It was just normal. And we walked up till we got to the actual turnstile area. It was just organised chaos. I mean, when I first came up I only remember seeing one horse and not many policemen. When you go to a match at Anfield I wouldn't say there was a massive police presence there but you do see the police and the police have got it all sussed out and whatever, but it wasn't like that. There was no organisation there whatsoever. When I saw this, I said to Adam 'Well, I'm not joining that.' Obviously I was thinking of him, and myself also. We stood to one side and I said to him 'Don't worry about it, we've got our tickets, there's no problem, if we miss five minutes we miss five minutes.' But it was just organised chaos.

While we were standing on the side, I actually bumped into the lad from work, Keith, who I gave the ticket to, so we were talking to him. We all call him Nookie Bear. So Adam's there and I'm talking to Keith, who had come down to see that his lad had got in all right. Keith said 'I'll have to go now, Eddie, I've got to get down the other end.' So I said 'OK, Nook, I'll see you.' So when Keith went, Adam said to me 'Why do you call him Nookie Bear?' I said 'He looks like Roger DeCourcey.' So again Adam was just falling about laughing and that's the way it was.

I had the attitude of 'I've got my tickets.' It would be totally different if you didn't have a ticket. Many a time at Anfield it hasn't been all-ticket and you get to a turnstile and you're saying to yourself 'What am I going to do if they close the gate?' It wasn't that situation. The pair of us had our tickets. The capacity had been set, we had our tickets, so there was no problem. I can't remember actually seeing it on the day, but on the video I've seen people climbing up. If I had been in there I would have been telling Adam to do that, to get out of it because unfortunately one of the problems is that once you join a crowd like that you can't get out. You can't say to the guy behind you 'Excuse me, I want to get out', because the guy behind you is in the same position. You're talking about a lot of people, and people are just coming at the back and they don't know. So that is one of the problems. I definitely would have been telling Adam to get up on the wall for his own safety and myself probably. I've spoken to mates who were actually in there and they say it was really bad.

Lord Justice Taylor, interim report, paragraph 62

Superintendent Marshall was on foot amongst the crowd. He became anxious about the numbers coming down Leppings Lane and spilling out onto the roadway where buses and cars were moving. At 2.17 pm he radioed to control to have motor traffic in Leppings Lane stopped. This was eventually done at about 2.30pm. Up to this time, despite the large mass outside the turnstiles and the numbers still approaching, there was still no panic in the crowd; no perception of crisis by the police. In the control room Mr Murray, who could see Leppings Lane on the video, advised Mr Duckenfield that they would get everyone in by 3 pm. Mr Duckenfield reaffirmed to him the policy about a delayed kick-off. It would be ordered only if there was some major external factor such as fog on the Pennines or delay on the motorway: not if spectators merely turned up late even in large numbers.

Rob White

I had read in the press before the game this year that the police were issuing a warning about pickpockets operating in the queues at the turnstiles, which had apparently been a problem at last year's semi-final. I had told my colleague to be aware of this, and I therefore expected to see an even greater police presence at the turnstiles this year to combat the problem. I was therefore particularly surprised to see so few policemen actually near the turnstiles, considering the warning that had been issued, and the fact that there did not seem to be any attempt being made to form orderly queues. This looked to me as though any pickpockets around would find the situation even more to their liking than the previous year. I again warned my colleague to be particularly careful with his ticket, because the article that I had read mentioned that last year some people had their tickets stolen while they were actually queuing. If this was indeed the case, it certainly seemed odd that the efficient marshalling that existed last year was not extended further. In fact, this year it did not seem to exist at all.

There was a mounted policeman by the blue entrance gates that we were approaching and he was allowing a few people at a time to pass through. However there were no queues in evidence at the turnstiles. There was just a single mass of people. The only other policemen that I could see were up by the turnstiles. As far as I could see, there was one mounted policeman further forward and only a few on foot. There were none between the mounted policeman at the blue entrance gates and the rear of the mass of people who had passed through those gates.

The area was certainly very congested when I was allowed past by the mounted policeman, but I did not think that it was dangerously so, at that time. I was, of course, at the back of those waiting to go through the turnstiles, though, so it was difficult for me to tell what the situation was like further forward. The atmosphere at the time was one of excited anticipation of seeing what we all hoped would be a great match. There was the usual pre-match singing as people waited to get into the ground, with the added sense of anticipation associated with the prospect of another Wembley Cup Final, should the team win. The underlying mood was certainly good-humoured and well-behaved. At the same time, inevitably, people were eager to get inside the ground.

As one would normally expect, I had seen people drinking from cans on the way to the ground, but I distinctly remember thinking to myself that I had not personally seen any drunkenness. I remember that because it was conspicuous by its absence. I'm sure that some people probably were drunk, but I did not see any evidence of it. Many of the side streets near to the ground were blocked off by policemen, and they did not seem to be having any trouble with drunken supporters, as far as I could see.

I'm sure that, like me, those responsible for crowd control had expected people to have been drinking. The large dustbins that are habitually placed at turnstiles to accept empty cans, and to serve as a reminder that no alcohol is allowed inside football grounds, certainly suggest that there is an expectation that some people will be drinking up to that point, otherwise they would not be put there. Having said that, personally I prefer not to drink before I go to a match. In any case, if I am driving to an away match, I would not even consider it.

Jill Thomas, outside the ground at the end allocated to Nottingham Forest fans

After two o'clock I remember there was a lot of drinking. There were Nottingham Forest fans walking up and down Penistone Road with cans, and I'd advised two of these lads earlier on that they weren't going to get in with this drink. It wasn't aggressive nastiness. It was like 'Look, we're telling you now, you're not coming in with those cans, so bugger off and don't let me see you with those cans again.' I remember these lads being a bit cheeky and that's why we arrested them. We'd turned our backs and they immediately doubled back and tried to sneak in at the turnstile, and that was immediately after we'd told them to clear off for half an hour. That was the main reason why they got locked up. They'd had one warning and they hadn't taken it. We went in and filled in the quick Gen 28s [police arrest forms] that we used to do at a football match and the two lads went into the police bus. It was about 2.40pm when we came out and the atmosphere had changed. I felt that there was more confusion and more buzzing than there normally was on a match-day. There were Liverpool fans coming up, trying to get in with Liverpool-end tickets. They were coming to the turnstiles on Penistone Road and saying 'Will you let us in here? We can't get in the other side.' 'No, you can't come in here.'

Lord Justice Taylor, interim report, paragraphs 55, 56 and 196

There were some 74 shops with off-licences in and around Sheffield. In general they opened at 8am. Liverpool supporters did visit them but the evidence did not suggest a great amount of alcoholic drink was bought there. Opening time at public houses was in general 11am. Some remained closed all day. Of the others, some 72, mostly in the city, were frequented by local patrons only. Some 23 public houses, however, served over a hundred Liverpool supporters each. Another 51 served more than 20 each. Little trouble was reported, but many supporters drank enough to affect their mood. At first excitement: later frustration. Of those who arrived at 2.30pm or after, very many had been drinking at public houses or had brought drink from home or an off-licence. I am satisfied on the evidence, however, that the great majority were not drunk nor even the worse for drink. The police witnesses varied on this. Some described a high proportion as drunk, as 'lager-louts' or even as 'animals'. Others described a generally normal crowd with an unco-operative minority who had drunk too much. In my view some officers, seeking to rationalise their loss of control, overestimated the drunken element in the crowd. There certainly was such an element. There were youngsters influenced by drink and bravado pushing impatiently at the rear of the crowd thereby exacerbating the crush. But the more convincing police witnesses, including especially Detective Superintendent McKay and Chief Inspector Creaser as well as a number of responsible civilian witnesses, were in my view right in describing this element as a minority. Those witnesses attributed the crush to the sheer numbers of fans all anxious to gain entry. There was no criticism of the crowd by any of the witnesses in the period up to 2.30pm or even 2.35pm. What happened then was not a sudden deterioration in the mood or sobriety of those assembled there. No doubt those coming behind would have had more to drink and would have included the unruly minority. But the crisis developed because this very large crowd became packed into a confined turnstile area and its very density hampered its passage through the turnstiles.

John Williams

The Liverpool end at Hillsborough was reachable only via Leppings Lane itself. Other approaches had been blocked off by the police to prevent rival fans mixing outside. By 2.30pm, crowds at the end of the road near the turnstiles were becoming uncontrollably large and the narrowing area around the turnstiles was choked with people. The police had made no attempt to isolate and filter out the unlucky ones who had travelled without tickets.

There were no identifiable queues to the entrances, just a claustrophobic free-for-all of fans fighting for access. At the £14-a-head North Stand entrances the single police officer we saw was helpless to intervene and stem the flow of events. (His senior was later in tears.) At the nearby terrace turnstiles a police horse could hardly move for crowd pressure. Older men were painfully squeezed inside; women were protected from the crush by their partners. It was already becoming frightening and dangerous outside. Chaotic.

Lord Justice Taylor, interim report, paragraphs 31 and 32

In summary, the south and east sides of the ground accommodated some 29,800 whose access on the day was through 60 turnstiles. The other two sides of the ground, north and west, with a capacity of 24,256 were fed solely from the Leppings Lane entrance where there were only 23 turnstiles.

Jenni Hicks, North Stand

I was sitting in my seat just before two o'clock. I can remember finding my seat and of course, as you do, you settle and look round the ground. And I can remember looking at the Leppings Lane end and thinking 'Where are all the Liverpool supporters?' I looked to the opposite end, to the Kop where the Nottingham Forest supporters were, and it was very full. That end was what I expected. The Liverpool end wasn't what I had expected. The only place that seemed to be packed were those two pens in the middle. (I didn't realise they were pens at the time, by the way.) At two o'clock, Pens 3 and 4 looked to me what you would expect. But you could have virtually parked cars in the side terracing. And it was such a contrast to the Forest end of the ground. And that, basically, was my first impression.

I sat down and I was slightly bored actually. I was on my own. I was just looking round and then, I think it was about half past two, I started to feel quite uncomfortable. I wasn't happy about the situation on the Leppings Lane end. I could see more and more people coming into that middle bit and the sides didn't seem to be filling up at the same rate. There were still massive gaps and spaces on the side terracing and the contrast became even greater. For some reason I assumed that they [Trevor, Sarah and Victoria] would be on the side, because I knew that Trevor wouldn't normally stand behind the goal. And I was looking round to see if I could see them because you could actually see individuals on the near side-terracing. I was looking round to see if I could spot them to give them a wave. I couldn't spot them and I thought 'Oh, that's strange, perhaps they've gone to the other side of the terrace', and the other end was quite a distance away whereas, because of the glass, I could lean over and see across to this side.

There was an elderly chap sitting next to me. I'd never met the guy in my life before and I was so concerned that I passed comment to him on the situation. I said 'This doesn't look right to me.' When you have been to a lot of matches, your instinct tells you when something is not right. I thought 'This just isn't right, it's coming up to twenty to three and this is not how it should be on a semi-final day.' We are not talking about a League game, we are talking about an FA Cup semi-final. This is a big game. And I just felt quite uncomfortable that this wasn't right. The swaying domino effect was going on and then I thought 'Why isn't the crowd moving out?' I didn't know there were pens. I assumed it to be like the Kop. And I thought 'Well, people aren't going to be there deliberately, they are going to move if they can, because there is a natural spread, isn't there?' The only time there isn't a natural spread is when there is something in the way to stop you going. And I kept thinking 'Why aren't they moving out?'

Lord Justice Taylor, interim report, paragraph 28

Unlike the Kop end, the West Terracing has not only crush barriers parallel with the goal line but radial fences at right angles to it, dividing the area into pens. This division was begun after an FA Cup semi-final in 1981 when crushing occurred due to overcrowding and gates had to be opened. It proceeded in stages . . . The first section of the West Terracing moving south to north contains gates 1 and 2 and is known as Pens 1 and 2 although in fact constituting only one pen. Next is Pen 3 with one gate; next Pen 4 with one gate; Pen 5, which is extremely narrow, was intended as a sterile area to divide Pen 4 from Pen 6. This was to isolate home and away fans on occasions when both might be accommodated on the West Terracing in separate pens. Finally there is Pen 7 at the north-west corner. Pens 5, 6 and

7 each have a perimeter gate. At the back of the pens, under the front of the west stand, there is a gate in each radial fence. When those gates are open, the back row of the terracing is intended to permit access from pen to pen along the whole west side. In practice, when substantial numbers are present, those gateways are not readily visible or accessible. The present layout of the pens, fences, crush barriers and gates has resulted from a series of piecemeal changes. The nature and effect of those changes must be considered later.

Simon Pinnington, Liverpool fan from Birkenhead

My friend is relatively short in height so we stood towards the front of Pen 4. At 2.30pm my friend became anxious that he would not be able to see clearly and suggested that we move back up the steps. We would occasionally say the same thing at the countless other games that we attended together and I would always say that once the crowd settled etc., he would be able to see perfectly. This time, however, I agreed with him and we moved back up the steps. I don't know why I agreed, it was just fate. Looking back, if we had stayed where we were we would have both probably been killed.

Trevor Hicks

I kept having a look over and obviously it was starting to get a bit busy in there. I'm almost convinced it was as early as 2.30 when it started to look naughty. Obviously you can appreciate that the trauma you go through on a day like that wrecks your memory banks a little bit, and what was a minute seems like an hour, but I have a recollection that it was perhaps as early as about twenty to three when I was starting to get concerned. I'd moved from my position by then because I was getting concerned. I knew roughly where the girls would be and that looked as though it was one of the worst areas in terms of being very tightly packed. The chap next to me, his son was also in Pen 4. We were chatting. We said it looked a bit bloody awful in there, and yet at our side it was still fairly light, particularly in the corner where we were. As you went towards the fence behind the goal it was busier. And it was quite tightly packed towards the back, I think. That's why I don't remember the gate being in the radial fence, because there was enough people to cover that, and yet down towards the front I remember there were several areas where you could actually see the blue painting of the fence. One of the things that really got me alarmed, around a quarter to three, was when I saw this old chap. He'd be in his sixties, I would have guessed, grey hair, and he was pressed against the fence, slightly twisted, and he wasn't moving. His face looked pale. I vaguely see him still to this day, stuck. I never saw him come out but I've seen him on some of the police video—I've been through that with a fine-tooth comb many times—so I know that he did and I know he lived, but at the time all I could see was what looked like a dead man pinned up against the railings. I have a recollection of his tongue hanging out and you could see he was in bother, and people against the fence were getting very agitated. This is when we had the incidents with the two police officers on the steps. I could have literally reached up and touched the toes of these police officers. Given that yard plus another six feet, it was my opinion they could see exactly what was going on.

Lord Justice Taylor, interim report, paragraphs 49 and 50

The nerve centre for police control is the control room or box situated at the south-west corner of the ground between the south stand and Pen 1 of the West Terracing. The box is elevated and reached by a number of steps. It has windows commanding views across the pitch and straight along the line of the west perimeter fence. The box is very small and has seats for only three officers. Superintendent Murray was in control of it and was advisor to Mr Duckenfield as he had been to Mr Mole the year before. Next to him sat Sergeant Goddard who operated the radios. The third seat was for Police Constable Ryan who operated the telephone and public address systems. At the back of the box stood Police Constable Bichard, who was in control of the police closed-circuit television system operated by a row of consoles on a bench in front of him and behind the three seated officers. There were five television screens showing views of five roving cameras fixed at high points on the stands and directed both inside and outside the ground. There was also a master screen which flicked in rotation from one camera view to another and which made a video recording. The cameras have a zoom facility to close in on any point of interest. Specifically, there were good camera views of the west terracing, of the Leppings Lane turnstiles and beyond them of Leppings Lane itself.

Trevor Hicks

I don't care what anybody tells me, I don't care if they all go to heaven afterwards, but I cannot see how those police officers, with the aid of CCTV [closed-circuit television] in particular, where you can pick out an individual at a great distance, didn't realise what was going on. We were actually pleading with these two officers on the steps. I'm shouting out 'Can't you see what's going on, for Christ's sake, there's a problem?' I had my leather jacket and jeans on and I remember I came out with a statement, roughly verbatim: 'If I had my sodding suit on you'd take notice of me, but because I've got my leather jacket on I'm just a bloody football supporter. Can't you see there's a problem? You must be able to fucking see.' I think those were the words I used. I'm a Freeman of the City of London, and I was given that honour for my work looking after civil buildings like the Old Bailey and loads of foreign embassies. I had nearly seven years of very close contact with the police at a very senior level, police security, the lot, so I'd seen the bad side of being a policeman, the family difficulties, the divorce rate, but I had the utmost respect for them. If I look back, I was very much an Establishment man. I was managing director of a company working for a household name in security. I'd become a Freeman of the City, and was very much a pillar of society, if I can use a cliché, and yet I was still a football supporter. Many of my peer group used to think I was crazy that I would go all the way to Liverpool to watch a game of football and drive all the way back again, but they don't realise how important it was to us as a family. It was the one thing that we shared totally. Vicki had her ice-skating, Sarah was going off to university, they all had their own groups of friends, I was away a lot with my job, so the football was the family trip together, at least every other Saturday and quite a few besides. Normally I had to wear a suit, so at weekends I like to get in my casual gear. It wasn't dressing for the occasion, it was more practical and in most cases more comfortable. I did like to be different at weekends. I remember saying that to this policeman and I remember feeling the despair that because I was a football fan my opinions didn't matter. I remember saying to him 'If I'd had my effing suit on you'd have took some notice of me.' All I wanted was for him to do something. Now it was clear to me, it was clear to most of the people in the small group around me. We were all calling up and nobody was taking any notice. The police were looking to the area where the problems were. This is why I can't understand that they didn't realise what was happening. Even if they made all the mistakes of letting people in and of opening the gates, the biggest mistake of all was to not to start the rescue operation quickly enough.

Graham Kelly

Primarily, the organisation of the match is delegated to the host club so you liaise with the secretary or the chief executive of the host club, making sure that all the wheels are moving round smoothly. You have people to meet at the host club, representatives of the two clubs, and specific functions are carried out by members of FA staff who will report to me if there are any problems. So other members of staff were there, carrying out particular functions, liaising with the referee, liaising with the club secretary and so on. I think every football match I go to is a working day. I don't pretend that I don't go to enjoy football matches but I'm always looking at games from a particular angle, either the referee or the law changes or the behaviour of the crowd or the behaviour of the players, so to that extent it is work, although I enjoy it as I enjoy most parts of my job.

I don't recall taking my seat particularly early. I can't recall what time it was. My seat was A25. It was on the front row of the directors' box, next to the chairman of the host club, who said to me as we watched the crowd and savoured the atmosphere of the rival chanting in the build-up to the game 'This is just what Maggie Thatcher cannot understand: the atmosphere, the feeling, the emotion, the actual feeling of being there at a big game. She's concerned about the identity-card issue and putting football in a box and hoping the problem will go away.' Or words to that effect. And I said 'Yes'. That was one reflection that remained with me for a long time. I don't recall any problems being reported to me. I can't recall at this stage whether there were any deliberations. It certainly doesn't figure large in my mind at this stage.

Rob White

Just after I went through the entrance gates (towards the turnstiles], the mounted policeman moved so as to hold up the crowd in the street and I could see that, gradually, the number of people waiting to get past him was building up. There did not appear to be any other assistance being given to control the number of people still in the street outside. Again, I thought how much better the situation had been with last year's marshalling. After a short pause, more people were let in behind me, but I had not moved at all because the crowd still in front of me seemed to be in exactly the same position as it had been when I was allowed through the entrance gates myself. This meant that I began to feel uneasy as the whole area was becoming very crowded indeed. Before long, a crush began to develop and people were then slowly being carried along in the general direction of the turnstiles.

I had earlier put my hand in my pocket to make sure that my ticket was safe, but within a few minutes, the crush had become so intense that I was unable to move my arm sufficiently to take my hand out of my pocket again. I could not move in any direction, other than that in which the crowd was slowly moving—towards the turnstiles. We seemed to be forced to take a couple of short steps forwards by the weight of people behind us, and then the crowd would stop for a while.

Because of my height, I was actually able to see where I was going, although I had no control whatsoever over the way that I was being carried forward. However, there were many shorter women and children all around me who were not even able to see where they were, or where they were going. What is more, because of their size they were in even more discomfort than I was, and I was becoming very anxious myself. The increasing number of screams, and the frantic shouting that was going on near me, indicated that I was not alone. However, further back many people seemed unaware of this and they continued their singing. I was able to see over most people's heads in front of me, and it did not appear as though there was a free-flow of people through the turnstiles at all. Instead, the build-up of people at the front of the worsening crush was hampering those people who were nearest to the turnstiles, as they tried to get through them. The reason that the crowd was moving forward did not seem to be because people were passing through the turnstiles, but rather that the pressure of people behind us was increasing. Certainly, the further forward I moved, the more painful the crush became. However, there was nothing that I, or anyone around me, could do about that because we simply could not move against the crowd. The only way to get out of the crush seemed to be to wait until we had reached the front and then had a chance to get through the turnstiles. Clearly, that was going to take some time, but we had no choice.

The mounted policeman near to the turnstiles was shouting very angrily at people near him to move back, but it was simply impossible for them to move at all. Those of us further back, towards the middle of the crush, could not move either. Action was required at the very back of the crush. People needed to be moved at the back so that the pressure in the middle, and then at the front, could be alleviated. There was nothing to be gained from directing instructions to those who were unable to move themselves. Only by sending people backwards, starting with those already at the back, would there have been any hope of easing the pressure further forward. However, once we had passed through the outer blue entrance gates, it was not possible to move back into the street due to the vast number of people still trying to get through those gates.

There was a brick wall a few feet to my left and many people were being forced up against it. They were calling out for the crowd to ease back away from them, but none of us were able to move in order to help them. My colleague had been standing slightly nearer to the wall than I had, and initially he had been almost next to me. However, as the crowd edged forwards, it seemed as though the people nearest to the wall were, in fact, moving at a slightly slower pace than those nearer to the centre of the crush. This meant that, as I finally neared the front, I had lost sight of my colleague as he was slightly behind me, as well as to the side.

As I reached the front, I had a clearer view of the actual turnstiles and I could see that many people were being forced up against the walls in between the individual turnstiles, as well as into each other. Furthermore, a large blue concertina gate to my left [Gate B] was causing a lot of pain for those who were being pushed up against it. Many people in the crowd were calling out for the concertina gate to be opened in order to provide people with an escape route from the crush, and also to prevent anyone from being seriously hurt. These calls had continued for several minutes as I had waited for my own chance to reach the turnstiles. Even when people were level with a turnstile, it was still extremely difficult to actually pass through because so many people were also trying at the same time. At the front, the crowd was swaying from side to side so that one minute I was facing a turnstile and the next minute, a brick wall next to it. I looked across to the far turnstile over to my right, and I noticed that a young boy was being carried out, on his back, above people's heads. He was wearing a Liverpool FC tracksuit top. He was passed to a policeman who, I suppose, may have been on horseback because he was clearly visible above everyone else, although he was not in the crush himself. He was, in fact, leaning around the end of the turnstile wall in an attempt to get hold of the boy. I have since seen television coverage which shows this boy being helped to safety, so that film would help to indicate the approximate time that I managed to get into the ground, because it took me a further two or three minutes to get in. I would guess that it was about 2.40–2.45, though.

Dennis Cerrone

Obviously as the kick-off approached it was getting crowded. I was stood near one of the horses and there were a lot of people around, not pushing, all walking towards the thing, and the horse was turning and I thought 'Get out of the way.' Horses don't look where they're turning, do they? So I walked away from that. He [the mounted policeman] shouted something to me: 'All right, I won't get you', because he saw the look on my face. This must have been getting on for about half-past two. Then, at a point between two-thirty and three, it was suddenly really swarming with people. At this point I was up where the turnstiles are. There was a crush-barrier [towards Gate C]. I got trapped against that crush-barrier and I couldn't get out. They were pressing and my back was up against it. My mate was behind me and I said 'It's hurting me, I can't get out.' And they obviously couldn't move. I were trying to push them, but they were being pushed from the back and they were pushing in. The only way I could get out was to knock my hat so it fell off, and I wriggled downwards and then got out underneath on my hands and knees. I was right on the edge of the crowd, but I had to get on my hands and knees to get under the barrier. I stood up and I said to my mate 'It's getting a bit hairy, this.'

The people were shouting by then: 'Open the gates, let us through, we're getting crushed.' You could hear these voices, and somebody was passed over the top. I can't remember now whether it was a boy or a girl, but I know it was somebody young and they were passed over the top and they'd obviously been crushed but were all right. I think that was the first time that I thought 'I don't like this.' I looked across at the police and they were looking round as though they didn't quite like what was happening, even the police on horses, and they're quite experienced blokes who do it all the time. They do it at Anfield, don't they, with the crowd? The people were pushing and the horses were actually getting moved. I started to feel 'This is dangerous, somebody could fall down and they could be crushed.' And still this mass of people was coming. I got a bit annoyed because it were obvious to me that they would know when they were pushing that there were people who couldn't get through the turnstiles fast enough to get out of the way, because you can only get through at a certain rate, can't you? I thought 'They're experienced people, the fans, they'd know they're pushing people who can't get through.' The horse was trained to stop this weight of people pressing people against the turnstiles, and that's why he was getting shoved. He did a good job actually. It could have been a lot worse without him. What crossed my mind again was: 'Why are they shoving? They know there's only a certain way they can go through, why aren't they waiting for their turn?' I couldn't understand why they were pushing. I'm sure there were voices saying 'Open the gates, open the gates, open the gates', shouting and bawling out. I did start to think 'If that side gate's opened a lot of these people could get round and take a lot of this weight off.' I started thinking that would be a good idea.

Lord Justice Taylor, interim report, paragraph 67

Superintendent Marshall realised the crowd had become unmanageable. Although loth to do so, since it was contrary to basic police strategy, he decided to request the exit gates be opened to relieve the pressure. Otherwise, he feared fatalities would occur. Other senior officers outside the ground agreed. At 2.47 pm he radioed control to permit the gates to be opened. At 2.48 pm, whilst Mr Duckenfield was considering the request, Gate C opened to eject a youth who had climbed in with no ticket. Immediately, fans outside took advantage and about 150 managed to get in before a mounted officer enabled the gate to be closed again. Mr Marshall repeated his request. Still no response from control. He repeated it a third time, adding that if the gates were not opened someone was going to be killed.

Rob White

It was a huge relief to get through the turnstile because the situation outside had been deteriorating all the time. I had to wait another several minutes before my colleague managed to get through the turnstile himself. I stood in the area between the turnstiles and the tunnel entrance to the centre terrace waiting for him.

The calls that I had heard when I was outside the ground, for the large concertina gate to be opened because of the danger of people being hurt, were still audible as I stood waiting inside. A number of fans had actually climbed up on top of a wall at the side of the crush outside, and had walked along to a ledge directly above the turnstiles. A number of policemen inside the ground, between the turnstiles and the entrance to the tunnel, looked concerned at this, so they went over to stand just below the ledge. I could not hear what was said, but the fans held up their still intact tickets and were then allowed to jump down to the safety of the area where I was waiting. I do not believe that, under normal circumstances, this type of action would have been permitted. I therefore presume that the policemen who allowed it to happen were sufficiently satisfied that the situation outside the turnstiles was such that it warranted their use of discretion as to how best to allow people into the ground. Sending those people who had climbed over the wall back outside the ground would only have added to confusion outside. I believe that this fact was recognised by the police officers inside the ground. Then I noticed my colleague come through one of the turnstiles, and we then proceeded towards the tunnel directly opposite the turnstiles which, I knew from previous visits, led to the terrace.

Lord Justice Taylor, interim report, paragraphs 44 and 45

Those entering through turnstiles A to G had three options once inside the ground. They could by moving to the right go round the south end of the West Stand and gain entry into Pens 1 and 2. They could go through the gap in the dividing wall towards the concourse behind turnstiles 11 to 16 and then round the north end of the West Stand into Pens 6 or 7. However, there were no conspicuous signs inviting them to take either of those courses. The obvious way in was straight ahead of the turnstiles where a tunnel under the middle of the West Stand gave access to Pens 3 and 4. Above the entrance in large letters was the word 'Standing' and a large letter 'B'. Thus B ticket holders were drawn towards the tunnel. The length of the tunnel is some 23 metres. It rises slightly at first then levels off but finally descends towards the terraces at a gradient of 1 in 6. As it emerges onto the terrace, the way ahead is bisected by the radial fence between Pen 3 on the right and Pen 4 on the left. A short spur of brick wall projects forward from each side of the tunnel at its mouth. Those emerging are thus guided straight forward rather than to either side.

Rob White

I only recall seeing one steward at the start of the tunnel and he was merely observing those people who were passing through the tunnel. However, there were two stewards at the foot of the steps to my right, which led to the seating in the West Stand, and they were checking tickets as people went past them and up the steps. No check was made of my ticket or, to my knowledge, of anyone else's ticket amongst those entering the tunnel.

On each of my previous visits to Hillsborough, I have stood in the area between the turnstiles and the tunnel for several minutes. Despite having looked around this area as I have waited each time, I have no recollection of any signs, or stewards, directing people to the terracing at the sides. This equally applies to my visit on 15 April [1989]. I have to say that I did not know that there was another way to gain access to the terracing, other than the way that I could actually see directly in front of me—namely through the tunnel that led to the centre section of the terracing.

I did not recall there being fencing at the sides actually on the terrace and, even if I had recalled that from my previous visits, as I could not see an alternative way onto the terrace, I'm sure I would still have walked through the tunnel. I remember that when I have visited other football grounds, such as Watford and Leicester City, which also have fences across the terraces, gates in them have been opened to allow people to pass through from one section to another. Indeed, I recall stewards at other matches using such a system to systematically fill sections of the terrace as they wanted, before closing certain side gates and then filling up another section. This prevented any one section from becoming too overcrowded. Such a system did not exist at Hillsborough. There were no gates in the side fences, as far as I could see.

The point I am making is that, despite having seen the ground before, its layout was certainly not clear to me and, in the absence of instructions or directions, I entered the terrace section by what amounted to the only way I thought was possible. I had time to survey the area, so I feel sure that someone who is in a hurry to enter the terracing, unless they were already aware of a route to the outer edges of the terrace, or were to be directed by someone, would also follow the route that I took. Of course, this route led to the most crowded part of the terrace, although from anywhere other than inside the ground it would not be possible to actually see this. Nevertheless, it is well known by anyone who has ever been to a football match, that the area directly behind a goal is a particularly popular place to stand, if that area is, of course, a terrace rather than a seating area. Consequently, such areas are always more crowded than the edges of a terrace.

As I started walking through the tunnel, I could see daylight above people's heads but I could see that the far end of the tunnel was obstructed by the sheer number of people congregated around it. Although I thought, at that moment, that this was only to be expected for such a big match just before kick-off, I remember thinking when I actually reached the far end of the tunnel, that I was completely surprised by just how full the area already was.

I found it difficult even getting through this wall of people onto the start of the terrace, but as I did, I soon realised that it would be best not to try and move directly towards the goal, because that area was already far too packed. It was also difficult to move to either side, so the only direction in which I could see any hope of finding a place to stand, in any degree of comfort, was to move diagonally forward. This is what I did. In fact, I moved diagonally to my right and my colleague followed behind me. As I edged my way forward, I could see that there appeared to be slightly more room nearer the front. In any case, I wanted to try and get a clearer view as much as anything at this time.

I was already aware that the area that I was standing in was almost certainly more densely populated than it had been at any stage of last year's semi-final. I was particularly worried about this, in view of the fact that I knew how many people were still trying to get into the ground. I thought that it would just not be possible to accommodate any more people in the centre section of the terrace. I reassured myself, however, that there did appear to be far more spaces on the side sections of the terracing and that, therefore, people still trying to get in would be directed to those areas, surely. It would be clear, at a glance, for anyone inside the ground that this centre-section was dangerously overcrowded, whereas there was still plenty of room on the side section beyond the side fence. This had not been visible before I had gone through the tunnel, though. I began to wish that I had been able to stand in the side section myself, but I could not see any way of getting to it.

Peter Jackson, outside the ground

It was tight on the chest because it was getting very packed. Pete Garrett was in front of me. He's taller than me. My nose was up against his back. If he moved, his elbows were going into my chest or whatever. It was not fun. Moira had given Pete the ticket she had. She'd wanted to go but hadn't gone because it was Sheffield Wednesday. This wasn't a premonition, it was 'This is not a particularly happy ground to go to.' Everyone knew that Leppings Lane was notorious for being a bad 'spec', if you can call it that. And I remember Pete to this day turning round and saying 'It's a good job Moira didn't come or she would be dead now.' And she would have been. There's no way that a pregnant woman could have coped with it. There were people who were passing out, people who were openly showing their discomfort, whose breathing was heavy, etc. Despite the closeness of the crowd we managed to make way for people who were in obvious discomfort. For example, we tried to get women in on one or two occasions. There was an old guy who was in trouble who we tried to get through to the front. But that was an effort to do that. There was a lot of discontent, as you'd expect, from the crowd: 'Where's the steward?' 'Where's the police?' 'What's going on?' But you couldn't see any policemen, you couldn't see any stewards, until you got to the turnstile. And I remember that there was one bobby situated between the two turnstiles that we went into. He wasn't doing anything. He was making no attempt to even organise the final thrust, if you like, and you had to set yourself up to get through the turnstile because if you didn't you were just as likely to end up against the wall and going back again. It was absolutely ridiculous. We got in and I lost Pete and Larry completely. I went the wrong way because there's no signs in Hillsborough to say 'Leppings Lane terrace that way', 'That way for the Stand entrance'. So I went the wrong way and realised I'd gone the wrong way. There were policemen inside and I remember I stopped to complain about what was going on outside. Other people were stopping to complain, and I think Pete stopped from what he told me afterwards, but by this time it was five to three, three minutes to three, and the inclination was to get in, which we did.

Eddie Spearritt

Because we had tickets, my attitude was 'Let them all go in, and once they're all in then Adam and I will go in.' Obviously people want to see all the game, but I don't think they're unduly bothered if they miss the first five minutes, or even ten minutes, provided they get in, in safety. So as I say we just stood to the side and met my mate. We were having a laugh with him and Adam and I were just talking. Obviously we were seeing what was going on but we weren't taking an awful lot of notice because we weren't actually involved in it.

Lord Justice Taylor, interim report, paragraph 67

In the control room, Mr Duckenfield had not made a decision. Mr Murray asked him 'Are you going to open the gates?' Mr Duckenfield gave the order and Sgt Goddard radioed to Mr Marshall 'Open the gates.' Neither the Club control room nor any police officers inside the turnstiles were told of this order before or after it was given or of any action it would require.

Eddie Spearritt

We stood there talking and the next thing this gate opened, which I now know to be Gate C, and we were allowed to go in. I think we must have been one of the first to go through the gate. Because as I say we got to the gate, the main gate at the turnstile at about half past two and we didn't enter the so-called queue for the turnstile . . . although there certainly weren't 'queues'. We must have been the first ones to go in. I hadn't been in that end, I didn't know the layout, and Adam hadn't, and as we walked through all that hit you was the tunnel, and you can see the pitch, so we went through there. We got to the front. I do not remember actually going down the tunnel. It's obvious that I did because I ended up in Pen 4, but that's one of the things that is blacked out in my mind. Even getting down to the front is basically blocked out. We ended up right at the front. The perimeter gate leading on to the pitch was within arm's length. And I'd said to Adam when we got there 'Well, this is OK.' Obviously with children the best place for them to see is when they're right at the front. I'd said to Adam that it was crazy that I still had my two tickets in my inside pocket. All the hassle we'd had in getting them and we hadn't gone through a turnstile. We hadn't seen any stewards or police to take them off us. And he said 'Yes, Dad, you know it's crazy.' Then the players came out and Alan Hansen was playing and of course he hadn't played all year and, apart from Dalglish himself, Adam and I both used to regard him as the boss man. He was really a class player. So we were really made up. I said to him 'Hansen's playing.' He said 'That's great, Dad.' And that was it then really, because we never actually saw the players coming down to the goal.

Dr Colin Flenley

We arrived at the ground with probably about twenty minutes to go and the atmosphere was different outside. There didn't seem to be any order to the queuing up at the turnstiles. There was no police cordon. It was quite crowded outside the turnstiles. It must have been about twenty to three, quarter to three. There was no queue and as more and more people tried to get in through the turnstiles we were getting more and more squashed. I'm quite tall, just over six foot, and I can remember feeling quite hot and het up. I mean, I'd been in the Kop many times and I'd never felt that crushed before and this was outside the ground.

There were two policemen on horseback, I remember, and some people were shouting to them 'Can't you do something?' They really didn't seem to know what to do. They were talking to each other, and I can remember one of the policemen raising his voice at the other policeman, because it seemed to be getting het up between the two of them. There were also kids climbing up on to the fence and going over into the crowd that way, trying to get out of the pressure. I remember actually thinking to myself 'Why don't they just open the turnstile and just let us in?' There was a little chap next to me who was feeling quite faint and we were trying to push back to make space for him to breathe. I'm quite tall and I got my head above so I could breathe quite easy, but I felt pressurized. I felt odd. Then all of a sudden the gate round the side opened and I thought 'Great, we're all right now', so we went in. I think there were two policemen, as far as I can remember, standing on either side of the gate.

Dennis Cerrone

When Gate C first opened, a couple of dozen fans ran through quickly, some even waving tickets and body-swerving past me. At this point I'm stood inside the gate with my arms out, saying 'Walk, walk!' I think it just goes against a policeman's grain: you don't like people running. But soon after, as everyone realised that the gate had been opened on purpose, to release the pressure outside, fans were just walking smartly through, again waving tickets. I wasn't making any attempt to take the tickets, because there were just too many of them. The only thing I did, I stopped one person who'd got a bottle, and I took it off him and threw it in the river. I thought 'I bet I'm on video throwing a bottle in the river and I'll be up answering questions.' You know how your mind works. I didn't want to put it down because somebody would pick it up again, and I didn't want to put it in the bin because somebody would take it out again, so I thought 'I'll throw it in the river and nobody can get it.' But I remember thinking 'I wish I hadn't thrown it, somebody's bound to clock me on video and they'll be wanting to know what I'm throwing in the river', but it shows you how the mind works, doesn't it?

Lord Justice Taylor, interim report, paragraph 70

The largest entry, however, was through Gate C. In the five minutes it was open about 2,000 fans passed through it steadily at a fast walk. Some may have had tickets for the stands. No doubt some had no tickets at all. The majority had tickets for the terraces. Of these, some found their way either right to Pens 1 and 2 or left through the dividing wall to 6 and 7. But a large proportion headed straight for the tunnel in front of them.

Dr Colin Flenley

I remember a teenager fell over in front of me and he got picked up. And I remember as you went through you got channelled towards the tunnel, because there were no signposts showing where to go, and I actually started to go down the tunnel and then I remembered and came back out and made my way round the side. If you didn't know there was a side entrance you wouldn't be able to find it. I have another memory of that. Just coming back out of the tunnel there were two staircases up to the stand, the seated area above, and they've got gates on them. And they had stewards at the bottom stopping people going in. That's a vivid memory of mine. So I went round the side and it was quite free and easy where I was. It wasn't crowded at all.

We were just standing below the police look-out box, and this must have been about five to three.

Rob White

With the match due to begin within a matter of minutes, I found myself standing with a barrier directly in front of me. I know, from past experience of capacity matches, that it is usually far more comfortable to stand with a barrier just behind rather than just in front of you. The only direction in which I could move was forward, so I decided to duck underneath the barrier. A number of other people did the same thing, and so although I stood up just the other side of the barrier, the additional people who followed me caused me to be pushed further forward, and nearer to the perimeter fence. At this stage, however, there still appeared to be more room where I was standing than where I had previously been standing, and I was relieved that the barrier was no longer immediately in front of me. There were no more barriers between me and the perimeter fence—only people. There is always some crowd movement during a match, and I feared that I would continually be pushed up against the barrier unless I moved. My colleague had not ducked under the barrier, though. Instead, he had managed to move backwards slightly and he was standing about 10 feet behind me.

Gradually, I was feeling the pressure of the crowd increasing all around and it was becoming very uncomfortable. I was now standing about three feet away from the perimeter fence in the centre section of the terrace slightly to the right of the goal. As I stood there, I was acutely aware that the situation was becoming rather desperate, and that it was in danger of becoming extremely serious. I had never experienced anything like it before. There seemed to be no control, whatsoever, on the number of people being allowed in.

Even before the teams were on the pitch, people all around me, but mainly in front of me, were calling out for someone to help them. Some were screaming and some who were able to move themselves were trying to climb out. Their attempts to escape were seemingly interpreted by the policemen on the other side of the fence as an attempt to invade the pitch. I could hear fans protesting as they were being restrained on top of the fences by policemen. Someone actually called out that he thought that some people at the front, by the fence, were dying, but he was pushed back off the top of the fence and onto the terrace again. Clearly, those early warnings were not being heeded, despite the increasingly widespread screams and pleas for assistance.

At this stage, although I could not move from the spot where I was standing, I had been able to raise my arms from by my sides to steady myself and so avoid falling over if the crowd began to sway. At the time, that seemed a natural reaction, although there were almost certainly too many people already packed in to enable such a sway to take place. Gradually, however, the situation seemed to be getting worse and worse, and I could feel that more and more people were being allowed onto the centre terrace, despite the already dangerous overcrowding. The crush was getting tighter all the time.

There were now more policemen and some St John ambulance men gathering on the other side of the fence obscuring my view of the pitch, so I did not see when the teams actually came out on the pitch, but I heard a roar from the crowd which signalled the moment that this did take place. I remember thinking 'God, no. Please don't bring them out now. Things will only get worse.'

Regrettably, that roar from the crowd coincided with an increase in pressure on the terrace as people who had not, at that time, taken up their positions, would have been alerted to the fact that the match was about to start, and they would be rushing so as not to miss anything. Unfortunately, my fears had been realised.

Stephen Hendry, aged 19, Liverpool fan from Birkenhead

Once inside the ground in the actual stadium itself the problem seemed much worse, there was lots of pushing and jostling, which we thought would settle down after about ten minutes. It didn't. What happened after the teams came out was a nightmare. More and more people started coming into the ground and the crushing got worse. We got pushed to the front of the ground, towards the barrier. People were screaming to push the crowd back. The situation became worse and worse, the crushing got worse as more people came in behind, and were now screaming in pain as they moved and got crushed against the barrier. Now people had been put on the floor under the barrier and were getting trampled by fans, helpless in the surge. The seriousness was now beginning to show, people were unable to breathe in the crowd, I for one could, but still the police did not open the gate at the front of the terrace. People were screaming and three fans climbed over the fence because of what was happening.

Rob White

From that moment on, I found myself pressed up against the person in front of me and both my arms were pinned between other people's bodies. That then meant that the only part of my own body that I was capable of moving was my head. Although my whole body was in severe discomfort, my left arm, left leg and back were in the most pain. In particular, a teenage girl who had been standing next to me had her head twisted round facing me, and the side of her face was being forced up against the upper part of my left arm. The excruciating pain in my arm was almost unbearable, and I feared that my arm was simply going to snap under the pressure. All I could see of the girl was her face, as the rest of her body was being smothered by other people. She was clearly in a great deal of pain. Her head was in a vice between my arm and the body of another man behind her. It was impossible for any of us to move at all.

I could tell that the poor girl was having difficulty breathing and she was incapable of speaking, because her face was being squeezed so tightly that it was being contorted. Her expression did not seem to change and her tear-filled eyes were just staring straight at me, pleading with me to help her. Although her eyes were full of tears, it was almost as though the pressure being exerted on her head was preventing those tears from flowing down her face. As I found myself captivated by this desperate sight next to me, I could feel a foot tapping on mine, gently at first, but soon it became more agitated, and I felt sure that it must have belonged to the girl because it had only started when I first looked at her. I knew that signal meant that she needed help urgently. I turned my head and saw a policewoman directly in front of me, so I called out to her. She looked at me as I started shouting, so I know that she heard me. I pleaded with her to do something for the girl next to me, either herself, or to call for assistance. She simply looked away.

I asked myself why there were so many people on the other side of the fence looking at the situation, but just standing still and not actually moving? We were the ones not able to move. We needed to be helped by those who could move. Then I noticed someone running towards the fence. At last, I thought, someone was going to help us. As the man reached the fence, he lifted up a camera to his face and then just walked away in search of another picture!

Lord Justice Taylor, interim report, paragraph 48

The club provided 376 stewards, gatemen and turnstile operators for duty on 15 April. The stewards were briefed as to their duties on the morning of the match by police inspectors and were allocated round the ground. They wore yellow tabards. The club's control room, situated below the south stand, could communicate by VHF radio with the stewards. Closed circuit television was installed by the club with screens in their control room showing all the turnstiles round the ground. A computerised counting system was incorporated in the turnstiles. This flashed onto a screen in the club control room the running total of spectators passing through the turnstiles section by section. Thus, at the Leppings Lane end, there would be separate running totals for turnstiles 1 to 10 (North Stand), turnstiles 11 to 16 (West Stand), and turnstiles A to G (West Terraces). When the total for any section was within 15 per cent of its permitted capacity a warning pulse showed on the screen. For the West Terracing that warning would occur when the numbers were within 15 per cent of the total terrace capacity of 10,100. What the system could not do was monitor the distribution of fans on the terracing, pen by pen. It could give no warning therefore if one pen was full beyond its safe capacity.

Anonymous Male Spectator

You've come through a tunnel and if you look back there is just a high wall, and you've got fencing in the front, so you were literally penned in and you knew there was no way out, panic began inside. That's when the horror began really. It was very hot, the sun made it worse, claustrophobic was an understatement and the pressure on your body was incredible really.

Eddie Spearritt

I've been in the Kop when there has been about 28,000 people and when you're in a surge you're hit from behind and you just flow with it. Hillsborough wasn't like that. Not for Adam and myself anyway. It was just like a vice which was getting slowly tighter and tighter, and Adam fainted. I tried to lift him up but I had this massive fence in front of me with spikes pointing in to you. There was a policeman on the track. He must have been five or six feet away and I was screaming and begging him to open the perimeter gate. You can scream your head off when you're screaming for your son's life. You really are screaming, and he didn't open that gate. The policeman was about five or six feet away from me. I'm right at the front. I'll be perfectly honest with you, I must have been like a lunatic anyway. I'm screaming at him that Adam had fainted and I think at one stage I even said he was dying and, as I say, the policeman didn't open the gate.

I couldn't lift Adam up because, one, possibly I was too weak, and two, it was that tight. So I started punching the fence in the hope that I could punch it down, which again was a futile gesture really. I didn't succeed in doing it. That was basically it. One of the things that annoyed me greatly is this magical six minutes past three. That's when the game was stopped and basically that to my mind is when the authorities finally said to themselves 'Oh, there is some problems here, we must do something about it.' Because of the time the players came out, I know basically what time it was when Adam fainted. It was 2.54 or 2.55 and no later than 2.55. It was just bedlam. I can remember someone actually walking over my head, his feet actually being on my head. Obviously panic comes into it, doesn't it? We're all human beings. It's not a daily occurrence when you're getting squashed to death, so people were panicking and, God forbid, I don't know what I did to other people, I just don't.

It was absolute bedlam and people were all screaming at the police to get the gates open and what-have-you, and begging for help. In the times that I'm talking about I didn't see any policemen responding. Since then the constable that I'm talking about has said that he actually opened the gate, and Lord Justice Taylor and Mr Andrew Collins QC [counsel to the Taylor Inquiry] said in the closing statements that he'd got questions to answer because there was other police that arrived at 2.58pm or 2.59pm, and they say that when they got there the gate was closed. The policeman that opened the gate said 'If I'm wrong I'm going to get a right rollicking over this', but it was at 2.59pm that that gate was opened. We're talking about Adam fainting at 2.54pm or 2.55pm so you're talking about quite a few minutes. And the next thing I remember, and again it's very vague—I'm only basically going on what people have told me—is that I woke up in hospital on the Sunday evening to find that Adam had died.

Anonymous Male Spectator

We couldn't get back through the tunnel. People were still trying to cram in [and others] were trying to get back out because they realised how bad a crush it was. So you sort of stayed put. It was then that kick-off time arrived. The crush seemed to be worse again and we saw people trying to climb up onto the fence, trying to get over the fence. They were being told by the police to get back in. We tried as much as we could to go backwards towards the stand. By then a couple of people had started to get pulled up into the stand which made a bit more room, so we edged towards the face of the stand. I boosted my brother up. I was lifted up and there was about four fellows leaning over the stand trying to pull me up. They got hold of my arms and lifted. As they lifted there was a bad crush again below me and my legs just jammed and these four able-bodied lads were trying to pull me up and they couldn't. I was sort of suspended there, and it seemed like about five minutes, but it must have been one minute. Once we were in the stand we turned and looked at the pitch. You could tell people were very badly injured to say the least.

Anonymous Female Spectator

There was a bloke dying next to me. He was a really big bloke, like a docker. His mate was holding him up, trying to stop him from falling. The pushing from the back just forced you down. I was looking at the ground and thinking 'If you go down there you're dead.' The smell was unbelievable I can tell you. I was only at armpit level of most people because of my size. I was trying to force my head up in order to breathe. I remember shouting at the bloke next to me: 'Move your arm, move your arm, you're killing me.' I looked around and it was obvious that he was dead. His eyes, his tongue, I could tell. I've still got scars from the fencing. I had a black eye for months and criss-cross marks on my back from the wire mesh fence for ages.

Dr Colin Flenley

There were players on the pitch. I can remember them kicking a ball around. But I was looking over to where the crowd was in the central area and I could see people being hauled up to the seated area above. I remember turning to the chap next to me, who I didn't know, and I said 'There's going to be another Heysel here, with the weight of the people being lifted up on to the seated area.' My vision was that the seated area was going to collapse. I wasn't interested in what was going on on the pitch. I kept looking in the central area, and there were people around me throwing coins and pebbles up at the police control box to tell them to have a look at what was going on. I remember someone shouting 'Can't you see what's going on over there?' and they didn't seem to be wanting to take any notice. The central section looked very packed. I'd got no idea what was going on underneath the heads and things. It just looked very packed to me. Especially from where I was standing. I was quite comfortable with plenty of space around me. And then a photographer went up the steps to the police stanchion and he seemed to be taking photographs. I remember he got coins thrown at him because I think the fans almost felt he was prying and perhaps would create a bad image of what was going on. Other fans were starting to go over onto the pitch and I had visions of the game being stopped or delayed and we'd get a bad name for what was going on. I just thought it was people trying to get out. I couldn't see why on earth it should be a pitch invasion, it was a nice happy day. I just thought 'These people wanted to get out because it's too crowded in there.'

Graham Kelly

My first recollection was of the people trying to scale the fence. Like the majority of people present, I immediately jumped to the wrong conclusion and thought it was a behaviour problem rather than a safety problem. And then it just developed from there.

Anonymous Male Spectator

I can still see them now. I saw this lad trying to pull himself up. He just sort of disappeared, then came back up and I said 'That kid's dead.' Then a girl, just like a piece of wood floating on water. The copper in front of us was just looking. I shouted at him to do something but he just sort of looked blank.

Jenni Hicks

I still wasn't happy about it. And then one or two people started coming over [the fence]. It started off with a trickle, one or two just coming over. And I thought 'Why are they coming over? They should be moving that way, not coming over.' They were coming over that way and being put into the side pens. I don't remember the kick-off. I didn't see any of the match at all. I was concerned because they started coming over and people round about were saying 'Oh no, we are not going to have trouble here.' And I thought 'No, if you are going to have a pitch invasion, you don't get a pitch invasion before the game. People have paid £6 for these tickets—a lot of money. They want to enjoy the match. They have come here to see a good game of football.' You get a pitch invasion with the exuberance at the end if you are going to get one. When you have won, you have had a great victory, everybody's happy. In my experience of going to football matches, if you are going to get a pitch invasion, that is when you are going to get it, at the end. They wouldn't want to do anything to stop the game starting. And, what I remember of it, nobody went on to the pitch. It wasn't a pitch invasion. The first time people went onto the pitch was when they were carried on unconscious.

I was very, very concerned and, obviously, from a totally selfish point of view, I was concerned most of all about my two daughters and my husband. I said to this chap next to me 'My two daughters and husband might be in there.' By this time he was an old friend. I had known him for virtually half an hour, but, because of the situation, he was looking for them, and he became my friend. He was asking 'What colour hair have they got? What are they wearing?' He was helping me look. And I ran down the steps to the first set of terracing. And there was no way I could get down to the bottom lot which led to the pitch. I didn't know the ground. If it had been at Anfield, I would have known exactly where to go. By this time I was starting to get very, very concerned, almost on the verge of panic. You know 'What is going on here? I have got to get down and see where Sarah, Vicki and Trevor are.' But, by this time, there was a line of police along the side and nobody, but nobody, was going to get on there from the seats. And I can remember thinking 'It will be all right, just keep calm.' I was trying to keep myself calm. And this chap said 'Now look, it will be all right.' I was just looking to see if I could spot them anywhere.

R. A. Knowles, Liverpool supporter
I saw the gate between the railings of the two sections being opened but could not believe my eyes when a policewoman grabbed my small 13-year-old son and pushed him through the gate back onto the terraces. She began to scream and shout at people to clear the pitch and became almost hysterical.

Jeff Rex, Liverpool supporter living in Bristol
My main memory is that everything seemed to happen so quickly. I firstly remember when a policeman opened the small exit gate at the front and I thought for a moment that we would all somehow get out. He let a dozen or so people out and then started pushing people back in. In the crush itself how I kept my emotions under control I shall never know—perhaps it was the shock of the moment and the fact that this whole situation had come right out of the blue. I can't imagine how long the intense pressure of the crush lasted. It seemed like an eternity.

Trevor Hicks
It was just at this time when people were starting to go over the fence. They were coming over the radial fence in with us and they were beginning to go

over [the fence at the front]. As I said, the details of it are a little blurred. I can remember some incidents vividly. I can remember the incident where there was a young lad trying to come over and a policeman literally put his hand on his forehead and shoved him back.

You could tell it wasn't a pitch invasion. Anyone who knew anything about football knew there was something wrong. It's strange, I don't know if it's a trick of my memory or if there was a funny atmosphere, but there was silence among the noise. The normal roar that you would expect from your bit of the crowd was subdued. It wasn't there. There was a feeling of concern. And that concern was rapidly changing from concern into something a lot worse. The police thought they had a pitch invasion on their hands. But everybody who managed to get over the fence just collapsed on the grass. There was nobody running up the pitch.

There was this guy on the steps who I believed was Chief Superintendent Greenwood. I'm now told it couldn't have been, but it was a senior policeman. I basically said a similar thing to him again: 'Look, can't you see what's going on? There's trouble down there. It's not a pitch invasion. For Christ's sake give them a hand.' And a serial of policemen ran across just in front of us, just before this incident, I think, but it was quite obvious they were going into a restraining position. It wasn't 'Help them out', it was 'Keep them in'. And I remember saying to this guy 'Look, for Christ's sake'—or worse than that because I was getting pretty agitated by this stage—'can't you see there's a problem?' He basically looked down at me. I'll never forget his face. It was one of almost total contempt. Yes, he was concerned and, yes, he was looking, and I was perhaps an irritant to him, but we weren't being listened to. He said 'Shut your fucking prattle.' That was the famous phrase and there's no way that I got that wrong. I will never forget that, and I think this was the point where I started to get almost desolate with concern, because here was I asking the police to look after everybody's safety and suddenly you realise how vulnerable and how small you are on this big earth of ours. I mean, I've had a pretty good career and I suppose I thought I was 'King Dick'. I'm a big head in many ways, or I was, I don't think I am now. But you don't believe anything can happen. You're almost invincible and almost any problem can be thrown at you and you can overcome it. I knew roughly where the girls would be because they were always just to the right of the goal. We now know that they had their backs to that fatal barrier. In fact one of their problems was that obviously having been on the Kop they had the sense to have the barrier at their back and not at their front and from all the video evidence that we went into after the disaster it does look as though they literally had their backs to the barrier that broke. When the sea of people were washed down the terraces, then the barrier gave way. I remember seeing the girls very early on after we got in but after that I didn't. I thought they'd be OK. I knew they'd be with their friends. I mean they were fifteen and nineteen. They were teenagers now, they weren't kids.

The worst you ever thought would happen would be perhaps a broken arm or a squashed foot or something. We just never ever thought you could lose your life at a football game. I'd been in a couple of incidents at big derby games and this type of thing at Anfield, and you come out and you've got pins and needles in your arms because you haven't been able to move them around but it's never been life-threatening. I think a risk of severe discomfort was about the level of risk that you had. We had had disagreements for many years. I'd been trying to talk the girls into coming into the seats with us. I'd offered to buy them seat tickets rather than standing tickets. They loved the atmosphere on the Kop. Now, all of a sudden, the things most dear to me, my two daughters, are in trouble, perhaps no more than thirty feet away, and I was really getting concerned now, and I'm looking down at what's going on. The game's kicked off. Nobody seemed to be watching the game as far as I could see. The crowd is the whole of our concern, certainly of this small group in this corner. Now if I could see it, the police were ten feet higher so they could see it. They had cameras. They had to know there was a major crushing problem and they had to know at at least quarter to three, if not sooner. So this is why I say, no matter what else, I can never forgive Murray and Duckenfield, in particular, the two guys in charge of that control room, for not getting the rescue operation underway.

Ian Battey, Accident & Emergency, Northern General Hospital, Sheffield

I went for my tea break at three o'clock, which was standard. The tea-break for afternoon staff would have been from three till half-three, or quarter-to-four if you were lucky and nothing came through the doors. At that point we had a two-and-a-half-hour wait in the department, which was getting to the point where we were trying to chivy the medical staff along. But at three o'clock we had no indications of what was going off. Most A & E departments now have a television or something. We didn't have a radio on or a TV on or anything of that nature, so I went for my break at three o'clock totally oblivious to what was going on.

Brian Barwick, BBC Television Centre, London

It became very obvious that something major was happening. 'Grandstand' were immediately alerted because we have a flow of information throughout the afternoon. On a normal afternoon we would be giving scores to 'Grandstand' from our outside broadcast, which they interpret and put on the screen. On that afternoon it was basically 'There seems to be a heck of a problem at Hillsborough, just keep an eye on it.' And then it became obvious that it really was a heck of a problem. They then went live to the pictures and we were able to give some information live on the air. John Shrewsbury, our major football producer, who has produced about the last ten Cup Finals, had gone to produce a major FA Cup semi-final and was producing something totally different. Live television is something that you've always got to respect. I've done thousands of hours of live television and you think you know all the answers and then something happens and you think 'Where are we going here?' This was one of those occasions.

Pat Nicol, at home in Liverpool

When Lee had gone to the match, I thought 'Well, I've got to let him go sometime', because he told me he was going to Bon Jovi concerts the next year. Well, I was more worried over that. I started washing, just doing whatever, and Lee always put a blank tape into the radio to tape the match. I had to switch on at five to three to get Radio Merseyside coverage of the match, you see, because there was only Radio Merseyside that could 'cover a match properly.' So I came in and for some reason, I don't know why, I put the television on and it showed pictures of a football ground. I thought 'I don't like the look of it, I wonder where that is', because I knew the match wasn't on the television and that there shouldn't have been cameras there. For some reason I thought 'That's Hillsborough, I know it is, I don't know why it should be on.' Well, I went sick then. I just sat down and pushed the video in to record. I had a sickly feeling and I looked at the clock and it was four minutes past three and I knew then that something had happened to Lee. I didn't know what but I knew. I thought it was a fight. I saw all the police lining up and I thought 'Why don't the police stop it?' I knew something had happened to him. That's why I know he died at four minutes past three. I just sat with the phone on my knee. I didn't know who to phone. I phoned the police. They said they didn't know what was going on.

Simon Pinnington

When the game kicked off, the pressure behind us was immense, more severe than in a capacity-filled Kop. I tried to put it to the back of my mind and concentrate on the game. The pressure then increased and despite being over six foot tall, I was struggling to see. My friend could not see and was being slightly crushed against the small fence which divided Pens 3 and 4. It was then that I began to fear for the people in front. I remember Peter Beardsley striking the Forest crossbar and then seeing a man climbing the fence to try to reach the pitch. Even at this stage I had no idea that people were being killed. At about this time my mind became a haze and I became shocked. The next thing I remember is hearing a man crying a few steps in front of me. He pointed to a girl lying face down to the left of the goal and said 'She's dead'. That comment just hit me like a stone. Up until that moment I had been naive enough to believe that no-one could die at a football match. I stared at her body, urging her to move a muscle, to prove that the man was wrong. She remained motionless. Then I knew she was dead. Looking back I feel ashamed that I just stood on the terrace, but I couldn't move. I was in shock.

Anonymous Male Spectator

You can't recapture the sounds on television. You can hear a deafening hum, but you can't hear the person next to you screaming in your ear and you can't hear people dying and you can't hear bones crushing and you can't smell the smells. You could smell people dying. Combined with the actual sensation of being crushed as well, you've got every sense bombarded at the same time.

Andy Williamson, directors' box

The match began, and obviously your mind and your attention turned to the game, but you were aware that something was happening at one end of the ground. And then Peter Beardsley hit the bar. Whether that was part of the surge that caused the barrier to collapse I don't honestly know, but it could well have been. But immediately afterwards there were people spilling out onto the pitch, there were people being hauled up on to the stand behind and there were people attempting to climb up the fences at both sides of the central section, even at the front as well.

At that stage we weren't aware of the extent of what was going on, particularly in the tunnel that led to the central section, but it was obvious that there was a problem at the front of that particular section because of the numbers of people and it was a great surprise to find ultimately that a barrier had broken and that had created some of the crushing at the front. At that particular time I didn't think that it was an incident of crowd disorder. That really didn't enter my head. It was obvious that there was an accident of some description. At that time nobody in the area we were in had any idea that it was quite so severe. And I think that people around tended to take the view, at least initially, that if the match carried on then the problem would get solved quietly and there wouldn't be too much of a difficulty. But within minutes, obviously, the referee was being encouraged to stop the game and the players became aware of what was going on behind Bruce Grobbelaar's goal.

Stephen Hendry

The game was now irrelevant, and as Liverpool had a shot deflected, a roar went up and that brought the final fatal surge. The play had been brought down to the Leppings Lane end and more and more people were spilling over the barrier onto the pitch, as other fans were screaming and panicking, three lads were on the floor still, looking up at the fans in the terrace for help. We couldn't move at all. Even by this time the gate still wasn't open. I was now unable to breathe as more and more fans streamed into the terrace. The gate still wasn't open and people were dying.

Peter Jackson, North Stand

As a regular fan will tell you, you can tell what a crowd looks like. You know when it's full, you know when there are gaps. You couldn't see gaps between the heads in Leppings Lane. You couldn't see scarves below, or red teeshirts, or yellow teeshirts, or whatever teeshirts we had then as the away kit. You couldn't see it. You could just see the heads and the crowd wasn't moving.

We were very close to the Leppings Lane end. We were in the first block of seats so we were maybe 50 yards from where the trouble was going on. What was so contrasting, while you had this mass of humanity that wasn't swaying and moving, the three wing sections were empty in the sense that there were no more than handfuls of people in them. You could see people climbing out, or attempting to climb out, being pulled up into the stand and going over the metal barriers at the side. As I say, I remember that, commenting upon it before the game started. I had a portable radio and I couldn't hear the radio for the noise from the crowd, but that's not unusual for a semi-final. Beardsley hit the bar within minutes and at this stage people were straggling onto the pitch in obvious discomfort. It was clear there was something going on there although you couldn't see what because you couldn't see past the heads.

Alan Hansen

The game started, and the first time I touched it the reception they gave me was just frightening. I was touched. The next thing I knew, Forest get a corner on the right-hand side, and I'm at the back post, and these two guys come on the pitch and I thought it was a pitch invasion. I'll tell you what one of the guys said to me. He said 'There are people dying in there.' And I said 'Get off, you're not doing yourself any favours. You're doing the club no favours.' He said 'Al, there's people dying in there.'

Steve Hanley, Kop end with Nottingham Forest supporters

Once again we [the Forest fans] were in good voice. The game kicked off and began really well, Psycho [Stuart Pearce] making his presence felt, Nigel [Clough] dispossessing Ablett and winning two corners, and Beardsley hitting the bar. This last event seemed to have coincided with the extra Liverpool fans pouring in, and the rush happened. Of course, we didn't know what was happening as people cascaded onto the pitch. The first fears were of a pitch invasion—more mindless nonsense. Even when the ambulances came on, it didn't click that people had died.

Steve Way, Kop end with Nottingham Forest supporters

Even with half an hour to kick-off, from the Forest end of the ground it was clear that the central area behind the Liverpool goal was overcrowded. We joked it was typical 'dumb Scouser' to be all huddled together in such an enclosed space, when there were clear gaps either side of their terrace. When the match began the eye followed both teams' swift passing of the ball, not the growing knot of bodies. Suddenly, six minutes into the game, you were aware of people clambering on the perimeter fence. It looked like a crowd invasion. A collective 'Oh no' went up. Then you noticed figures trying to climb into the upper seating section. Eager hands tried to help haul them up. Instantly all realised something had gone wrong. Our end went immediately silent.

Jill Thomas, outside the ground at the Kop end

I remember very soon after the kick-off, a woman and her two children came to me and they were trying to get out of the gate. She had two boys, and they were only about seven, eight or nine. I said 'Where are you going? What are you doing? Why are you going out?' And she said 'I'm not staying in here a minute longer, I want to get out.' It must only have been about five past or ten past three. I thought 'What the hell's she going on about? Why does she want to go out?' She had been in the Nottingham Forest end on the Kop, so she must have seen something that had frightened her or her kids. I don't know what she'd seen, or what she'd sensed, but she came and said 'I'm not staying in there.' The turnstile wouldn't let her out so we had to open the barrier gate to let her out.

Rob White

The pressure of the crowd had been building up gradually to the point where I could no longer move at all, and I did think that it could not possibly increase any more. However, I do recall a sudden instance when the pain became even more intense, and the pressure on my body even greater. I remember yelling out at this moment and many other people, particularly behind me, also called out at the same time. I believe that the match was still in progress because I could still hear much of the crowd reacting to the play on the pitch with cheers and applause, unaware of what was happening all around me. I could not actually see the players, though, because my view was still obstructed by the motionless people on the other side of the fence.

I thought because so many other people had called out at the same time as me, particularly in the area behind me, indicating a widespread increase in the level of pain being endured, that there must have been a surge at the back and that even more people were trying to get in. It was the suddenness of that pain and the simultaneous shouts and screams that I remember vividly.

This did seem to prompt some action on the pitch in front of me. The police were beginning to look more anxiously towards the back of the terrace, whereas before their gaze seemed to have been fixed upon those who were suffering at the front. Some of them actually climbed onto the fence themselves to try and get a clear view of the rear of the terrace. This then created a gap in my line of vision, which enabled me to see the pitch and some of the players. They were standing still. The match appeared to have been halted.

Peter Jackson

Superintendent Murray came on to the pitch to stop the game. I remember Steve Nicol going to the referee to draw his attention to it. There were people on the pitch at that stage, on the playing arena. The Liverpool fans who were on the arena were religiously trying to avoid the pitch. Those who were walking at this stage were walking round the sides on the track. Nobody actually went on to the pitch itself until I think the game was stopped. Nicol had gone to the referee and then there was the lad who started the ball rolling for people to get onto the pitch itself. He went to Grobbelaar or somebody to speak to. So it obviously wasn't a pitch invasion. There was obviously something very drastically wrong going on. That was six minutes past three, as history tells us.

Bruce Grobbelaar

Two or three shots went in. One shot went over the bar. I went up to pick up the ball. All they said was 'They're killing us, Bruce, they're killing us.' And I thought 'Who?' I took the kick and kicked it away. Voices through the fence. I looked round, and I could see the fright on the people's faces through the fence, and I said to the policeman: 'Is there any chance that you can open the gate here?' Then a shot went past, and the ball was away in the corner. I went to retrieve it, and I said to the policewoman—I thought it was a policeman—'Get the effing gate open. Can't you see that they need it?' And there were screams coming at the time. I kicked the ball upfield, and I went back and said 'Get the fucking gate open.' I turned back and the ball went out of play on the left, and that's when I shouted to the referee. The policeman came on to the field, and the game stopped. Six minutes.

Steve McMahon

The match was halted by a policeman running on to the pitch, although I didn't see him. But within seconds of spotting dozens of fans climbing over the high fences and pouring on to the pitch, I knew the truth. I was standing there on the pitch when a lad I knew from where I used to live in Halewood ran over to me and was clearly so distressed and agitated that I was sure straight away that something ghastly was going on. This lad was shouting at me in terrible fear, the fear was visible on his features; he shouted at me: 'There are people dying in that crush in there.' He pleaded with me to do something about it. I didn't know what to do. I didn't really know what was going on in there, or how I could help. I felt so helpless, there was nothing I could do.

Ray Lewis, referee

It wasn't until about six minutes past three that a policeman actually came onto the field of play. Prior to that I must admit that there were things that were going on in that Liverpool end which I was aware of but I wasn't necessarily concerned with. I don't think the linesman at that end was in a position that it was causing him a problem to supervise the line at that time because the police were keeping the crowd well behind that goal and it wasn't affecting anyone at that stage. What was going through my mind was that they were just evacuating certain areas and spreading the load of supporters from one pen to another, which happens in a lot of games.

The first time I thought anything was wrong was when the police inspector came on the field of play and said 'We've got problems down at this end, we'd like you to take the players off.' That was the first time that I had any inclination that there were major problems. At that time, when the policeman said that, my view was that it was literally going to be only five minutes until they sorted out the problem. We went back up the tunnel. I think at the time there were players thinking 'What is actually happening, why do we have to go off?' I think the Notts Forest players probably went off quicker than some of the Liverpool players because I can remember turning and I saw Ronnie Whelan and Stevie Nicol, I think, sort of standing around. And I said 'Look, the police do want us off, will you come?' And we finally went off. I went into the dressing-rooms and said to them 'Keep warm, the police have informed us that it's likely to be five minutes or ten at the outside. OK, I will keep you informed. You will have the opportunity of going to do a warm-up before restarting the game, and we'll go from there.'

Steve McMahon

The FA's chief executive, Graham Kelly, was at the match and a lot of the players delivered a few harsh words in his direction as we were coming off the pitch, myself included. I told him: 'Now you know why we should have had the other end of the ground.' There was a barrage of abuse from other players behind me, and most of them were spitting their venom towards Kelly in the general frustration of their situation.

Mike Lewis, Studio B9, Broadcasting House, London

We had a horse-race around about three o'clock and we were just settling back to go round the football and do the rest of the sport in between 3 pm and 3.45 and then make a decision which game to go to, and about five past three Peter Jones came on the talkback and said that something was quite seriously wrong, so we went straight over and he did a description of about a couple of hundred people on the pitch and police coming on and ambulancemen, and it was obviously very serious and very chaotic. The referee had taken the players off. Peter could see that it was going to be very serious and that the game was going to be delayed for some time. He said it was mayhem.

Rob White

There were quite a few people now standing on the touchline and some were also on the pitch. Some were policemen, some St John ambulancemen and some spectators who had been able to climb out. They appeared to be arguing with each other and then they pointed at us.

The players then turned and walked off the pitch and, as this was happening, I saw a man lying on his back in front of me, just on the edge of the pitch. Some policemen were kneeling down next to him. Someone had taken off the man's shirt and pulled down his trousers, and the policemen were giving him the kiss-of-life. I am sure that was the first time that I saw someone being attended to on the pitch, because I remember it having such an impression upon me. It only served to confirm my fears that people were in real trouble. The man on his back did not appear to be moving at all. He was a large man, and that showed me that even size and strength could not save people from being crushed. I knew that I had to try and keep my rib-cage above the crush and keep breathing. In that respect, my height of 6ft 2½in was absolutely invaluable.

As attempts to revive the man on his back continued, the number of people moving onto the pitch steadily increased. Fans, policemen and ambulancemen alike were carrying limp bodies onto the playing area. Some were pummelling hearts with their hands, others were giving mouth-to-mouth resuscitation.

I could see that a very narrow gate in the perimeter fence several yards to the left of where I was standing had been opened, and policemen were trying to extricate those nearest to it from the tangle of bodies. Their efforts proved largely fruitless, because even when they seemed to have hold of people, the sheer compression that existed at the front of the terrace served only to thwart attempts to release them. This was the only gate in the fence that I could see. There were none near to where I was standing. Only the people nearest to that gate had any chance of getting through it. Still the only thing that I could move was my head, so I knew that there was no prospect of being able to reach the gate myself. A number of people behind me had been able to raise themselves above the crush and they literally climbed over the heads and shoulders of those still trapped around me until they reached the perimeter fence, and then jumped down on the other side to safety. Even at this stage, many policemen were still lined up along the touchline and were restraining some of those who had been able to free themselves from encroaching onto the pitch. Those fans would have been aware of what was happening on the terraces where they had just been standing, and so they seemed anxious to get onto the pitch to help those who were lying injured. Gradually, however, many of those policemen began to realise that their help was needed in trying to evacuate the terrace area, rather than preventing those who had escaped from walking on the pitch. When this realisation did sink in, the trickle of people being carried onto the pitch to receive attention soon became a flood. Unfortunately, though, judging by the number of heads which were being covered with discarded items of clothing, it was already far too late.

Anonymous Spectator, West Stand

It was as if you were looking through binoculars. You could see people crushed, you could see the shoulders coming close together and you could see them reaching out, sort of for help, and dragging other people down because they wanted to get up and get some air.

Rob White

Then I noticed that an ambulance was slowly moving in front of the perimeter fence until it reached an area just behind the goal, slightly to my left. It was then forced to stop because there were a number of people lying on the ground in its path. These people were completely still.

I looked back at the girl standing next to me. Her foot was no longer tapping on mine, and the grimace on her face had been replaced by a ghastly vacant expression. I realised that she had died. Not only were people dying up against the fence, but they were dying next to where I was standing as well. Although the girl was dead, the pressure being exerted on my arm by her jaw-bone was still causing me to wince with pain. She was still in exactly the same position that she had been when she was alive.

The continuing pain in my arm, combined with having to withstand the force being exerted on the remainder of my body, was necessitating much heavier than normal breathing and I was beginning to feel quite exhausted.

I did not think that I would be able to cope for much longer with my frightful predicament and I could see no sign of any forthcoming assistance to ease my plight. I then thought that I too would suffer the same fate as the girl on my arm and that, before long, I would also be dead.

Knowing that I was totally unable to help myself or, indeed, anyone else around me, and having seen no signs of encouragement in front of me, I had accepted the fact that soon my pain and suffering would stop and that I would not feel anything at all.

At that time, my sense of panic seemed to disappear as it merely seemed futile. Instead my thoughts turned to my family and my girlfriend. I could see their faces in my mind, but the images were blurred. I felt desperately sad as I thought of how distraught they would be. I just wanted to be with them again, so that I could say goodbye 'properly'. I tried to bring their images into focus so that I could be with them in spirit, but they merely faded.

Somehow I was becoming oblivious of the situation I was in, and strangely I was distancing myself from it as if I had played my part in it, but that it was about to come to an end. I began to feel that I was merely a bystander watching a rather shocking film that I could turn off anytime I wanted. However, I looked up at the top of the stand to my right and saw a row of television cameras which were pointed towards us. I then came out of the trance that I had allowed myself to fall into, and realised that I was very much part of the horror that was going on all around. I had kidded myself that I was looking through a camera at the terrible scenes in front of me, but in fact they were trained on me as well.

Trevor Hicks

Of course there were the famous gates in the perimeter fence on the pitch and I just got a flash of what I believed to be Victoria. She had long black shiny hair and it looked as though she was being passed up onto the pitch. We were getting into the chaos stakes now. There were people coming over and my concern was for Sarah and Victoria and obviously everybody else. As far as I can remember, I went on to the pitch through the nearest gate. I got on to the pitch and spent perhaps a minute looking around, trying to find Victoria, because I thought she had gone straight onto the pitch. I since know that she hadn't. She'd been passed into Pen 3 and gone out through the next gate along from the one I went through. And by some miracle, I suppose you'd call it, it ended up with Sarah and Victoria side by side on the pitch just inside the touch-line. I remember the St John ambulance, because it actually ran over my feet, when I was kneeling down giving attention to Sarah and Vicki. Again, it's well documented that there were no medical facilities. I remember the young boy who was in some of the newspaper photographs. I've a terrible memory for names but I have excellent visual memory. I can see a face once and I will remember it for an awful long time, and I remember the young ambulance lad. He couldn't have been more than about fourteen and he had a brand new little white bag. But the bag was empty. There was nothing in it. Perhaps his folks had bought it him for the big match, so his uniform looked right or whatever. I've since found out afterwards that Sheffield Wednesday paid the St John Ambulance £42. Now that works out at less than a £1 a thousand spectators, and that's pretty cheap. That is first-aid cover on the cheap.

Lord Justice Taylor, interim report, paragraphs 87 and 88

The St John Ambulance Brigade had some 30 personnel posted round the ground for the match—25 adults and five junior cadets. They were quickly on the scene when the first casualties emerged and sought to revive them. Their divisional superintendent, Mr Wells, tried unsuccessfully to help those pressed against the fencing by feeding oxygen to them through the mesh until they could be got out. Dr Purcell, Sheffield Wednesday's doctor, came from his seat in the South Stand and attempted resuscitation. Assisted by a male nurse from the crowd, he moved from patient to patient doing what he could, but in most cases it was too late.

Peter Wells, divisional superintendent, St John Ambulance, Woodseats branch

We just could not get to them, however many staff or however much equipment we had. People were just pressing down on each other and suffocating but there was no way we could get in there. They had their hands tied to their sides. They were vomiting and could not get the vomit out of their mouths. We tried to free the airways with our hands and give them oxygen. It was a terrible experience which I hope I will never ever see again. They were completely helpless. I was helping one young girl in her 20s and trying to hold her mouth through the wire mesh to keep her breathing going but there was nothing we could do. My wife Kathy was working on another casualty, a little boy. His father was watching as she tried everything to revive him, but a doctor walked past and said 'There's nothing more you can do for him, try the others.' It was so frustrating—we could not get them out for want of a set of bolt cutters, and because we could not get them back from the fencing.

Mike Lewis, Broadcasting House, London

We didn't know what was going on, so we went off to some other games and talked to the cricket. We had the BBC TV pictures as well, and it was quite obvious that something was wrong, but we didn't know the extent. You think the players will come back on when it calms down and the game will resume. When we went back John Inverdale cued it by saying 'It looks like there's been some crowd trouble at Hillsborough', and Peter Jones very quickly made it clear that it was not crowd trouble at all. He said 'It is not crowd trouble, the crowd were packed in far too tight', and then he did some descriptions about stretchers coming out and he said they were 'awful scenes'.

Dennis Cerrone

I was talking to somebody outside, and this message came over saying: 'Everybody get round to the pitch, everybody get round to the pitch.' And, of course, your first thought is 'They're fighting.' That's what you always think, isn't it, at a football match? So we all ran round and we came on from the side. Not behind the goal area, but the side of the pitch. If you're looking at Liverpool's goal, I came in from the left, running like hell, and a sergeant stopped me and said 'It's horrible, there's all dead people over there.' I thought he must be crackers: 'Dead people? What are you talking about?' I didn't say anything to him, I just carried on running—he was going the other way.

Graham Kelly

When the referee took the players off the pitch I went down and the next hour was probably the longest hour of my life. It seemed like half a day, it seemed so long.

Andy Williamson

I kept my seat initially. Because it wasn't the Football League's game, it really wasn't my business to stick my oar in. There were enough experienced people around to try to resolve the problem that was occurring. I stayed there and then ultimately after five or ten minutes descended into the bowels of the stand, just to try and find out what the problem was.

Initially, there was a wild suggestion that gates had been broken down at the rear of the stand. To be perfectly honest, I can't remember how that rumour came to my attention, but that was certainly the initial impression that was given. Obviously accusations were subsequently made that it was actually the police that began those suggestions, but whether that's true or not I've no idea. But that certainly was the initial vibes that were coming through both to the club officials and to the Football Association officials who were there.

Dr Colin Flenley

I wasn't interested in the game at all because I was still looking at these people trying to be dragged up. Then a fair-haired young boy was being taken to one side by the police in a state of collapse. He was taken round the side of the pitch and I thought 'There's something wrong here.' And then they started to do mouth-to-mouth with him, so I made my way through the crowd quite easily down to the front. There was a policeman standing on the other side of the fence, and I said to him 'I'm a doctor, somebody needs help.' And he opened the gate and let me onto the pitch.

I got visions of ten or twelve bodies, just lying on the pitch, and I went up to the first one and tried some mouth-to-mouth and cardiac massage, checking if there was any pulse and if they were breathing. If my memory serves me, it was an older man I started on first and I can remember shouting for oxygen or a suction machine. Apparently there was none available or someone had gone to get some. There was a little St John Ambulance boy with me, trying mouth-to-mouth while I did cardiac massage. I showed somebody else what to do and left that to them. I went over to what turned out to be one of the Hicks' daughters. Her face was blue, she wasn't breathing, so I started mouth-to-mouth and cardiac massage on her, and the thing that stuck in my mind with her was her father. He was standing over her, just shouting 'Sarah, come on, Sarah, you've got to breathe.' That will stick in my mind forever really.

Trevor Hicks

By this time it was panic stations. I found Sarah and Victoria. As I said, they almost had their heads together and the first recollection I have was of two guys, one of whom I now know was Dr Colin Flenley, but of course I didn't know who he was at the time—he was just another Liverpool fan. He was looking at Sarah, so I started looking at Vicki. I'd had a quick look at Sarah, obviously, and she looked in a pretty tough way, as did Victoria, and there was another couple of chaps and it was all happening so quickly it's very difficult to remember which was which. I left Sarah because it was quite obvious that the guy I now know as Dr Flenley knew what he was doing. I thought he was a first-aider of some kind and he was looking after Sarah, so I left him to it. I had a quick look at Vicki and there is this enormous feeling of inadequacy. The time they need you most. What can you do? You're not a first-aider, you're not this, you're not that, you haven't got a bag of kit in your pocket, you haven't got what you know that they desperately need now.

I've since found out that somebody had already attempted to revive Victoria but I didn't know that then. All you know is that you've got to keep them alive long enough. (I used to work on an oil refinery back in my ICI days and in survival training the trick was to keep the guy alive long enough for the experts to take over.) There were about three or four guys, and the one I remember is Colin Flenley. I spent most of my time trying to suck vomit out of Vicki's mouth. Sorry to give it you straight but her airway was blocked and I'd had my finger in. She'd obviously vomited or had the contents of her stomach pushed up into her windpipe, who can say, but there's no way that you can get anything into her till its cleared so literally I had to suck mouthfuls of vomit out of her mouth and throat and spit it on the ground. That gave me a problem for about six months afterwards. I then got a few puffs into her and then I was trying to get some attention so I went off. There were some firemen around. And this is when my other hero of the day, the PC from Sheffield, was trying to give me a hand as well.

Dr Colin Flenley

While I was trying to resuscitate her I remember a St John ambulance reversing up and I remember it reversing over this bloke's foot. The bloke was obviously dead, lying on the floor, and I thought 'This is just like a farce.' Anyway, somebody took Sarah away on a makeshift stretcher, so I went over to a young lad who had a Liverpool Candy teeshirt on. I got his heart going but he wasn't breathing, and then I left him to a policeman and somebody else and they carried on with him. I have distinct memories of attending to about four or five people but, after the event, Trevor Hicks showed me the police video film and you could actually see me going between about ten or twelve people. I'd got no idea that I'd done this because I was obviously doing this automatically, and I'd got no idea of the time I'd been on the pitch.

There was a GP from Nottingham who happened to be in the crowd and he was on the pitch helping to resuscitate, but I saw no other professionals there. Just St John Ambulance and policemen and policewomen. That was another vision of mine, the look on the faces of the policemen and policewomen, almost a look of disbelief and sort of standing around not knowing what to do. I presume it was disbelief really and shock perhaps, having thought that what was initially crowd trouble wasn't, and perhaps a feeling of guilt. That's what I can think of. My vision was mainly that the fans themselves were actually doing the work, and the St John Ambulance Brigade, who themselves were completely unprepared for it. There were young lads expecting to take out a few people who had fainted in the game but that was all.

I was surprised how everybody wanted to help, even to the extent that there were five or six people trying to hold on to a makeshift stretcher. Everybody seemed to want to help. There were a few people standing around or sitting down, obviously confused, looking for their friends, but most of the fans were eager and willing to help. Looking back, I think the people were already dead and it was just too late for all of them. If something had happened five or ten minutes beforehand then, yes, people could have been saved. But I'm sure these people were already dead or too far gone. I felt what I was doing was futile, but you've got to try. I assumed only ten or twelve people had actually got crushed to death. The ones right up at the fence must have been able to see all those bodies piled up. I thought I'd seen most things in my life working in Casualty, and I didn't think anything could shock me any more, but nothing in my professional life could have prepared me for what I saw on that day.

Lord Justice Taylor, interim report, paragraph 105

Before 1986 there had been no SYMAS [South Yorkshire Metropolitan Ambulance Service] representative routinely present at Hillsborough matches. The club was content, as indeed are many other clubs, to rely upon the St John Ambulance Brigade and a 999 call if necessary. From 1986 onwards, after representations, the club provided two seats in the South Stand for SYMAS staff at League matches. At one stage it was suggested that they would be best placed in the North Stand close to the gymnasium which had been designated as the casualty centre in the event of a major incident. The South Stand seats were allotted as they placed the SYMAS staff closer to the players' tunnel should a player be injured. These seats were, however, not available at Cup semi-finals. SYMAS representatives nevertheless attended at the semi-finals by arrangement with the police in 1988 and again in 1989. The SYMAS officers stood on the ramp leading to the pitch at the north-east corner. They had one ambulance outside the ground and one on standby.

Ian Battey

One of the staff nurses who was actually working the early shift, came through to me about five-past or ten-past three, something of that nature, and said that she'd had a very strange phone call from switchboard which was to relay a message, apparently from the police, saying that 'there was some trouble at Hillsborough' (to paraphrase what was said). The message that she gave to me was: 'We've had a phone call from the Police that there's some trouble at Hillsborough.' There was no indication that this was a major incident and we needed to do anything different.

Now, Hillsborough, as far as we were concerned, can cover anything. It's not just a ground, it's a shopping centre, it's an area of Sheffield with quite a large housing population and so on. So you wouldn't automatically consider that it was something at the ground, and at that point we didn't. Alongside that, we had an ambulance crew pulling up about the same time, delivering a normal, routine casualty patient, and one of the ambulance men said to me: 'Oh, we've just seen the Police Incident Unit heading down towards Hillsborough.' Now, my initial reaction was that we were talking about a road traffic accident, that we'd got a smash-up at the main junction down at Hillsborough and we were likely to have a number of casualties coming from that. On the strength of that supposition, I actually made a phone call to Jim Wardrope, who's the A & E consultant, at home, to say to him that we had a two-and-a-half-hour wait, that we were likely to be expecting something from down there—I didn't know what, the impression I got was that it was likely to be a road traffic accident—and I didn't feel that the two medical officers that we had at the time could cope with the sheer numbers that we had waiting in the department. Basically, we needed some senior back-up and an extra pair of hands. So fortuitous or not, I'd actually been in touch with Jim. He said he would come in, and he was on his way to the hospital.

It was standard routine practice—if we got a problem that we didn't feel we were going to cope with then we got the boss in and got the thing moving. My gut feeling was that something was not right. That's a very personal thing, experiencing what was going off. Because we're so close to the Herries Road which links Hillsborough to the hospital, we could hear sirens outside and we didn't know whether these were fire-engines, ambulances, police cars or whatever, but something deep down inside me said 'Something's not right here, something's worse than I'm being told.'

Rob White

There were, by now, large numbers of people on the pitch clustered in small groups attending to an ever-increasing number of casualties. Many advertisement hoardings had been ripped down and were being used as makeshift stretchers to carry those who were injured. Most of these 'stretchers' that I saw were being carried by spectators rather than ambulancemen, and their faces showed clear signs of strain as they ran towards the area below the television gantry on the right-hand side of the pitch as I looked, before returning to carry other injured fans.

There were many bodies lying covered all over the place, but still some of the injured were receiving mouth-to-mouth resuscitation and still people were using their bare hands to try and force hearts to beat again.

Eventually, I noticed that the crush seemed to be easing slightly behind me, and I was able to move my arms for the first time since the initial surge had rendered them useless. Then whoever had been forced up against my back moved away from me slightly, and I was able to stand upright. Gaps started appearing in the terrace and I was able to take a step backwards. At that moment, I looked down at my feet and I noticed two bodies face down, one lying across the other, at almost the exact spot where I had been standing all that time.

A man came over towards me and he helped me to lift up a young boy. We turned him over and then I felt ill. The boy's face was blue and his mouth was a dark shade of purple. He must have been dead for some time. He had probably been lying on the ground ever since the crush began, unknown to everyone, not that anybody would have been able to pick him up even if they had known that he was lying there. He was probably in his mid-teens with dark hair and, I think, wearing a dark blue anorak. This is the body that was lying on top of the other one. I had to just help the man lift his body onto the perimeter fence and two other men took him from us.

Jeff Rex

My own memory is a bit hazy of when the pressure eased. I can remember thinking to myself that I could actually move the upper part of my body although my legs felt like they were surrounded by concrete. I remember falling back onto the terrace and then getting up to look at what now resembled a battlefield. After an unsuccessful search to find my two mates I was pulled into the seats above (although by then there was no longer any danger on the terraces). Here I stayed until everyone was told to go back to their transport.

Rob White

During the time that I was in a trance, my recollection of events is somewhat vague and by the time that I had come out of that trance, and was able to move slightly, I do not recall seeing the girl that had died on my arm.

There was now space to move almost right up to the fence, although there were many bodies lined up against it, and people were beginning to lift them too. I managed to lift one more child's body over the fence, although I am unable to describe this child because, although I did lift the body, I have absolutely no recollection of any physical features whatsoever. I seem to recall almost seeing a mere outline of this person in my mind, and no more. I had been so shocked by the sight of the young boy, that it was almost as though my mind refused to accept any more punishment for the time being.

The effects of the crush on my arm made the grim task physically very difficult. The other men that were helping in the lifting operation could see that I had been hurt, and there was no way that I would have been able to lift heavier bodies than those that I had already struggled with, so they insisted that I was helped out of the centre terrace section myself. However, I could not get over the perimeter fence at the front, because its height meant that, even with assistance, I would have needed to pull myself up and over in order to get onto the pitch, which I would not have been able to do with my injury. So instead, someone helped me over the lower fence at the side which led to the sparsely populated side terrace section. Even though this fence was lower than the one at the front, I had difficulty negotiating it because of my arm and also because the sheer exhaustion caused by the crush had made me feel giddy.

Because I felt unsteady on the top of the fence, I did not want to jump over until I felt I could land safely on my feet, because the terrace was obviously solid concrete. The man who still had hold of me called to two men on the side terrace for help, and they came over to try and catch me. They told me to jump but, unfortunately, they only succeeded in breaking my fall, and I actually landed on my left knee. They checked that I was not too badly injured and helped me to stand up. The red stain on my trouser leg betrayed the fact that my knee was bleeding. I was able to stand, though, and although it certainly hurt, at least I thought that meant I had not broken anything.

The two men then went off to see who else they could help as I leaned against a barrier and just tried to catch my breath and compose myself as best I could. My nose was also bleeding, but I was just so relieved to have got out alive. I really had not thought that I was going to.

I looked around at the stunned faces on the terrace. Many were crying unashamedly. After a few minutes, I managed to get my nose-bleed under control, and I limped back to the side fence that I had escaped over. By this time, the front of the area where I had been trapped had been virtually cleared. However, a few yards further back there were still many people congregated in the centre section of the terrace, but they were able to move freely by now. I could not see any remaining injured fans in this area and the danger appeared to have passed. As I began to reflect upon what had happened, I stared at the nearly-empty front section of the terrace and found that I could no longer hold back my own tears. Yes—it really had happened.

Lord Justice Taylor, interim report, paragraphs 111 and 112

Although the great majority of those who died were in Pen 3, at least five were in Pen 4. Most deaths occurred at the front of the pens but there were a few fatalities further back. In all, some 730 people complained of being injured inside the ground and 36 outside it. Of the 730, about 30 per cent are thought to have entered through Gate C after 2.52pm. The largest category of injury was bruising, especially to the ribs and chest.

Ian Battey

We're now talking about 17 or 18 minutes past three. The exact times elude me. We had a phone call direct from the ambulance service via a dedicated phone line to say we were to expect a child cardiac arrest and would we prepare for that particular casualty. Apart from the fact that that child would be with us within two to three minutes, there was no mention of where that child was coming from and the circumstances of that particular casualty. (A dedicated phone line, at that time in our hospital, was a normal ex-directory GPO line, but we only used it for contact from the ambulance service, unless we got people who dialled it as a wrong number, which used to happen. It rings a large bell in the department which tells you that something's going off and the ambulance service want you.) As would be routine in that situation, we prepared the department. In that particular instance, we emergency-bleeped an anaesthetist and the paediatric registrar.

A minute or so after that, I said to the staff in the department 'I may appear a fool afterwards, but we're going to open all these emergency cupboards.' My instinct said that something wasn't right and I got the staff to start opening the major-catastrophe cupboards, where we keep all the equipment, and to set up resuscitation points. As I got my key in the door to open the first cupboard, the ambulance with that child arrived. As that child was being unloaded from the ambulance, the ambulance man who'd brought them up said 'This is what we're dealing with, we've got an incident inside the ground, we're probably talking about crush injuries, this is your first casualty.' We were talking 'a lot of casualties', but we'd got no idea of numbers or anything.

I can only go on impressions rather than the fine details of ages, but I would say this child was 13 or 14 years of age. He was being resuscitated by the ambulance crew. He had a mask on his face and the ambulance crew were putting oxygen into him and he was moribund, in effect, on an ambulance cot. We rushed him straight through into the resuscitation bay to start resuscitation. I have a very vivid picture of this child coming in, and all the activity. I mean, enough activity goes alongside that anyway, but there was the extra activity of the dawning of what we were actually going to be dealing with. That meant a lot of thought on behalf of the staff as to exactly what we needed to put into operation. It's one of those things that you practise for. You can tell people what they should do in those situations, but when it actually occurs you hope it falls into automatic pilot, and I'm glad to say that that happened with the bulk of the staff.

My role normally was to make sure there were enough staff to do the job, that they had the equipment they needed, and to be in there, hands on. My role in that situation changed immediately to co-ordinating everything: What do we do about the casualties in the waiting room—30-plus people with a two-and-a-half-hour wait? How do we get extra staff? Have we got enough equipment to deal with what's going to be thrown at us? At that point the child had been taken into the resuscitation room with two of my experienced staff nurses. I got one of my other staff nurses to contact switchboard and tell them that we were putting the major-disaster plan into operation, leaving switchboard then to do their cascade system of 'phoning people and getting people down to the department. I also allocated a member of staff to start 'phoning round our permanent A & E staff. That, as I subsequently found out, was one of the areas where things didn't go to plan—if it's a nice day people are not at home. I think we contacted three people by phone, and they said 'Yes, of course we'll come in, we'll be there as soon as possible.'

At almost at the same time, I went through into the waiting-room and stood in the corner and asked people if I could have their attention. I said that, due to unforeseen circumstances, we were unable to see them unless they didn't feel they could go home without being seen. Everybody bar two people left and went home. I went back to setting up a triage area for the prioritising of patients and trying to make sure that we had enough staff, medically, nursing and otherwise, to take care of the patients as they came in.

After the arrival of the child, we had three ambulances arrive in very, very quick succession. All three of those ambulances were carrying at least two patients, one on either cot. I do remember one ambulance coming in with a third person in there. That's a little hazy because I was dealing with them as they were coming through the doors rather than watching them coming out of the ambulance. At that point we had one of our Casualty senior house officers [SHOs] and myself attempting to sift and prioritise the patients, regarding their injuries. About that time, four or five minutes after the child had arrived, Jim Wardrope, the consultant, arrived. The situation was explained to him, and he took over the management of the triage area, which released the senior house officer to move on and start treating the casualties. Luckily, we then had four members of medical staff—two Casualty SHOs, a paediatric registrar and an anaesthetist—but we were short of pairs of hands. The casualties were coming in thick and fast and one thing still strikes me about those casualties—they were unmarked. When we practise major disasters and things of that nature, you are dealing with people with limbs off, loss of blood, a lot of things whereby you can say immediately 'That person's decapitated, therefore there's nothing we can do with them.' But when you're getting young, previously fit casualties in with no apparent markings, but with no signs of life, the dilemma you have is 'Do we try and spend time on this casualty or do we say "No, there's nothing we can do", and maybe save the life of somebody who's less critically injured?' That was the great dilemma that we had when casualties started arriving.

I was trying to co-ordinate staff coming into the department from one direction and patients coming into the department from the other. We've got medical staff coming in and we've got people volunteering. I had to make decisions very quickly. Having worked in the hospital for nine or ten years, at that point, I was in a position to say 'Well, I know you, I know what your experience is, I don't think you'll be any good in that situation, but we need you in this particular area.' As staff were heading towards A & E, I then had to say 'We need extra staff in resuscitation, we need extra staff in physio for the minor walking wounded, we need extra staff on the wards.' I vividly remember some of the more senior nursing-management people coming down and saying to me 'Ian, where do you want us, what do you want us to do?' That was difficult—it's almost a turn-around in roles—but everybody was very willing to do whatever they were asked to do.

Dennis Cerrone

I went over to behind the goal. I can't remember seeing those people [who were crushed against the fence] so I must have either blocked that out or I didn't get there at that time, but I've seen since [on the police video] where they're all on the railings and people are getting a lift over and people are getting pulled out. I can remember seeing this twisted crush-barrier. The crush side was twisted and it immediately struck me that it was rusty at the bottom and the paint was off. At that time there was space on the terrace, but there were people laid down, and I went with somebody else—I don't know who it was—and I picked this bloke up and I took him through the tunnel to an ambulance that was at Leppings Lane, and we left him with the ambulance men, and then we came back in. And at that point, as I was walking back in, this lad got hold of me and he's shouting in my face—he put his face as close to me as he could—and he's shouting and swearing at me. Really, really obscene. I just pushed him out of the way. I didn't know what he was on about. He were obviously in a state of shock as well. I just pushed him out of the way and walked on.

I think we picked another chap up and took him out to the same ambulance. I'm not too sure about that. I don't recall seeing any more people laid on the terrace, but I went on to the pitch and they were all laid in a big line, and I went up to the corner and in my head I thought 'Oh, they'll be coming round soon. Why have some of them got their faces covered up, because when they come round they're going to be frightened, when they've put the thing over their head?' Because I thought they weren't dead—I couldn't accept they were dead. I were waiting for them to start going 'Oh', like you do, when you come round. You shake your head and think 'Oh, that was naughty.' And slowly it dawned on me that they weren't going to come out of it. I'm now at the right corner-flag, as you look at the Liverpool goal. They were all laid there and people were working.

There were ambulancemen there and others, and there were people bringing buckets of water on, and fans breaking bits of board up and getting people on them and carrying them off. It gets a bit hazy then because all my instincts were telling me to run away. You think 'It's really dangerous here, it's really horrible, there's dead people everywhere', and you don't want to be there, you want to go off and get home and get out of it. I've asked other people afterwards if they had that sort of feeling running through their mind, and one or two have said 'Yes'. I don't know whether others have said 'No', but they did have and don't like admitting it, or what. I don't know. But certainly that was really strong with me: 'Run away, get out of here because it's bad.' Obviously I didn't. The other side of me said 'Well, you can't, because there's so much to do here. You can't leave it, you've got to do something, you've got to help.'

There's a joke in the police about the famous exam question: 'You're walking down the town and a train crashes and a jumbo-jet crashes on top of that—what do you do?' The joke answer is 'You take your hat off, run away and leave it to somebody else.' I didn't think of that at the time, I thought of that afterwards, because I got this urge to leave the place. I wasn't scared because there was nothing actually threatening me, but it's just you didn't want to be there. The atmosphere of the party had changed to a horrible atmosphere. At that point it was like I was going in and out of reality. I felt as if I were seeing things and then drifting off into not noticing things even though they were happening—I just couldn't register them. I later spoke to the doctor about this and he said that that urge I had to run away, when you get that, your body produces this adrenalin to enable you to run away as fast as you can, but because you don't, it goes to your brain and it starts to make you hallucinate and have all these daft ideas. I think that's what I was doing, because I can only remember in patches. I can remember helping people and moving people, and at other times I probably just stood there thinking 'What do I do now?'

Graham Kelly

After a short while I went along to the police control box to ascertain what had happened. As I made my way along there, I don't think I realised the enormity of what had happened. I think probably once I got there, having run the gauntlet of the fans' abuse on the way, I realised there was a serious problem. I walked at the back, and, when I say I ran the gauntlet of the fans, it was only for a short period for one small section at the back: 'This is your fault, you're to blame for this sort of thing.' I can't recall the exact words.

They [the police] said that there had been a forced entry. As I recall I think I would have been addressing myself to the chief of operations, which would be Mr Duckenfield, in the knowledge that his ACC [assistant chief constable] was in the box at that time in the background. The police in the box indicated that it was likely that the match would have to be abandoned. I then went back to the boardroom and convened a meeting of the two club chairmen, the referee, a representative of the police and a representative of the club (Graham Mackrell, the secretary) and apprised them of the situation as I knew it. My feeling in part of the early stages was to deal with it properly and to make sure that everything was handled correctly. It was obviously a serious problem by then, and there were obviously fatalities. I'd no idea there were many fatalities so it wasn't a disaster of that magnitude. I didn't think deeply into the general implications of another problem for football. I was just upset by it. I knew there had been injuries. I had no idea that there were very many fatalities. I don't think that the police actually would say that to me, but they would say that the match looked like having to be abandoned: 'There's been a forced entry.' So I go back and have a meeting in the boardroom a bit later. At that stage, the idea was that the match might not have to be abandoned. Now in retrospect this was the police saying 'I don't want to announce it too soon, we don't want to cause more problems by abandoning it and having people all over the place which we can't control.' So that hour carried on and we just didn't know. I just didn't know. You have got to bear in mind the situation behind the scenes. There are a lot of people [on the pitch] doing a lot of brilliant things out in full view. I was not able to be part of that. I was under the stand, doing little really. You've got television there, you've got radio, you've got all the media, you've got an immense number of people who might be saying or doing anything. My prime consideration was to keep a certain amount of control of the situation from the FA's point of view. We weren't in control of the actual event. That was delegated etc. And you tried to keep the clubs happy and the teams happy. You just get together and say 'The matter's in the hands of the police, we've got to hold it and we're in the hands of the police. We'll come back to all of you as soon as we can.' In effect the referee would communicate it to the players and managers. I would say I was not available to the media. I can't recall speaking to anybody in particular. Until I knew more there was no point in my saying anything. The press weren't actually in the boardroom, they were in another corridor, away behind a door, so it wasn't an immediate problem. Presumably they'd be trying to get access. We would say something when we could.

John Aldridge

I just thought a barrier had collapsed or something and we'd be taken off for only 10 or 15 minutes. No one knew what was going on. We just went in the dressing-room, and we got to know the consequences gradually. We were just trying to psych ourselves up again for the restart of the match. We didn't have a clue what was going on. You just wish it would hurry up because you're nervous and you don't even dream of what's going on outside. You didn't have the slightest idea. I think the staff knew but they didn't want to tell us. We didn't know for about 45 minutes or so, a long time, and it was only when we heard screaming outside that we started to realise. Kenny [Dalglish] went out, and you could hear people shouting in the corridor: 'People dying'; 'Kenny'. I can't even remember who told us, to be fair, because I think everything went a blank that day. I can't remember who told us 'There's people dead.' We were told we couldn't do anything.

Steve McMahon

Several fans filtered through to the dressing-room area, and there were a few desperately anxious to get into our changing-rooms; they urgently wanted to, not only to inform the players what was going on, but to register their protests that there was a suggestion that the game would continue. Clearly, they remembered the indignity of Heysel when the European Cup Final went ahead.

They were upset and desperately wanted to let us know that the game *could not* go on after what had happened. A few were screaming: 'There are a couple of my mates dead out there, and you lot are still thinking of playing on.' I could hear another shout: 'If you play this match with our supporters lying dead it will be an absolute disgrace.' One lad, who was determined that the game must not carry on, actually got through the door to the dressing-room, but he was quickly ushered out by either Kenny Dalglish or Ronnie Moran.

By this time, there were a couple of supporters sitting on the floor outside our dressing-room crying their eyes out. Kenny Dalglish went outside to console them. But the manager wouldn't let us leave the sanctuary of our dressing-room. He issued strict instructions to that effect. You've got to remember that at this stage the game had not been officially called off, and the manager simply wanted to calm us down, in case we were told to play on. Kenny spoke to the supporters and found out precisely what had occurred.

Ray Lewis

I don't think we were aware of the severity of it until nearly half-past three. I think the word came through to us at probably twenty-five past three that they thought there was a fatality there. That, without a shadow of doubt, then put it in a completely different light. My control in that game had finished when the police had taken over.

The club got us some sweaters to wear to keep us warm. I was down the end of the tunnel wanting to know that I would be informed of the developments. At that time we were seeing people that were coming back injured. Our referee's room was converted into a first-aid room. They were taking people in there who were in a state of shock. That was more or less from straight after we'd come off the park. I don't know if you're aware of the dressing-room layout at Hillsborough. When you come up the tunnel you turn left for the referee's room and the home dressing-room is on the opposite side. It's quite a broad passageway, so there was plenty of space. The first-aiders were saying 'Can we just bring these people in?' They were in a state of shock more than anything. I don't think there was any broken bones or anything like that. They were the walking wounded. We were in and out of that room. Quite a few people were in there as well at that time, as there were in the corridors, and it was around that time that the chief superintendent of police and, I think, the two chairmen and the chairman or a representative of Sheffield Wednesday went into the boardroom and I followed them through. I was then told that there was possibly more than one fatality. They didn't want to announce anything there and then because they wanted to get all the services to the crowd. They didn't want 50,000 people out on to the road, which would cause a problem there. So the decision was made, as I understood at the time, not to say anything to anyone, but the view was taken that, because of the fatalities, there was no way the game was going to be played. I think it was about twenty to four when I went into both dressing-rooms and said 'I haven't heard it officially but I don't think it's going to happen.' And some lads had already changed. Now whether the word had already got to them by then I don't know, but they were in the showers. Then it was basically seeing what you could do and where you could help. There were still the people in the rooms, etc.

Steve McMahon

The referee came into the dressing-rooms and officially informed us that the game had been called off, but we already knew that there was no chance of the match carrying on. The news had filtered through, all right. We had heard that there were ten people dead, then it was twenty, then thirty. It just went up and up in stages. Even if the FA wanted the game to go on, even if the referee had walked in and said play on, I don't think there was a single player in our dressing-room who had the stomach, who had the guts to walk back on to that football pitch to play a game of soccer. Half the players were in a state of shock, half had been slowly getting changed in any case.

Andy Williamson

The fans reacted far more quickly than the emergency services in some respects and took the matter into their own hands. It was not initially a surprise that the police were very conscious of an outbreak of trouble because, let's be honest, football did have a reputation for trouble at matches, albeit a reducing amount. By the late eighties those problems had diminished, but there was always a risk of an outbreak, so it was not that much of a surprise that the police reacted in a defensive way, concerned that there could be an outbreak of trouble. On the other hand, the personnel present weren't deployed to try and help the situation. It was a considerable time really before the situation was eased and a considerable number of people trapped in that central section were actually got out. When there was all the commotion going on, with people being stretchered off with the advertising boards and so on, I wasn't really sure what use I could be. That's something that really dwells with you afterwards: Why did I not get involved? Why did I not draw people's attention to the obvious crush? It was so obvious that you would have thought everybody could have seen it, but nevertheless it's a feeling that I'm sure does continue to dwell with most people who were there. Whether it would have been welcomed is not the point. It's something I regret not doing when it was as apparent as it was to everybody, not only myself and the chap I was with, that there were far too many people in that area of the ground.

I think it was some considerable time afterwards, probably what would have been around half-time, before it became apparent that there were actually a number of deaths. Initially the suggestion was that there had been two or three deaths, which obviously everybody was appalled with, but subsequent events showed that was woefully underestimated. Around that time I went on to the pitch with the Sheffield Wednesday chairman, Bert McGee, who I knew because he had previously been a member of the Football League Management Committee. He was obviously distressed at what had occurred, and was in tears at that particular time. But it was very difficult getting accurate information.

Mike Lewis, Broadcasting House, London

We were very worried about how to deal with it. We had something very serious and yet we had a full afternoon of sport ahead, so it was quite difficult. But we still weren't sure how serious it was. We went off round the other games and then back to Peter Jones, and he started talking about ambulances coming in and oxygen cylinders coming on to the pitch. Then he talked about how he had a tap on the shoulder as he was sitting there watching it and it was Emlyn Hughes. (Emlyn had been the summariser with Peter at Heysel, and Emlyn was magnificent that night. He was very deeply affected by it all, as was Peter.) Emlyn just tapped Peter on the shoulder and said 'This is ghastly, I can't believe what is happening here.'

Peter talked about an incident when a Liverpool fan ran down to the Nottingham Forest end and was baiting the Nottingham Forest fans before being led away by the police, and there were some arguments between fans and the police, but that was out of frustration, and I think we were pretty convinced that it wasn't a hooligan story. Peter ended his report and we went back to John Inverdale and he talked about how it was not crowd trouble, it was crowd scenes, and we were not quite sure how serious it was.

Alan Green, who was meant to be the other commentator, had by this time gone down to the dressing-room with producer Pat Murphy to find out what they could. Alan said that it was obviously total chaos and there were reports about a door being broken down by crushing fans trying to get in, and that Liverpool before the game had been very unhappy with their ticket allocation because it seemed that Forest had had the better allocation of tickets. Peter Jones talked about the stretchers on the pitch and ambulances and 250 policemen, and he was saying that he didn't believe the game could take place. It was about twenty to four now.

We're having to take all this in and John Inverdale is trying to balance the news from Hillsborough with all the rest of the news. I thought he did a superb job. He left little pauses as we went backwards and forwards, because John was the break between what was happening at Hillsborough and what was happening everywhere else, and he was trying to find the right words to get in and out of everything. We were still being quite cautious. We were telling the story but we didn't want to use emotive language until we really knew what was going on.

We went back to Peter Jones and he said that Hillsborough looked like a vast hospital ward, and then he talked about unconfirmed reports of deaths. We then went out of that to Bryon Butler, who was commentating at Villa Park, and he suddenly sounded very, very down. It was remarkable listening to that. The Villa Park boys had just been doing their job and getting on with it, and the full enormity of what could have been happening up at Hillsborough suddenly started to get to them. So John Inverdale is walking this difficult tightrope. We then went back to Hillsborough again, for an interview with a doctor, Glyn Phillips, who had been on the terraces. He talked about the sheer mayhem and said the police had lost control. He talked about how people had died on the pitch and how he'd tried to resuscitate somebody who was clinically dead and he'd got their heart beating again but he didn't know whether their brain had been affected and how long oxygen had been lost to the brain. Then John Inverdale came back in and said that Jimmy Armfield had commented before the game that the end behind the Liverpool goal looked to be very, very packed in comparison to the two sides behind the goal. We came back and John said 'Everything else pales into insignificance, but there has been lots of other sport. Here are all the half-time scores.'

Steve Way, Kop end

Anyone who runs on to a soccer pitch and is not a footballer seems to be running slowly. The police seemed to take ages to reach the corner of the overspill. Initially they tried to contain it, but they rapidly merged with the mass. A third of the pitch was now swarming with people and we all knew the match would be abandoned.

Hillsborough had become a disaster area. Fans ripped down hoardings, improvising stretchers—acts of vandalism sanctioned by the police. Stopped from getting on the pitch by our barriers we stood in the Spion Kop end, solemn, serious. My ticket read 'Spion Kop—standing'. I added the word 'helpless'.

A few Liverpool fans resorted to more traditional soccer tribe behaviour. They strode towards the Nottingham Forest end saluting us with masturbatory gestures and the ubiquitous clenched fist. This led the police to usher in a new battalion. They formed a solid line of black across the halfway-line, over which we could see very little. Their ranks would constantly part, allowing the DIY stretchers through. This was now a regular and increasingly ghoulish convoy. The flimsy metal frames now had bodies on them; very still bodies lying in awkward positions, contrasting with the jerky bouncing motion of the straining bearers.

Those true supporters made a diagonal run to our corner, the ambulances' only access to the pitch. Yet no one was really thinking. All too often the bodies were placed in the path of an ambulance. As a result its entrance was staggered, and not at all triumphant.

Meanwhile fans, clearly numbed, outmanoeuvred St John ambulancemen, clustered over bodies, trying to start hearts. It was only when the firemen arrived with the resuscitation equipment and the know-how that the success-rate improved. Each success was applauded by the Forest fans, though the sound of clapping was lost in the silence: 52,000 in shock is very quiet. There was nothing to hear on the PA.

Policy decisions were made. Those they thought they could save were given valuable ambulance space. The others were just left in the goalmouth to die. Of all the images of the day, the most vivid is the sight of a considerable beer belly being pounded to no avail. Eventually left, it carried on wobbling under its own momentum.

Dennis Cerrone

One thing that does stick in my mind is that at the other end of the ground they obviously thought at first that there was fighting on the terraces, and I think they were a bit annoyed because it was holding the match up—they didn't realise what had happened. Anyway, somebody decided that the people at the other end of the ground were going to try and get over and come to the end we were at, which would have been horrendous, and we formed a line.

It was a Chief Superintendent that organised the line, when they thought the people at the other end might come over and cause trouble. I was near to him and I heard him saying 'Get in a line, get in a line, just in case they come.' I was in that line. I can remember being in that line, walking, and I thought 'This is ridiculous', not because we were doing that, but because there were 30,000 people there. And I thought: 'Well they're not going to, are they, because they're normal people? They're just going to stand there.' You can think the strangest things when all that adrenalin is whizzing round your brain. And, anyway, after the years we'd had of football hooliganism, if there's a problem at a match, that's what you're expecting. You're kind of conditioned to it.

Barry Devonside, Liverpool fan, father of 18-year-old Chris

To say there was a coldness, a fear about the place—it was something I'd never experienced or ever want to again. People were absolutely shellshocked. You were standing there watching people collapse and people who were dead on the pitch, people being carried off on boards every minute, people running across the pitch—supporters—carrying boards with arms just flopping down and bodies lying there motionless. And right in front of your eyes you had about 150 coppers lined across the pitch in front of the North Stand doing absolutely nothing, and that generated a lot of hatred within the stand.

Jill Thomas

I can't remember how I got into the line. I don't know whether anybody ordered me to do it or whether I saw the line forming. I just ran straight down on to the pitch from the ramp, where the emergency vehicles come down, near the gym. I remember being very frightened because I thought that the Nottingham Forest fans were going to rush and try to get to the Liverpool end. We were in a line in the middle of the pitch and there was 20,000 people at that end and 20,000 people at the other end. I remember thinking 'Oh, yeah, we're going to do a right lot of good, aren't we, if they decide they are going to start rushing at each other?' We must have stood there in a line for about five minutes and somebody realised that there wasn't going to be any rushing. I might have just walked off from the line myself and thought 'I'm not standing here like a lemon any more.' I realised that something was going on down at the Leppings Lane end, and I ran down there, and I saw Paul Eason [an ambulanceman] and he said 'Get back, Jill, go away.' Then I realised that they were actually bringing bodies out. He was being protective towards me because he'd known me for a long time—we'd grown up together. I did go right down and I saw them carrying somebody out. One of the crowd said 'They've all been crushed to death, they've all been crushed to death.' That's how I found out. I think I got back up to the north end because I got somebody up off the pitch and helped them to walk, with my arm round them, back up to the North Stand. I didn't go back down to Leppings Lane. Whether that was subconsciously because I didn't want to, I don't know, but I didn't go back down to Leppings Lane.

I remember hitting a policewoman, a 'special' policewoman, on the way back up to the North Stand. She was just screaming and having hysterics. I remember slapping her across the face and telling her to pull herself together because she was no good to anybody in that state. I remember that very vividly. I remember her standing there, absolutely screaming and having hysterics. I remember slapping her and shaking her by the shoulders and telling her to calm down and pull herself together.

Dennis Cerrone

I saw a mate of mine, and I went up to him and asked him if he were all right and he said 'No, I'm not', and he burst into tears. Two or three other bobbies were crying. It was just a release for them. I just stood with him for a few minutes and I thought 'Oh, I'm going to start crying soon', but I didn't for some reason. I wanted to, because I think it's better to get it out, but I didn't.

I've forgotten what we did then. I think I walked back with this lad to see if there was something we could do. But it was getting a bit more organised then. I think an ambulance came round the pitch and was in that corner. I can remember that, but I can't remember how all the bodies got from the pitch to the gym. I can't remember who took them, although I must have been on the pitch when it was all happening. I were either looking the other way, or talking to somebody else or doing something else. But it didn't seem to be long before they had all been moved.

Dr R. A. Lawson, Leytonstone, London

Like the other doctors present, my overwhelming impression was of chaos. Whilst it will always be impossible to foresee and plan for such tragedy, I found it disturbing that the police did not take more control of the situation. When I initially went on the pitch to help, efforts to identify those in immediate need of attention were hampered by the number of fans, with no or minor injuries, who were penned at the Liverpool end by a double line of police. Those neither directly involved in rescue efforts nor seriously hurt should have been allowed clear to allow access. There was no attempt made to identify the main medical centre. Thus, despite repeated enquiries, it was over an hour after the tragedy before I tracked down even the barest of medical supplies.

James Wardrope, consultant in Accident and Emergency, Northern General Hospital, and colleagues

First aid was administered by police and St John Ambulance personnel together with seven or eight doctors and a few nurses who had been spectators. The resuscitation equipment available was very limited and included only a single oxygen cylinder. The nine available stretchers were quickly used up, and spectators resorted to using advertising hoardings to carry bodies to the gymnasium, which served as a makeshift mortuary.

Help was not summoned over the public address system until 15.30. By then some doctors had left the ground thinking that the match had been abandoned because of hooliganism.

Dennis Cerrone

Dalglish went on the loudspeaker to get the people to be calm. At the Kop end I don't think they realised what was going off, and I don't think they believed it anyway, because I find it hard. You know 'It's a football match, a nice sunny day, you don't get people who are dying and being killed.' I do remember having a daft thought on the pitch, when I realised the enormity of it. I thought 'It's gonna be ages now, because when we've sorted all this out, we're going to have to play the match and I'm going to be really late getting home.' It's a stupid thing to come to your head, isn't it? But you're still thinking that it's going to get back to normal and carry on as normal. The daft thoughts that go through your head. They're not thoughts from you, I don't how they get there. I met a bobby from Liverpool and he said a stupid thing as well. He said 'When I get back I'm going to put a complaint in about this.' I must have been on my sensible mode then because I thought 'Do you think nobody's going to do owt about it, that it's going to be left to an officer putting a complaint in to his superintendent and saying they'll look into it?' But he must have been like I was, up and down with adrenalin. I didn't say anything to him because there was no point. He didn't know. He was like me. 'I'm gonna complain about this when I get back', he said. Afterwards, when I realised what he'd said, it made me feel a bit better about some of the daft thoughts I had had.

At the side of the pitch, where the managers and cameras were, people were coming and going and bringing water on. People went on with big buckets of water. My mouth was like a desert, everybody's must have been, because I saw people gulping the water. But that's one of the signs of extreme pressure, isn't it? Water goes from your throat, so I've been told, and you get a dryness.

I can't remember the people inside the new stand, and I'm sure they must have just sat there waiting and watching. When I've watched the video I don't even remember so many people being on the pitch. I'm surprised when I look at them: 'There's hundreds on there', and it seemed like there were me and a few dozen others at the time. For some reason, I didn't take in that amount of people.

Tony Ensor, watching from the directors' box

I was sitting, as it happened, next to the deputy chief constable of Merseyside, and it was clear to me from the halfway-line, where we were sitting, that this was not a law-and-order problem. There was something seriously wrong. It wasn't clear of course to the Nottingham supporters at the far end.

They thought that this was another act of hooliganism. I don't criticise them for that because on the face of it it may have appeared like that. But early on, almost immediately, I decided, along with Peter Robinson, that we'd better go and investigate.

We went down to the pitch, by which time the players had come off and the police were there, and the police were lined up [across the pitch], believing there was a law-and-order problem, and their training and reactions were channelled into that. It was some time before they realised that one of the greatest tragedies that one was likely to envisage was occurring around them. I remember thinking to myself that I could not believe that I would be attending a football match twice in my life when I would be seeing a lot of people dead or dying. It was a very sobering, extraordinary feeling which of course doesn't leave you.

As the situation developed it became more and more horrific. We could see that people had died, but we didn't know the scale of it. As far as I was concerned I was not a person who could render first-aid or offer any useful practical help. I felt my duty was not to get in the way, so I didn't linger after I had established the initial situation on the pitch. But as we waited for developments and the news came through of the mounting death toll it was quite unbelievable and it left quite a mark upon us. At Hillsborough, I didn't feel any of the shame that I'd felt at Heysel. It was a totally different feeling. I felt that something had gone wrong at Hillsborough, which has since been admitted. The organisation there was woeful.

Peter Robinson, chief executive of Liverpool Football Club, watching from the directors' box

It's a sad thing to say but as a result of my involvement with the Heysel Disaster I was initially better equipped to deal with this one. As I saw it happening, I knew that something was terribly wrong. I think that one or two people around me were thinking that it was possibly an outbreak of hooliganism, but my immediate reaction was that it certainly wasn't, because nobody was coming onto the pitch. I was sat in the directors' box, which is some 70/80 yards away, so I couldn't see clearly, but it was evident to me that something was very wrong and I was greatly concerned. It quickly came through that there had been a disaster.

With the experience I'd had at Heysel, I was determined to find out for myself exactly what had happened. Stories were circulating that Liverpool supporters had charged down the gates. I thought that it was essential to remain calm and collected and to find out for myself. I went to the Leppings Lane end with Mr Ensor, our club solicitor, and spoke to as many supporters as possible and gathered as much information as I could. One thing clearly apparent to me was that the gates were intact. They had most certainly not been forced and what had initially been said was untrue. I then returned to the directors' area and was able to relate to a number of officials and press representatives what I had seen and been told by supporters on my visit to the Leppings Lane end of the ground.

Jenni Hicks

I can't remember any announcements being made until Kenny Dalglish spoke. And then the next one I heard was when he said that the game had been abandoned or whatever. I was watching the pitch. And I was trying to see if it was Sarah or Vicki in the ambulance. There was a St John ambulance first, and then a second ambulance. And I didn't realise that my youngest daughter was in the second ambulance. It was the only South Yorkshire ambulance that actually was allowed onto the pitch, because the access was apparently absolutely appalling. That is something else I have learnt since. Trevor and my youngest daughter were in that ambulance. And I remember watching it going across the pitch and thinking 'Oh my God, this is more serious than anybody had ever envisaged.' You think it is not going to happen to you. You think that because the authorities are there they are going to take charge, and, if everyone runs on and starts panicking, you are going to muck up whatever they are trying to do to alleviate the problem. You try to behave, and trust that the experts will know what they are doing and whatever should be done will be done, and obviously it didn't turn out that way. I can remember a chap running up the steps back to whoever he was with and saying 'There are dead people down there.' And at that point, I knew that if I wasn't going to be on the verge of hysteria, I had to really think 'Now it is going to be OK. It has got to be OK.' Because at that point, I don't know what would have happened. I thought 'It can't be true. This can't be true. We are at a football match here. This is a Saturday afternoon. A lovely sunny Saturday afternoon. This just doesn't happen.'

There is a strange feeling of unreality, especially if you know you have got people in there. They are your whole world. And you just can't bear to think of what might be. I stayed there and I can't believe that I stayed there and did as I was instructed: to keep calm, to stay where you are, not to go on the pitch. I did that exactly, because I thought that if I did exactly as I was told, and I behaved, obviously somebody was in charge, things would be taken care of and it would be OK. It is strange looking back on it now. It was all so unreal. I just thought 'I don't believe this is happening.' I couldn't work out why it should be happening. 'What's going on?'

Anonymous Female Spectator

I came to on the pitch. I wasn't quite sure where, but I do remember having white paint from the pitch markings on my jeans. I got up and tried to walk, but I kept falling over. I was barely conscious. I just couldn't do it. I could see the line of police across the pitch. I could barely breathe. They weren't allowed to break ranks. Anyway, eventually one did and his sergeant or whatever tried to stop him, but he came over anyway. He asked if I was all right. I said I was and he rolled me over on to my side to see if I could be sick. I was moved over to the side of the pitch near the Forest end. Despite being in that state I got up, and with a lad started to break down the [advertising] boards to use as stretchers. I was carrying the stretcher with what turned out to be my crushed arm. I was taken to the gym and there were like these three piles there: the dead, the nearly dead and the 'injured but going to be OK' like me. I was sat on this table, together with a lad who had broken his leg, and this St John Ambulance lady comes up. She looked terrible, she was really upset. I put my arm around her and said, you know 'It's terrible, isn't it? You'll be OK.'

Jill Thomas

I've been casualty-bureau trained since I was a cadet, so my initial reaction was 'This is just chaos, injured people are walking out into Transit vans, nobody's going to know where anybody is', so I took out my pad and started taking down names and addresses. These were the ones who had broken arms and cracked ribs and the ones who were hyperventilating and in shock. They were just getting in the back of vans themselves. Some were being helped in by officers. I remember there being a doctor there who was saying 'Lay them down here, lay them down there.' I did that for a while, trying to get people's names and addresses, but I just got deluged by people wanting to find other people. They were saying 'That policewoman's got a list', and the next thing they were all shouting out—'Where's Paul Morton?' 'Where's David France?'—and I was trying to look down the list and it was just chaos. Then an inspector came over and I had to hand the list over to him because they were setting up an information point.

Dr Tom Heller

I switched on the television just after 3pm and saw the coverage of the snooker being interrupted by scenes from Hillsborough. Like almost everyone else, I imagine, I thought that there had been a pitch invasion and worried about how this might affect the chances of English clubs being allowed back into Europe. I then got into my car and took my daughter to a party that she was due to attend. At about 3.20pm I heard on Radio Sheffield the call for doctors to go to Hillsborough, so I hurried to drop off my daughter and go to the ground. The party was about 2km from Hillsborough, and on my way to the ground I followed a fire engine with flashing lights and siren that was going through red traffic lights and on the wrong side of keep-left signs. I kept my car glued to the back of the fire engine and was at the ground within a few minutes of hearing the announcement. I parked in Leppings Lane, about 20m from the blue gate that became such a focus of attention later. I had no notion of the significance of the gate at the time.

As I was parking on the forecourt of a garage that fitted tyres I was approached by some policemen. I told them that there had been a call for doctors on the radio. One of them immediately used his radio to find out where doctors were being asked to go, and we set off, running through the corridors, round the stadium, and towards the sports hall. The stadium was familiar to me as I had often been to matches there. The concrete beneath the grandstands is unusual: it is stained grey, cold and unyielding; the light is always poor beneath the stands, even on sunny afternoons like that one. As we rushed along the atmosphere was all wrong: there were lots of people but there was no noise. We got to the sports hall in about two minutes, and I entered by stepping through a cordon of police officers who were holding back people who were crowding around the outside of the door.

Lord Justice Taylor, interim report, paragraph 107

The gymnasium had been in use for serving meals to the police. When the Major Disaster Plan was ordered, it was cleared and divided into two. One end became a temporary mortuary; the other was used as a casualty clearing area for the injured. As the stretchers, designed and improvised, brought in more and more casualties, the scene was initially and inevitably chaotic and harrowing. There was intense distress amongst the injured and bereaved; relatives were reluctant to be parted from the dead and sought to revive them. There were people looking for missing friends and relations;

there were recriminations, there were scuffles. Some of those involved were the worse for drink. Doctors and nurses had followed the casualties in from the pitch and sought to attend the injured as best they could in the adverse circumstances. Those in most urgent need of hospital treatment were taken to ambulances as they arrived, triage being employed to determine priorities. Doctors were requested by the police to examine each person thought to be deceased to confirm and certify death.

Jill Thomas

I was on duty at the gymnasium door. There was another police officer with me. The gym door was really narrow—it's just a single opening door—and I remember being stood there with him, and we let in anybody who was high-ranking or who said they were medical, but nobody else. It took a long time for it to sink in. Before they moved the bodies to the mortuary they laid them on the floor behind the stand. I couldn't believe that they were dead. I thought 'They're all going to get up in a minute, it's just some sort of trick, some sort of joke, they can't be dead, all these people can't possibly be dead.' For ages and ages I thought 'They're not dead, they're just asleep, they're going to get up and start talking to me and walking about.'

We deal with death all the time, and I've dealt with loads of sudden deaths—babies, car accidents, old people who have died at home in bed—and when it's one it's acceptable. It's just one dead body and you realise that we're not going to live forever, and you just deal with it and comfort the family and do the job as best you can. But when you see about eighty bodies laying there you just can't take it in. It's just incomprehensible. Especially after it had been such a beautiful day as well. It was such a beautiful, sunny, bubbling, highly-charged day, and for it just to change, just like that, that's what made it seem so unreal.

I remember an Asian doctor who was absolutely wonderful. He was a fan—I don't know whether he was Nottingham, Sheffield or Liverpool. He came up to me on the door, and he said 'I'm a doctor, can I come in and see if there's anybody I can help?' I said 'Yeah, come in', and somebody near to the door made an involuntary muscle reaction and I thought 'Oh, my God, he's alive.' I remember running after this Asian doctor who was going around checking if there was any sign of life from anybody. I said 'That man there, that man there, he just moved.' He had to calm me down a bit then because I was thinking 'He's not dead and he's laid in here and we could be helping him.' He went to him and I remember him touching his neck and pulling his eyes back. He said 'He's not, dear, he's gone. We can't help him any more.' And then I went back on the door.

Dr Tom Heller

Nothing could have prepared me for the scenes inside. I had thought vaguely that there might be a couple of members of St John Ambulance standing over a man with his head between his knees, telling him to take deep breaths. I had thought that they might have been overwhelmed because four people fainting was more than they could cope with and that I'd join in their exhortations and be back at my daughter's party in time for the second round of the Marmite sandwiches. This was not normal though. There were bodies everywhere. Who was alive and who was dead? They couldn't all be dead. It had to be a mistake; this just didn't happen on sunny afternoons. Blotchy faces against the floor, not disfigured but apparently peaceful. Bodies higgledy-piggledy just inside the door, the line stretching over to the far wall. I asked a policeman what was to be done. Thankfully he pointed away from the bodies to a section of the hall that was separated from them by a long, low screen of the type used to divide sports halls when two different sports are being played at the same time. There were more bodies here though. My God, what could I do? Who was going to tell me what to do?

Without directions I ran along the line of crumpled bodies. At least this lot were alive. I stopped between two bodies, took out my stethoscope, and lifted up a teeshirt and listened, grateful to have the time at last to do something that I knew how to do. I often use 'stethoscope on the chest time' to think during consultations. It's a good ploy really; the patient thinks that I am being ever so thoughtful and thorough, and I have time to think about what the hell to do next. Panic overtook me on this occasion. How could I be sure that this person was the one who needed help most? What was going to happen to all of the others if I stayed with this bloke? I could hear his heartbeat and breath sounds. For some reason I took my stethoscope out of my ears and crawled up to his face. 'What's your name, mate?' I asked. 'Terry' was the reply. 'OK, Terry, how are you feeling?' No answer. Silly question really. His leg was at the wrong angle somehow, and so was one of his arms; he looked terrible, and where I had rested my stethoscope earlier was obviously not all right at all: it was moving wrongly and was not the right colour either. Although I could hear breath sounds, they were hard to interpret. I think I was just panicking. I remembered how to do a tracheostomy with a Biro. Would this be my opportunity? I turned him over on to his side and pushed my fingers on to the top of his tongue to establish an airway. This seemed to help, and his breathing started again. I had pulled him over on to his bad leg though—there didn't seem much alternative. His face was against the floor, so I reached out and found a leather jacket on the floor and picked up his head and rested it on the jacket. What medical equipment could enable this man to survive? If only someone would arrive who knew what to do. What did I know about anything? I turned around and looked at the man behind me; he was immobile and a terrible blue-grey colour . . . and so it went on.

Stephen Hendry

I had managed to get away over the rail to the other terrace, my mate finally got hoisted up to the stands above. Then, at last, the gate was opened. Fans spilled onto the pitch, only to be blocked by awaiting cameramen. I had managed to get to the front of the terrace, to the gate, as by now I had been hardly able to breathe. I saw five bodies get handed out to awaiting police or St John Ambulance. Next I remember I was on the pitch myself, getting my chest pumped for some reason. What followed was absolute mayhem. I saw at least eight dead people, confirmed dead there and then. People were still climbing up to the stand; there were people in tears on the pitch because relatives and friends were injured or dead. This was about 3.30pm.

Rob White

Then I looked towards the back of the right-hand side section of terrace that I was standing in, and noticed that the people at the front of the stand above were ripping down the advertisement hoardings just in front of their seats, and were passing them down onto the terrace. I had earlier seen the use to which similar hoardings had been put while I was still trapped myself, so I thought that more 'stretchers' were needed on the pitch.

There were not many people standing near the side fence (that I had escaped over) but this is where the hoardings were being passed to. I, and three others, got hold of one of the hoardings and carried it above our heads, a short way up to the perimeter fence. I was careful to take the weight mainly with my right arm, being mindful of the injury that I had sustained to my other arm. As we were passing the hoarding over the fence, some people just behind were waiting to pass another one to us. At the same time, some other hoardings were being passed over the side fence into the centre section of the terrace.

Since the events at Hillsborough, I have seen a photograph in the *Liverpool*

Echo which showed what, I am certain, is this very moment. Although the camera is too far away for it to be possible to positively identify myself, the number and the position of the hoardings is just how I remember them. The official ground clock, clearly visible in the photograph, shows the time as 15.37. From this, I am able to deduce that I was probably trapped on the centre terrace until about 15.30, or thereabouts.

Trevor Hicks

This takes longer to tell than the time it takes to happen. As it turns out, we were on that pitch until about three thirty-six, so it was something like twenty minutes. Anything that could probably have been done was done but it was too late. Jenni was a born worrier and I was thinking 'She'll be demented.' If it doesn't sound ridiculous, I at least knew where the girls were. So one element I didn't have was the worry of 'Where are they?' That obviously changes later but, at this time, I'm on the pitch, I'm with them both and obviously I'm surrounded by other people. But my only thoughts are looking after my own. I know that sounds selfish. Nobody is thinking that anybody is dead. Everybody thinks 'We've got a load of people where if we can get them first-aid they will live.' I think if we had got first-aid for everybody, some of them would have lived, and some of them did. I've talked to Colin Flenley, the doctor, and he remembers a couple of people he worked on who were revived. There's a genuine hero in my view. He saved a couple of lives. He certainly saved one and possibly two. I'd tried to get help. The first-aiders couldn't be blamed. There wasn't enough of them. A number of them were young kids who were almost in a blue funk and I don't blame them. It was a horrible, horrible sight, and suddenly I got brought down to earth with a bump. The 'Great Invincible' that I am is suddenly a 'no-mark'. There is no way that you can do what is required. I did my best. As I understood it, I'd kept Vicki alive long enough and this was when the ambulance came on to the pitch. This was the only ambulance that got on to the pitch, other than the St John's one which came round the perimeter. I have this recollection of all the policemen stood around not giving a lot of help. Still trying to usher people off, even then. That's not true. It's a gross generalisation. As I said, I'll never forget the young PC who gave me a hand. He's got a young family of his own. He tried to help me. There's no question of it. But I think probably the worst moment of all was when the ambulance pulled up on the pitch about five or ten yards from us. Me and the PC and somebody else picked Vicki up and took her across to the ambulance and put her on the right-hand-side bed and then came back to get Sarah, but in that half a minute the ambulance was full. There were perhaps three or four people on the floor, which we later found out were dead bodies. There was somebody on the other seat with a woman with him, and there was an ambulance man. We picked up Sarah to take her and we actually got there and there was no way we could put her in, so we had to put her back down on the pitch. But I'm then faced with what I think gave me most of the nightmares: 'Do I go in the ambulance with Vicki or do I stay on the pitch with Sarah?' It's some sort of invisible reckoning process. I knew that one of the guys looking after Sarah was a medic of some kind and he knew what he was doing, so it was my feeling that with one ambulance man and six people, I'd better go with Vicki. I got into the ambulance and it started to move off but the PC got in with me, still holding this oxygen bottle, and we were trying to give Vicki mouth-to-mouth. You could feel the people on the floor rolling against your legs. I was seeing to Vicki again, mouth-to-mouth, trying to keep the oxygen going. The ambulance man was busy checking and he'd already said that there were three, or it might have been two, people on the floor that were dead. I have a very vivid recollection that one of them had actually got one of those breathing tubes in, one of the very few people who had obviously had proper medical attention. So we were in the ambulance and we were hurtling towards what I found out later was the Northern General, which is a journey of about ten minutes in the ambulance. At one stage the ambulance man thought he felt a pulse and you can imagine, my thought was 'Oh, thank God, we've kept her alive.' PC McGuiness gave me a hand and we arrived at the hospital and again it was absolute bedlam.

Ian Battey

The geographical structure of the A & E department caused us some problems. Where ambulance patients come in we store trolleys, so that patients can be placed on a trolley immediately they come out of the ambulance. In a major-incident situation we had to keep those trolleys topped up with trolleys from elsewhere, so that limited the space available. And the storage cupboards for major-incident equipment were in that same location.

You're talking half-a-dozen people, plus the ambulance crew, plus the patient, all in a very confined area of about 11 or 12 feet square. The patients are immediately examined by the medical staff, in this case the consultant; they are labelled by a receptionist; there's a porter there ready to take them to the appropriate area when they've been triaged; and there's myself who's trying to keep a handle on where these people are going and how many staff we need in that area. At one point we actually had three or four patients per resuscitation bay; we'd got so many patients and not enough equipment that we were actually taking them into other areas. We took over the waiting room as an extra resuscitation area. They have piped oxygen suction on the wall and so on, even in the waiting area.

Access to the temporary mortuary from the triage bay was through the waiting area into what would be 'Orthopaedic Outpatients' on a normal weekday. While accepting the initial influx of patients you're almost on auto-pilot. You're hoping everything you've been prepared for falls into place, and hoping that decisions that you make at that time are the right decisions. But there isn't time to stand back and think.

Peter Jackson

It must have been at least 45 minutes before we in the stand fully appreciated what was going on, because even radio reports at the time weren't really telling us what was happening. It was 45 minutes before we really saw that people had been killed. We could see that it was an overcrowding problem and that people were distressed, and that they were trying to get people out. People were walking around and lying down, but within 15 minutes there was a convergence of the emergency services round the end of the pitch and you couldn't actually see. We've subsequently seen, in videos, people being resuscitated, dragged out, etc. You couldn't actually see that. Fortunately, perhaps. What you could see, of course, were people running up and down with stretchers and I'd say it was about 45 minutes before it was obvious that somebody was dead (because the stretcher bearers walked). I remember it being a very small body. Then we appreciated that there were deaths, but again we didn't know what had happened or what had caused this. We'd been instructed by the police to stay where we were. We didn't have relatives that we knew who were in there. We could see that there was no point in us getting involved. Peter [Garrett] was in a moral dilemma because he's a trained first-aid man, but, to be frank, there was no point in him getting involved. It was getting done as fast as it could, so we stayed put until we were finally told to leave the stadium.

David Fairclough, former Liverpool footballer

I was living in Belgium at the time, because I played for SK Beveren. Normally we played on Saturday evening or Sunday afternoon. On this occasion we were playing at home on Saturday evening. Luckily we received BBC television so it was usual for me to watch the 'Grandstand' programme while I relaxed before going to play. On this afternoon I was expecting to watch the rugby and hopefully keep in touch with the news at the Cup semi-final. But it was surprising to find them going over to Hillsborough live at three o'clock. Obviously something major had happened, this wasn't normal. The pictures were numbing, an enormous tragedy evolving, live and on TV. No-one I'm sure could fully understand the implications, or the scenes that were unfolding. It was just incredible to think 'Jesus, people are dying there, at a football match', not knowing how many would be killed by the end of that fateful afternoon.

Peter Johnson, chairman of Tranmere Rovers

I was with Tranmere. I was up at Hartlepool, and shortly after the kick-off, someone came out and said the match at Hillsborough had been delayed. There were some 'crowd problems', as I think it was described at the time. Shortly afterwards, someone came and said 'One person's been killed.' And my mind went back to Heysel. I had been at Heysel, and the game couldn't start, you may recall, and people were rushing around in a Kop with very few people on it. That was the terrible thing about it. The people died at Heysel on an almost vacant Kop, whereas at the end where the Juventus fans were packed, jam-full, there was no problem. I was sitting at Hartlepool and my mind went back to that match at Heysel. And then at half-time, of course, the horror scenes were on television.

Pat Nicol

I had the television on and, after about half an hour, something told me to stop recording and turn the sound off. I don't know why. There's no reason for it. So I stopped recording. It had recorded for about thirty-five minutes. And then about half-past three a number to ring came up on the screen. I rang that number from half past threeish, from when it came up on that screen. (I was ringing until about half past five and they never answered that phone once.) I put the phone down and the phone rang and it was my son. He said 'Mum, where's Lee?' He had heard about it in work, and he came down then. On television you could see the bodies on the pitch, and the body I was looking at was my son and I didn't know. When I was watching it, I could see a red bundle being passed over the side of the goal-post and I thought 'That person's dead. Whoever it is is dead.' It looked to me like a boy of about eight or nine in red but Lee was very blond and the boy's hair looked dark. I thought 'He's got Lee's shoes on', but only because they were new shoes and they were these horrible big Hi-Tec silver things and Lee was only five foot and five stone and, God, these shoes looked enormous on him. I didn't think it was Lee, to be honest. It didn't enter my head. I knew something had happened to him but I thought 'That little boy's dead.' They put him on the side of the pitch. Then they were going into the ambulances and one thing and another. There was that much going on. Andrew had arrived by then and I said 'I've got to go to Sheffield, I don't know how to get there. You stay here and answer the phone.' I rang the police here, and they were useless. I know it was a tragedy, an emergency, but it was awful.

Rob White

Having passed the hoardings over the fence, my thoughts turned to my colleague who I had become separated from even before the teams had come onto the pitch. The last time that I had seen him, he was about 10 feet behind me and I felt sure that he would not have been in the same danger that I had been in, because the worst part of the crush seemed to have been congregated along the length of the perimeter fence, and back just as far as the first set of barriers which were nearest to it. This had at least seemed the case when I had been trapped, because some people behind me had been able to climb out over the top of those of us at the front.

Nevertheless, I was naturally concerned to find him, in view of what I had seen happening to other people. I stood and scanned the centre terrace section to see if he was still amongst those who had remained in that part of the ground, and then likewise around the side section of the terrace where I was standing myself, but to no avail.

I then hobbled down towards a gate in the perimeter fence and a policeman on the other side helped to lift me through it and onto the pitch. He asked if I needed my leg seeing to, but as that was not of immediate concern to me, I replied that I would be all right.

I started looking at people on the pitch in an attempt to reunite myself with my colleague. By this time, most people were standing around and it appeared that most of the injured fans had already been taken care of. There were still a few injured people receiving attention, but for most people on the pitch there did not seem to be any further assistance that they could give. As I walked across the pitch, grown men who had been reunited with their friends were standing with their arms round each other, crying on each other's shoulders. Everyone around knew just how they felt and shared in their sense of relief at finding each other, but at the same time there was an atmosphere of numbness at the shock of seeing so many who had suffered so much.

Despite having earlier convinced myself that my colleague would have been safe where he was standing, I began to feel anxious that maybe something had happened to him. I looked back at the terraces behind the goal and walked along the touchline to try and catch sight of him, but there was no sign of him anywhere. I walked around the perimeter of the pitch in front of the stands and then backwards and forwards across the pitch, but still nothing.

Then I also remembered that the media were covering the match, and feared that my family and my girlfriend would be sitting at home aware of the tragedy that had just occurred, and would be fearing for my safety. I thought that I would have to let them know that I was all right as soon as I possibly could, to stop them worrying about me. I thought about trying to get to a telephone outside, but nobody appeared to be leaving the ground and, indeed, there had been an announcement over the public address system requesting that people did not leave the ground in order to avoid causing congestion in the streets around the stadium, which needed to be kept clear to allow ambulances to gain access. So I thought that I would have to stay where I was. I knew that I had to get in touch with those at home—but how could I?

Steve McMahon
There was precious little conversation in our dressing-room, which is usually alive with banter, but on this occasion no one had anything to say.

John Aldridge
When we did get told the match had been abandoned, we went upstairs to the players' lounge, out of the way, and the telly was on there. It kept on coming over that 'so many' more were dead, and it was just horrendous. A horrible feeling. You couldn't take it in. We just felt so helpless. I sat down and thought 'It shouldn't have happened. They came to watch Liverpool—a game of football—and now they're dead.' I couldn't take it in. They only came to watch a game of football.

Alan Hansen
I'm sitting there, and, probably because I'm so hyped up, it has not hit me at all. We got upstairs and the girls upstairs, in the players' lounge, they're all

crying their eyes out, because they're watching it on television. It still hasnae hit me.

Steve McMahon

John Barnes was in a terrible state. He couldn't say anything to anybody. He was inconsolable; he was in tears. Even Susie couldn't calm him down, she just put her arm around him in an effort to comfort him. The full impact of what had happened just seemed to hit Barnsie right away, yet it didn't really strike home to the rest of us until the next day, or maybe, in some cases, even a day or two later, perhaps because we were in such a state of shock.

Paul Edwards, Liverpool supporter

I went to the match with three friends. I remember shouting to a policeman even before we went into the ground because the crush was so bad. Within seconds of getting into the terrace I lost sight of all three friends. I scrambled up a wall so I was standing above the terrace. I spent the next hour trying to attract the attention of my friends who by this time were on the pitch. I could see them crying and looking for me among the dead bodies. My Dad and the rest of my family were sitting in stands to the side and they didn't know what had happened to me. My Mum was waiting at home for the phone call, so it affected everybody.

Dr Colin Flenley

After there appeared to be no more bodies on the pitch I was then in a state of disbelief again. I was wandering around the pitch really. Somebody came up and gave me a cup of water. My mouth was parched. I remember looking back behind the goal and seeing this pile of clothes. That struck me. They were clothes from the dead, or they may have been clothes from fans who'd got out but had had coats ripped off them in the pressure. They'd been collected from the Leppings Lane end and put there, presumably by policemen or fans. That's something that will stick in my mind. That was what struck me. That looked like Auschwitz. When you see pictures of these piles of shoes, you think of Auschwitz.

I can remember chatting to a policeman at that time. There was one motor-bike policeman who said to me 'We were afraid something like this would happen at some stage.' He said there was an FA Cup semi-final [at Hillsborough] quite a few years ago, Tottenham and somebody [Wolves in 1981]. He said 'We nearly had something like this then. We were saying to the people that you shouldn't really have a big semi-final like this here.' So that made me annoyed.

I wandered round and started chatting to other people to share what had gone on and what they'd done and what I'd done. People were beginning to say 'The Liverpool fans should never have been at this end, we should have been down the other end.' There was that. There was also 'You know, it wasn't like this last year, it was a bit more organised last year.' The number of fans like myself who had got in without having their tickets taken. I got in through the side door, which was freely open.

Dr Tom Heller, in the gymnasium

I had taken my bags full of the equipment and drugs that I usually use. Not much call for antibiotics or infant paracetamol this afternoon. After some time—how long?—I became aware of a friend of mine going between the bodies doing the same as I was. Another general practitioner. We had worked together in the past but not on anything like this, nor are we likely to again. A smile of recognition. I wonder if I looked as lost as he did.

The first large scale equipment arrived, and we started working together, putting up drips on everyone. We intubated as many patients and established as many airways as we possibly could. We needed scissors to cut through clothes. Why didn't I carry them in my bags? We started giving intravenous diamorphine, and some sort of routine and organisation began to be established. I'm quite proud in a funny sort of way to be able to put up so many intravenous drips so quickly without missing a vein. More doctors had arrived by now, and around every body there was a little huddle of workers. Someone said that he was an anaesthetist—a man of gold dust. Come over here and look at Terry for me, mate. He's still alive, but he keeps stopping breathing. 'Hang on, Terry'. The anaesthetist took out the airway, and it was blocked with blood. Not a good sign. One rib seemed to be almost through the chest and was certainly at the wrong angles. The ambulance stretchers arrived, and we put in a passionate bid for Terry to be taken off first. By now six people were around him, holding the drip bottle, his head, and his legs, which were at all angles. He was rested on to a low trolley. I checked that the ambulance was waiting and could get through to the hospital. The anaesthetist went with Terry to the ambulance. Thank God for anaesthetists. I'll never tell an anti-anaesthetist joke again.

Now that I had no one to work on I wandered around and could see the dead bodies again at the other side of the sports hall. Among the doctors I recognised many of my friends and colleagues who had also answered the call of duty. One of them gave me a hug, bless him—a friend for life after what we went through that day. The police were much in evidence, but nobody was in charge of the medical tasks. What should I do next? Where would I be most useful? I decided to use my newly refound skills to put up drips on everybody who was going to be transferred to hospital. I somehow remembered that this was the thing to do in case the patients suffered more collapse on the way to hospital. It was also a sign to the hospital doctors that we general practitioners could do something right after all. I used up all of my diamorphine on those in need.

Ian Battey

One of the overwhelming things that I remember from that whole episode was that people were volunteering and were willing to do anything. People who had heard it on the radio had come to the hospital. The only place they knew to go to was Casualty. They didn't know where relatives' bases or staff-reporting bases were, or anything like that, so they went to Casualty. So they were coming in the same doors as the casualties were coming in. You've got people there who are coming from the Red Cross or St John's or just people off the street who were saying 'Do you need me to donate my blood?' or 'Can I come in and make you all a cup of tea?' or 'Can we mop the floors?' or 'What needs doing?' I said 'Thanks for coming, but this is the wrong place. If you want to help I suggest you go to the next entrance down.' We had GPs volunteering, we had people travelling in, we had people on the motorway between Leeds and Sheffield who, instead of going home, came straight to the hospital. We had people from all over the place: nurses who worked at different hospitals who just came to offer any kind of help as a pair of hands: 'I can work on a medical ward if you need to release staff to go and work elsewhere.' It makes your heart feel good that people do respond in that kind of situation. But it did cause me a severe headache, just dealing with the sheer volume of people, and all I really wanted to deal with was the casualties coming through the door.

We then had a dilemma with the fact that we didn't have enough equipment. We had 17 or 18 people who were in need of ventilated support. Now, the A & E department only holds three ventilators. Where do you find ventilators? We were calling on intensive care, we were calling on the operating theatre, to try to send equipment down so we could support the staff. Simple things like drip-stands. Somebody turned up in an estate car from somewhere with a pile of brand new drip-stands, which were fine, but it took people 15 minutes to unwrap them because of the cellophane and the Sellotape. These are the small things which stick in my mind. Looking back, they're almost comical, seeing people sat in a car-park trying to unwrap drip-stands. Alongside that, people were coming in the back of ambulances, policemen and all sorts of people, travelling to the hospital with casualties, having assisted in the resuscitation at the scene, and they were actually standing in resuscitation rooms holding bags of fluids above their heads because there were no drip-stands to hang them on.

Dr Tom Heller

By this time the routines were more established. Someone was writing down the obvious major damage to each person and what he or she had received in the way of drugs, etc. Then suddenly there was nobody left in the hall who was in need of attention and who wasn't dead. I noticed a close friend amid the sea of dead faces. He was comforting someone who was leaning over a body. I stepped over some bodies to speak to him and offer some help; there weren't any words, just a look of rare empathy and comradeship. The doctors in the hall grouped together, almost silent, all wondering what to do next. I left the hall and walked through the silent crowds back to my car. I went home stunned and numbed. My children were playing in the garden; it was all so lovely and normal. Sandpits and skipping-ropes.

Ian Battey

We received the first casualty about twenty past three, and we're probably talking somewhere in the region of quarter-to-four or four o'clock when all the services that the hospital mobilises really started to impact. Volunteers were there almost as soon as the casualties started arriving. My feeling is that, because of the high media impact, people were aware of it before we were. We couldn't get hold of our own A & E specialist staff on the phone because they were out shopping or enjoying the sun or whatever, but within an hour of us needing them we had a complement. Those not there weren't in Sheffield. A colleague of mine subsequently told me that she was on a weekend away in Blackpool and she said they came back after being out for the day; they were watching it on the TV and she was literally running round the hotel room at seven or eight o'clock at night like a headless chicken, wondering whether she should come back to Sheffield, whether there was anything she could do if she came back, and almost feeling guilty that she wasn't there.

One of the other things about the way in which the hospital mobilises was the fact we mobilise operating theatres. There are staff called in, we put operating theatres on standby and they cancel operations, which on a Saturday were only emergency operations anyway. There were people put on standby in operating theatres who never did a thing, and who subsequently felt guilty because they could have come down to A & E or they could have been in a ward area. They were needed where they were, just in case, but I think there was one broken wrist that was set and that was about it.

The majority of injuries that we had were consistent with crush injuries, people who just did not have enough room to expand their chests. To take a breath you obviously have to expand your chest at least an inch or so. We did have people coming in with the more overt crush injuries, like broken ribs, but the predominance were people who'd stopped breathing, and they'd stopped breathing because they literally couldn't breathe. And because they'd stopped breathing then their hearts had stopped. So the majority of people needed immediate resuscitation, and were in effect in a cardiac-arrest situation—their hearts had stopped, they had no spontaneous breathing and therefore needed full life support to actually do that. There were very, very few other injuries that were actually sustained by the people that we saw, but I'm aware that some people crushed at the bottom of the fence, for example, had sustained broken bones. The rest of it was bruised limbs, those kind of things.

I think there were two occasions when the triage system let us down. The way we were actually prioritising patients, we'd actually sent two patients round to the immediate treatment area who were not requiring immediate resuscitation. It was difficult to distinguish between the hysteria which goes with a situation like this and those suffering from a lack of oxygen to the brain. They had to come back because their condition deteriorated, either in transit between A & E and that area or while they were actually there. They came back for ventilating. So even the best laid plans of mice and men don't always work to the best of our ability.

Other things were going on at the same time, like the setting-up of police reporting bases. We set up a temporary mortuary and we had 11 or 12 patients who were either dead on arrival or who died despite resuscitation attempts. They were labelled with a hospital number and colour-coded to go to that area. As things started to quieten down, one of the reception staff was asked if she would go and document as far as possible who these people were, and she had got no training and no idea what she was going to walk into in that room. Somebody had said, just off the top of their head 'Would you mind checking that room and marking.' She opened the door and there were 12 bodies. They were on the couches, they were on the floor, and that was very difficult for her to cope with, and caused some anxiety in dealing with that.

Rob White, on the Hillsborough pitch

I wandered around not knowing what to do, and I was getting increasingly worried about not being able to allay the fears of my loved ones. Then I noticed that the Nottingham Forest manager had come onto the pitch, and was being interviewed by a television crew. There was a cordon of police across the width of the pitch between me and the impromptu gathering of newsmen by the players' tunnel entrance, but I thought that here was my chance to pass my message home, so I casually walked through the police line, expecting to be questioned, but I was allowed to pass through unchallenged. I was confused as to why it had been deemed necessary for there to be such a line there anyway at this time. I then went over towards the group of people who had converged around Brian Clough and noticed that there was another hand-held television camera on the pitch nearer to me, filming two fans who had escaped the crush. Out of desperation, I walked up behind them and put my head between theirs in an attempt to get myself seen on television and show everyone at home that I was alive. I just mouthed the words 'I'm all right, I'm all right' as if I was talking directly to my family and the cameraman was providing a link-up service. Then I realised, however, that any pictures were probably being recorded and edited, so the chances were, that idea would not have had the desired effect, so I frantically tried to think of something else.

Then I noticed a ground official nearby with a portable telephone. I thought that my prayers had been answered, so I walked over to where he was standing and gave him my phone number and pleaded with him to ring it for me. He dialled the first half of the number and then the screen went blank. The battery had gone because he had phoned for so many other people before I had reached him. I was becoming increasingly perturbed over the fact that the nightmare that I thought had ended when I managed to escape from the crush, was continuing for different reasons.

I then walked back to the Leppings Lane end of the ground, where I had originally been trapped. The centre section of the terracing was now occupied by a number of policemen who were sitting down with their helmets in their hands, looking just as dazed and shocked as everyone else.

Some of them were crying as they reflected upon the awfulness of what they had witnessed.

Dennis Cerrone

I did go over to the gym at one point, but I didn't go in. I stopped at the door and I thought 'I'm not going to go in unless somebody's got a job for me in there, because I don't want to go in and see all that.' I stood there for a bit— people were going in and out—and I thought 'I'll go and ask somebody', but I don't know whether I did or not. If they wanted me in to do a job, I'd go in and do it, but there were loads of people already in there and some of them were just wandering round, not actually organised. It's a bit vague from there on.

Rob White

I could not decide what to do next. Should I stay in the ground and try and find my colleague, or should I try and leave and look for a public telephone to phone home? I again reassured myself that my colleague would have been in a far better position than me, and, as I had survived, so I felt sure that no harm would have come to him. In any case, when we had first arrived we had agreed to meet back at the car if we were separated for any reason, although obviously at that time we did not envisage the circumstances which were to lead to that becoming a reality. That's it, I thought. He'll be back at the car wondering where I am.

I went over to the corner of the pitch, where I saw someone going through a gate back onto the terrace. I asked a policeman who was standing by the gate whether it was possible to get out of the ground, even though the vast majority of people were still in their places. He directed me down a side passage which led away from the side section of the terrace, having told me that it led to the exit. This was the first time that I had realised that there was another entrance/exit leading to the terrace, other than the tunnel by which I had gained access to the terrace myself.

Halfway along the passage, I came across a supporter who was walking in the opposite direction, back towards the terrace. He actually asked me if I knew whether the match was still going to be played or not! I just hope that he had not been aware of the scale of what had happened if he was able to ask such a question. He could not possibly have seen the sort of scenes that I had witnessed, surely. I half looked at him and muttered 'I sincerely hope not', before continuing along the passage to the exit.

The game was over as far as I was concerned. How could they possibly play a match now? I thought of the young victims that I had seen crushed to death. It wasn't just their ages and the number of bodies that I had seen that distressed me, it was the way they had died that was so terrible. They had known what was happening to them, just as I had known what was happening to me. The only difference was that I still knew, and always would—but they knew no more.

Match? What match?

Ian Battey

The press were starting to arrive. I remember one particular situation. There was a lull in the casualties that were actually arriving. We seemed to have had ambulances non-stop, and then the ambulances stopped coming and we had a breathing space. It must have only been a matter of four or five minutes, but there was time to stop, take a breath, mop the brow, and I remember going outside into the sunshine. I squatted down with my back against the A & E doors and it was then, as my body physically relaxed slightly, that the magnitude of what we were dealing with actually struck me. I was squatting down, my back against the wall, and I put my head in my hands and I thought 'What on earth has happened here?' I still didn't know what had gone off at the ground. 'Why are all these people here?' was going through my mind.

Somebody from inside asked for something and it was kind of a subliminal thing; I wasn't really listening to it, but knew that I had to get up and do something about it. I moved my hands out of the way and there was a TV camera right in front of me and at that point I had great problems in restraining myself. I could have very easily stood up and hit that man. All right, he was doing his job, but that brought home to me some of the sharper edges of what we were actually dealing with, the media issues, and the fact that people obviously need to know about what goes on. Having that camera pointing at my face and seeing this bloke stood there was something I found very difficult to cope with emotionally. And then I had to go back in as the next few ambulances arrived and put my professional head back on and get back on with the job at hand.

Mike Lewis

There were lots of rumours flying around, but I was checking PA [Press Association] wires, monitoring television, and monitoring everything we could, and we were absolutely convinced by that time that people had died. We would normally have been deciding which semi-final to go to, but we were concentrating on Hillsborough and balancing that with the other sport. We didn't feel it was right for Peter [Jones] to just hold it because he didn't really have a lot to say—he was sitting up in the stand. We had a reporter and a producer downstairs in the dressing-room area but obviously it was difficult for them to get on the pitch. So we went off to Villa Park, did some commentary, back to Hillsborough, where Peter's saying 'There's no way this game can go ahead', then back to Villa Park, back to Hillsborough, back to Villa Park, and after about 20 minutes into the second half, Peter reported that the game had been officially abandoned.

Steve Hanley, Kop end

The match was called off at about 4.20 and someone with a radio said they'd heard that five were dead. By the time I reached my car, the number was fifty. Since then, everybody has been blamed—the FA, the police, the host club, the fans. It's not my place to assign blame, all I can do is express the shock, horror and sympathy that fell upon me. We've been in that end before and know how cramped it is. We went to see Liverpool FC get hammered and we saw people, the same as ourselves, die. Those of us at Hillsborough on 15 April 1989 spent 100 minutes staring at the most awful event of our lives.

Steve Way, Kop end

Not all Forest fans were angels. One lout cheered another Liverpool death. He was set upon. The man in front of us had to be violently restrained by his mates from mutilating him. 'He's scum.' 'He's not worth it', they cried. Indeed he wasn't.

The watching role was not easy. By now Forest fans were drifting out of the ground. Their exit lines were estimates of the fatalities, gleaned from the transistor radios which some fans carry to hear half-time scores. They all turned out to be too low.

The police, fearing that emotions would turn to violence, brought in the dogs. They added to the horror by continually barking or playing dead, echoing the corpses beside them. Though the police were doing their job, their apparent indifference to those around them was hard to stomach. In the end, having done our 90 minutes, my friend and I left.

Simon Pinnington

When we left the ground the feeling of helplessness became worse. We walked back towards the coaches with scores of people in an eerie silence, broken only by the sound of weeping.

Jenni Hicks

I left with everyone else. I walked out of that place like a zombie and walked and stood in this little shop doorway [where the Hicks family had arranged to meet]. It was just yards away from the Leppings Lane gate. As I stood there the people from the Leppings Lane terraces were coming out and I was scanning the crowd for Sarah and Vicki and Trevor. There were police standing around, I suppose to make sure that the crowd got out without any problems. There were an awful lot of people shouting abuse at the police. I am standing there trying to think 'It is going to be OK', and I could hear the fans coming out and shouting to the police: 'Fucking well people dead in there. There are women and kids dying in there. It's all your fault.' And they were shouting this abuse at the police, and I was trying to cut off from that because I didn't want to know that people were dead, because that was too frightening a prospect. The police just stood there, almost in a zombie-like position, like I was in. They just stood there. They didn't retaliate at all. They stood there. They knew that they had a big problem. I think they were grateful that that was all they were getting—verbal abuse. Because, let's face it, the people who had just come off those terraces had been fighting for their lives. They couldn't breathe and one thing or another. I didn't realise it at the time, but looking back on it, it could have been a much worse problem. The only thing that was happening was verbal. There was nobody throwing punches or getting hold of them. If you had struggled in there and you thought the police hadn't done enough for you, it could well have happened. And it didn't.

Rob White

I walked out into the street and saw that other people had already left the ground. A man was banging his hand on the side of a police car which had parked on the other side of the road, directly opposite the Leppings Lane turnstiles. He was shouting at the driver. No attempt was made by other police officers around to restrain the man. He was not being aggressive or threatening, he was rather expressing his anger and frustration. Whilst I would not wish to condone his actions in any way, I could understand that an experience such as that endured by so many people that day, and maybe also by the man I saw in front of me, could quite easily provoke such an unbalanced response. Although I could understand his emotion, I did not agree with what he was doing and I could not see it achieving anything. However, I do think that his state of despair was responsible for his behaviour.

I believe that this was also recognised by those people around the man who were calmly trying to defuse the situation, and so prevent it from becoming confrontational. Although I did not wait to see if there were any further developments, I would not consider what I saw to be interpretable as a criminal offence. I would stress, most strongly, that the incident I have just described was the only time during the whole afternoon that I had personally seen any action which I would describe as 'disagreeable'. Prior to that, every action of the fans that I had seen had been totally admirable, beyond reproach and, at times, quite heroic. From the time that I was trapped on the terrace, until I actually left the ground, the impression that I had was that most of the initiative was being shown by fans themselves who had been aware of the scale of the problem far sooner than those people who had been on the other side of the fence from the beginning.

Ian Battey

We had a particular problem—and again it's one of those things that, in hindsight, should never have happened—whereby relatives of casualties were funnelled away from the A & E department to a 'relative reception base' (a) to allow people to get on with the resuscitation side and the treatment of the casualties, but (b) to also offer support to friends, relatives, whoever it may be as they should arrive. And that meant that we had to lock a set of doors, which were the normal walking wounded entrance to the casualty department, and just use the ambulance entrance for that department. Unfortunately, it took 20 or 25 minutes for the penny to drop that we hadn't locked those doors, and we'd got relatives in the waiting-area for A & E, which we were having to start using for the spill-over of casualties.

Trevor Hicks

I remember the charge nurse. It was a hot day and the sweat was pouring out of his face. There was a lot going on but the guy was stood still, sweating profusely, running this like a military operation. They call this triage, as I now understand it. They quickly whipped Vicki into one of the crash rooms at the side. I was with her. I'd identified her, tied a little tag to her foot, and they immediately started injecting her with adrenalin and then I was asked to go outside. The police constable and the medical team worked on her for what seemed about ten or fifteen minutes. This is all a case of overdrive. I know I sound as though I'm busy thinking all this out. I'm not. It's almost like being in your own little time-capsule. All this is going around you. You're not going through the normal thought processes: 'Must do this, must do that.' You're working on auto-pilot. I was still functioning but very practically I suppose, not deliberately. It was not 'Oh, I must do this.' You're living on your instinct, I suppose. Then another moment I remember very clearly was when PC McGuiness had to come back out, and he actually told me that Vicki had been pronounced dead. Then it was as if a switch went and all I was bothered about was Sarah. I knew I'd got Vicki to hospital. She'd got attention, they couldn't do anything. Obviously I was crying by this time but then all I wanted to do was to find Sarah. It seemed natural to me that she'd end up at the hospital. She'd been on the pitch, the ambulances started coming, and we were in the first one, as I understood it. I didn't know what was going on outside the ground, of course, or that casualties were also going to the Hallamshire. As far as I was concerned, she was going to hospital, so I went off wandering round the wards.

Ian Battey

I vividly remember one gentleman who came up to me and said 'I'm trying to find my daughter.' This transpired to be Trevor Hicks. And my first priority really was to try and encourage that gentleman to leave the A & E department and go to the relatives' base, and I made this suggestion to him and he was quite adamant that he wanted to stay around, he was looking for his daughter. And I said: 'Well at the moment there's nothing I can do. If they are here they'll be having treatment, and if they're not here then I don't know where they'll be going', because obviously in that kind of instance there'll be more than one hospital receiving casualties. I eventually got a member of staff who'd come down to assist Mr Hicks to the staff base.

Trevor Hicks

It sounds impossible but it was just bedlam. I have no criticism of the medical staff. I mean, they were flat out. The disaster plan had obviously collapsed, they were just overwhelmed with people, and I spend half an hour or three quarters of an hour wandering around talking to administrators, giving descriptions, doing this, doing that. Eventually I ended up in the casualty area and I'm still looking for Sarah, because I knew she was in a bad way as well. What I didn't know, of course, was just how bad. If I remember rightly, they were using one of the side wards as a temporary mortuary and a nurse, I think, took me to this police officer who was busy setting up a casualty bureau, if you like. I was asked for another description—it was probably the fifth or the sixth—and I described her: white teeshirt and jeans, brown boots, Swatch watch, that kind of thing. Sarah had fairly short blonde hair, shoulder length. Vicki had hip-length, dark, curly hair, so they were very dissimilar in that sense. Anyway, the police officer said 'I think I might have someone who fits that description.' Bear in mind that all I've heard is that there are about seven to eleven people dead. And I'm thinking that surely Sarah can't be one of them. Vicki's one of them, but there can't be any more. The odds are against it. To be honest, it hadn't entered into my head at this time that Sarah could be dead. She was injured somewhere. That was it as far as I knew. Anyway, it's a bit of a long story so I'll keep it short but I was shown a Swatch watch. One had a dark grey watch, the other had a black one. I said 'It looks as though it could be hers', so I was then taken by a young PC and a female padre across to the hospital mortuary. From the hubbub of everything else, the bedlam, there was this peaceful situation where the trolley came out with some sort of frame over it. It looked like a tent arrangement and they peeled back this dark wine coloured cover and it was Vicki. I had steeled myself for thinking it was Sarah and it was Vicki again. I couldn't believe it. I remember swearing: 'For fuck's sake, I've identified her three times already.'

With hindsight you have to accept that things can go wrong, but they'd already tied a label on her—how could they possibly think it wasn't her? Anyway, I got over that, but you can imagine the trauma. I'm getting to my wits' end now. There's no sign of Sarah. By this time, I've come to the conclusion she's not at the Northern General. No sign of Jenni. I'm worried sick where she is. I know she isn't injured because she was up in the stand but as far as I'm concerned she's probably gone off her trolley by this time. She doesn't know where I am. In fact I now know that I was reported missing as well, because Jenni didn't know that I wasn't in that pen.

Jenni Hicks, waiting outside the Leppings Lane tobacconist

The most awful feeling was when nobody else came out of the ground. As the people were coming out, I was hoping, waiting for them, and they are all coming. Each one is a chance. They are coming and coming, and then it thins out and thins out, and eventually nobody comes. And I am still standing in the doorway. I suddenly thought 'Oh, my God.'

I did what we were always brought up to do—I went and asked a policeman. I'd brought my daughters up the same way: If you have got a problem and you are not sure what to do, or if you have run out of money, go and find a policeman. That is what they are there for, isn't it? I went up to a policeman and a policewoman. I explained my situation. I said 'My two daughters and my husband were on the Leppings Lane stand where you have had the problems. I have got no money and no car keys. What do I do?' And they said 'Oh, just walk round to the back of the stand. Somebody is sorting out names and descriptions of people.' I was totally on my own from then on.

I walked round to the back of the North Stand, where they had got a trestle-table set up. I found my way round there eventually. I had to walk right round this area and eventually saw this table set up underneath, where they said it would be. Police were there taking names and descriptions of people. I gave names and descriptions of Sarah, Vicki and Trevor and I was assured they were 'not in'. Well, I didn't know it was a temporary mortuary. It didn't sink in.

So I said the same again: 'I am in a strange city, I have got no car keys, no money and I am on my own.' And he just said 'Where's your car parked?' I said 'Well, it is in the car-park about ten minutes walk away, but what is the point in going to the car? I can't even touch the car because the alarm is on.' So he said 'Well, that's where they will be, you have got split up.' He didn't seem to be listening to what I was saying. That's when I said 'No, these are my family, they said they would meet me in that shop doorway. They know I will have seen what has gone on and I would be terribly worried. No way are they—one or all of them—not going to be at the appointed meeting-place unless they are injured and they can't physically be there. If they could physically be there, they would be there.' But he didn't want to know this. He wasn't interested in that. Again, I did as he said. I walked to the car-park. Walked halfway round the ground. By this time the hysteria was starting. I couldn't control it any more.

On my way to the car-park I passed a Scottish couple, and they said 'Are you all right?' I said 'I've lost my husband and two daughters, I can't find them and they were on that Leppings Lane end.' These two had obviously been to the match, and I said that I was just running to the car-park: 'I just want to find them.'

I could see the car-park in the distance and the thing that still sticks in my mind is that our car was the only one left there. And there was nobody there. And I still ran to the car. I knew I mustn't touch it, because if I touched it I would have set the alarm off. And I just stood there looking around this empty car-park with our silver Granada standing there, and I thought 'What am I going to do? What do I do now? I haven't even got any money for bus fare. Where do I go from here? I will have to go back to the ground and tell these people "Look, they are not at the car-park".'

Steve Way

Outside was equally chaotic. Hillsborough is about two miles out of the centre of Sheffield down a straight road punctuated every hundred yards by junctions and traffic lights. It was an end-of-the-world snarl-up. Cars which had moved out of the lanes to allow the emergency services through had got wedged. People had tried to filter out of parking spaces and side roads only to get stuck. Lights went from red to green but nothing moved. Fleets of football buses stood in broken lines. Shocked fans sat inside them not caring that they weren't moving. Eventually everyone, like refugees, started to walk. Forest fans walked with Liverpool fans.

Peter Jackson

I think at about 4.30 it was Rogan Taylor who said 'I think we'll just hang around here, let's find out precisely what's happened.' And I think we went on the pitch straight away. We went onto the terrace and we started talking to people who were in obvious states of distress. People were telling us that the police had just opened the gate and let people just walk in willy-nilly without tickets, whatever. And Peter Garrett [a Liverpool policeman] said at that stage 'Well, if that's what they've done it's murder.' He said it to a policeman and we had to drag him off the policeman.

We went onto the terrace and saw the debris left behind—the spectacles, the programmes, the scarves, the clothes. We then went outside. When we went outside we were accosted by several people who were pointing out to us the gate that had been opened and were keen to give us phone numbers and addresses for eye-witness accounts. It was at that point that we thought that we had better get to a media outlet of some sort. Thinking about it, we were hard-faced at the time because we just went round to the main entrance and walked in. We weren't just doing it for the hell of it, we had a purpose. John Williams, for instance, was an academic in football. I remember that as we walked round an ambulance arrived and we almost walked into body-bags. We went in through the main entrance into the press box. It was at that point that we were told about the allegation that fans had kicked the door down and it had been a fan-induced riot, if you want to call it that. It was a good job really that we did make the media communications that we did. Rogan was whisked off for one of the local radio stations. I think it was Graham Beecroft, who was at Radio Merseyside at the time, and I did Radio City with Liam O'Donoghue, and then I think it was the 'stringer' [freelance] who was doing all the local radio down in the South Midlands. Whilst I was being interviewed with him, a guy who writes for the *Mail*, Bob Cass, came back in and said 'The fans are telling us that the police opened the gates and there was a big influx and what do you expect?' He'd gone outside and started asking people himself, because at that stage he didn't know us. I remember him coming back while I was being interviewed and saying 'Well, actually, this appears to be true. This is what the fans are saying.'

Graham Kelly

I don't know what the immediate hospitality area, the directors' box holds, say, 100 people. These 100 people were all around. Anyone might be asking me a question at any time and I would be telling them what was going on as far as I could. The referee made his room available to us somehow, although it wasn't very large, and it just dragged on and on and on and we couldn't get any information. It went on for over an hour.

During that time, while we were waiting, a limited number of supporters were coming through, down the players' tunnel, and I was getting a competing story from them, either direct or second-hand, that a gate had been opened. That led to confusion. You just don't know what is the truth. To this day, I don't think we were told that the match had been abandoned. I think that the announcement went out over the tannoy before 4.30. Obviously the teams had given up by then. I certainly wasn't officially informed. I don't know what was said to the club secretary or to the referee. But again it's one of those situations when somebody's here and somebody's there and you just don't know. Nobody came to me and said the match has been abandoned. It was passed on and passed on by word of mouth that an announcement had been made. I was underneath the stand virtually all the time.

I don't recall specifically anyone saying 'There's twenty lost' or 'There's thirty lost'. My only recollection is of the time when I eventually had to face the media. I think the first one was live BBC television and then BBC Radio, maybe BBC Radio Merseyside, I'm not sure. And then the written press. That series of interviews started at about twenty to five and I think the number quoted to me at that time was about fifty. That's the figure I gave, so obviously it was. I don't recall what was said before that, I'm not sure what numbers I heard after that. On my first interview, at twenty to five on television, I went straight in front of the camera and said what I'd heard, that there were two stories [about the gate] and I didn't know which was correct, if either.

Mike Lewis

Score updates. Back to Villa Park. Then Alan Green did an interview with Graham Kelly. It was a good interview in very difficult circumstances. Graham Kelly explained as much as he knew about what had happened. By that time there was about a quarter of an hour left at Villa Park. Back to Villa Park for a bit of commentary. Back to John Inverdale, who gave out some emergency numbers that we'd got by then. We were trying to piece together the story, and by that time we were thinking about how to do the top of 'Sports Report' and how to tell this story.

You're just trying to do the best programme you can, to tell the story the best you can and not to hide anything. We kept thinking 'Are we right to be doing the other game? What else should we be doing?' You don't really have time to take stock. You're just trying to keep the programme going and make decisions about what to do in the future and make decisions about taste and decency, check the facts, try not to go over the top and try to keep a sense of balance in the coverage. Pat Thornton was holding the programme together, keeping calm and talking about the next moves. I was talking to reporters at Hillsborough, talking to Peter Jones, trying to see what he wanted to do. You have to be guided very much by the people there. Obviously there were scores coming in from all over the place. There was of course the other semi-final, with Everton one up through Pat Nevin in the first half, and the crowd there were basically unaware of what was going on.

We went back to Peter, who said 'There's a sense of peace now.' By that time there were only about 50 or 60 people left on the pitch. The game had been abandoned and the majority of fans had left the stadium. Then he told this story about how a young Liverpool fan had climbed up the stairs and asked to use the phone to call his mother. And Jonesy said 'He was pale and he was crying', and he ended the report by saying 'And of course he can, of course he can.'

Dr Colin Flenley

After a period of time I thought 'Well, I'd better go and find my friends.' I got out of the ground and first of all I thought 'I'd better go and phone my wife and tell her I'm all right.' I knocked on the door of the first house I could see, and an old lady opened the door. She was a bit deaf and she hadn't got a clue what had gone on. I said 'Do you mind if I phone my family because there's been a disaster at the football ground?' She said 'Yes, come in.' That was another memory, knocking on the door of this lady's house, because there was a queue of Liverpool fans outside virtually every other house up and down the road. People were letting them use their phones and people were coming out wanting to know if you wanted a cup of tea or a biscuit or anything like that. They were wanting to know if you were all right.

I phoned my wife. She'd already been told by our next-door neighbours that there'd been a problem. She didn't know where I was in the ground but she knew there was a problem, and the neighbours had come round to sit with her until I phoned. After I made that phone call I started to walk up the road and I saw my mates driving down. They were trying to look for me. They didn't know where I was. They had been in the stands. They'd been told by the police to leave the ground, which they'd done. So they'd been driving up and down trying to find me. We got in the car and none of us talked, apart from me. My friend said to me afterwards that all he could remember was me just going over what had happened and what I'd seen. But the others were just speechless.

Anonymous Male Spectator

We went back to the car, drove out of the housing estate that we were parked in and found a phone, and luckily after what I've heard since, we must have been so lucky, but we got through to my sister's house, and we left a message with her to say that we were all right and that the mates that were with us were all right.

Anonymous Male Spectator

The security guy at the factory across the road [from the ground] said 'We've opened up. If you want to use the phones and the toilets, come on in.'

Jill Thomas, on duty at the gymnasium door

Relatives were coming over and saying 'I want to go in, I want to go in, I want to see if my son's there.' I was on the door, just stopping anybody going in if they were not doctors or medical people. I seemed to do that for ages. I stood there till about half past four. Eventually they did clear the family and people away from that area outside the gym. They were just hysterical, like anybody would be if they didn't know where their loved ones were. I remember that all the time all I wanted to do was to go home. I just wanted to go home and see my baby and make sure that she was all right. I felt so much loss and suffering with other people, it just made me think that if all those people can die just like that then maybe my little girl was dead. Perhaps she'd had a road accident or something like that. At about five o'clock I managed to get out on to Penistone Road, and I wanted to ring my husband and make sure my little girl was all right. I went and knocked on somebody's door. I said 'I just want to ring home to make sure my little girl's all right.' I don't think the woman could understand because everyone else was wanting to ring home to let everyone know that *they* were all right, and I wanted to ring home to make sure my little girl was all right. I remember going in and her letting me use the phone and I couldn't get through because no one was at home.

Rob White

As I walked away from the ground, my immediate problem was to find a telephone. Having turned left and walked up a hill, the first public telephone that I came to had a queue of about a dozen or more people waiting to use it. I realised that I needed to phone as quickly as possible, so I went in search of another one. Regrettably, I found a similar situation at the next one also. Many of the shops nearby were closed, but I came across one which was open and I asked the assistant if there was a phone that I could use. She showed me to the back room and I joined a short queue of fans waiting to use it. Recognising everyone's sense of urgency, all calls were kept as brief as possible and, for the benefit of those behind me in the queue, I asked my father to ring my girlfriend for me when I eventually reached the front of the queue. Everyone else seemed to be making just one call and listing other people that should be contacted on their behalf. It was only fair.

Having left the shop, I still felt that I wanted to speak to my girlfriend myself, so that I would know whether or not the message had been passed on, in order to ease my mind. I carried on walking, but each queue in the little shops seemed to be getting longer and longer. Everyone seemed to have had the same idea.

I noticed some residents had come into their front gardens and were chatting to each other over their fences. They seemed to be aware that something was going on, so I asked a lady whether I could use her phone. She kindly allowed me to, and I was able to speak to my girlfriend [now wife]. After expressing my gratitude to the lady, I then realised that my plea for help had prompted others to follow, and a queue had already formed in her hallway. I hope that she did not mind. She did not seem to, fortunately. I think that she could see the relief on my face and no doubt on those who phoned after me. I had just made the two most precious phone calls of my life.

That was one great weight off my mind, but now I had to try and get back to the car and check that my colleague was there. I did not know exactly where I was, because I had approached the ground from a totally different direction to the way that I had walked in search of a telephone. I decided that the best thing to do was to walk back to the ground and then I knew that I would be able to find my way back from there.

After about five minutes, I arrived back at the ground and by this time people had clearly been asked to leave the stadium and many people were filing out into the streets. It took me about another 20 minutes to walk back to the car, and when I finally reached it there was no sign of anyone waiting there. A family were standing in their driveway nearby, so I gave them a brief description of my colleague and asked if they had seen anybody waiting by the car, and they confirmed that somebody had been, but that he had walked back in the direction that he had come from after a few minutes. The family could see that I was very upset and that I had been injured, so they took me into their house. Fortunately, one of them was a nurse and she looked at my injured arm for me. She thought that the injury was not too serious, although since the full extent of crush injuries are not visible, she could not give a full diagnosis. She did, however, put some cream on it for me, which she said would help until I was able to have a proper examination.

The time must have been about 4.40–4.45, because the television was on in the house and the football scores were being shown on BBC1. I could not believe that these were deemed to have been of any signficance whatso-ever, considering what had just happened, but then I did not know what coverage, if any, had already been given to the scenes at Hillsborough that I had witnessed. I did not have to wait long, as the programme switched to a scene which was already indelibly etched in my mind. The talk was of at least 50 fatalities and over 100 injured. At the very least, I thought.

Someone in the house tried to ring the emergency number on the screen to enquire about my colleague, to reassure me that he had not been hurt, and to convince me that it was quite likely that he had been the man that they had seen earlier by the car. Inevitably, the line was engaged each time they tried. After ten minutes or so, there was a call from the road outside to say that the man they had seen earlier had returned. I looked out of the window. Yes—it was him. Thank God.

Fortunately, my colleague did not appear to have been injured or too badly affected by what he had witnessed either. However, at that time, neither of us were aware of each other's circumstances in the crush, and it did not seem an appropriate time to begin a discussion to establish such details. Personally, I felt that I had seen far too much to be able to describe events with any degree of clarity so soon afterwards.

My overriding priority was to get myself home as soon as possible to show my family that I really was all right. The car that I had driven to Sheffield was not insured for any other driver, so I knew that I would have to drive myself. I felt that I was physically capable of doing so, despite my injuries, and I made sure that I felt sufficiently composed in my mind as well, before setting off. Naturally, I avoided talking about my experience on the return journey, for I knew that if I began recalling the horrendous scenes that I had witnessed, I would break down emotionally and would not be able to continue driving. In any case, I deliberately stopped the car and had a walk round a number of times along the way, to make sure that I was able to continue.

Looking back, I am amazed myself that I was able to drive home under the circumstances and, perhaps, had I been more rational about my dilemma, I may have acted differently. However, after such an experience, how could anyone have made a rational decision? Fortunately, we both got back safely and I felt that I, and everyone who was concerned about me, could best cope with what had happened with me at home.

Shirley Beer, mother of 17-year-old Paul, a Liverpool supporter living in Exeter

My son had gone to Sheffield to watch his beloved Liverpool play. I was worried about the long journey [from Exeter], and my husband wasn't too pleased as he wasn't too keen on him going to football matches. I usually persuaded him to let our son go as I know how much he loves Liverpool. About half-time I turned on the TV to see how Liverpool were doing. All of a sudden there was a football pitch with lots of policemen. I thought 'Oh, no, not more trouble.' Then I heard the commentator say something and I realised it was more than a pitch invasion. I thought my heart was going to stop, and I said 'Oh, no, Paul's in there.' Then the TV went to something else. We sat there in stunned silence till our daughter walked in. She could see something was wrong. I blurted out 'Something terrible is happening at the Liverpool game.' Then some more scenes came on TV, then an emergency number to ring, which I could hear my daughter trying in the background. Of course it was engaged. The more she tried the more frustrated she got, banging the telephone down with such force. Then they were saying that people were dead and dying before our very eyes. At first it was about four people, then I thought it would never stop. I had watched the Bradford Disaster on TV and felt awful then for the people and families. Now we were involved. Then I saw a young man on a stretcher which looked like my son. I went hysterical and rushed to my Mum's, only four doors down. I could hear my daughter saying 'Don't tell Gran, she'll have a heart attack', but I knew she would find out sometime. I let myself in sobbing uncontrollably, blurting out that people were being killed at the Liverpool match. She grabbed hold of my hand and made me sit down and said 'We must pray.' This calmed me down and after a while of praying we went back to our place. No news, more dead. I was offered a cigarette. I'd given up 12 months ago, but I took it. Then one of Paul's mates at work had heard the radio and came in and sat with us. One of my friends rang, then another one, and she said she didn't like to ring in case we were using the phone or even Paul may be trying to get through. She was afraid to knock on the door, but she said she had to know. We didn't bother to use the phone anymore so we just sat and waited and prayed. Then the phone rang and we rushed to pick it up. It's Paul, he's all right, he can't talk for long as he's ringing from someone's house and there are more waiting to use the phone. Relief, prayers of thanks, phone calls to let people know he was all right. Then the guilt that we are fortunate. Our son is all right. But what about those other poor families?

Pat Nicol

I didn't know anything until Austin rang me at five o'clock on Saturday to say that he couldn't find Lee. They'd got off the train and made their way there. They were shown into Pen 3. They always stood in the same spot, at the back of the goal. That was the lucky spot. They got their places early. It wasn't crowded and then it started to fill up. When they'd all surged forward, he said that it got very crowded. They were all pushing forward and he said Lee slipped off the step but he was all right. Austin was standing behind him. Then, he said, the next thing they pushed again and Lee said 'Ow, get off me, I can't breathe.' He said 'I couldn't see Lee then because there was a very big man standing behind him and Lee fell and that man fell on top of him.' That man fell on top of him and actually crushed Lee to death, so it all happened quickly. But Austin thought he'd just passed out because he went 'Get off, I can't breathe.' When Austin rang me at five o'clock he said 'Lee's passed out but he's OK—they passed him over and they took him in an ambulance and he was fighting them.' Austin assumed that he was fighting because he didn't want to go in that ambulance, but he was convulsing. A policeman had given him the kiss of life and that caused his body to convulse repeatedly, giving the appearance of fighting. Lee had been crushed to death in Pen 3 at 3.04pm.

Mike Lewis
Mike Ingham commentated on the end of the game at Villa Park. Everton were through. They didn't know what was happening at Hillsborough, so there were lots of celebrations on the pitch. We came out of that very, very quickly. John Inverdale did an excellent link back to Alan Green, who said there could be 50 dead and there were many, many more injured. Suddenly you're aware of the enormity of it.

Mike Graham, Everton supporter, at Villa Park
The game against Norwich was a terrible affair and we won it by a nicked goal, but that's by the by. I remember during the course of the first half people with transistor radios, and bulletins came across that Liverpool and Forest hadn't kicked off yet. Come half-time, and we still had no concrete news, but there was talk about 'trouble', in inverted commas, and people griping: 'Here we go, we'll be in the fucking Sherpa Van trophy next year.' And then the second half followed, and we won, and as we were walking away, still quite buoyant, there's rumours flying around left, right and centre.

Pat Nevin, Everton footballer
As soon as the game was finished we just jumped up and down celebrating, having a great time. I'd scored the winning goal and that was one of the biggest moments of my career and the boys were on an incredible high. We went into the dressing-room expecting the champagne. I just looked

around and there was a quietness, a kind of hush. The press wanted to talk to me because I'd scored the winner but you could see it in their faces, a kind of haunted look, and I knew there was something amiss. One of the radio chaps said to me 'It's bad over there, there's quite a few dead.' I couldn't believe it. It didn't sink in, and then someone whispered in my ear 'Look it's high, over 60.' I was trying to speak to the nation on Radio 2 about our semi-final when all of that was happening. It was coming through my head and it was just impossible to talk. I can't remember what I said but it was along the lines of 'I can't talk about football now. I just don't care.'

Mike Lewis

By this time John and I are trying to write the headlines for five o'clock. Alan was explaining what had happened. We said that through a surge of Liverpool fans at the Leppings Lane end, a gate was forced and it led to the crush. John talked about it being a terrible tragedy and a major disaster. Then we updated on the other scores. At five o'clock, John would normally say 'It's five o'clock, "Sports Report" ' and then we would play the signature tune, but we dropped the music because we didn't think it was right. For the last ten or 15 minutes John and I and the producer were talking about what we should do and how we should do it. You're trying to get it right and not let people down.

So, at five o'clock, John said something like 'Good evening. This is a tragic day for sport. It is thought that around 50 fans have been crushed to death at Hillsborough, where Liverpool and Nottingham Forest were playing the FA Cup semi-final. It appears that too many Liverpool fans were crushed behind one goal, and five minutes after kick-off a surge forward caused mayhem and many deaths.' He then gave the Everton result, and then we played a clip of Peter Jones's original description of why play was stopped. John Inverdale then said 'It's now been confirmed that 74 fans have died' and he gave the emergency number again.

Mike Graham

I remember we stopped at some traffic lights, at a pelican crossing there, and a car pulled up in front of us with the window rolled down, and he had Radio 2 on, and I heard somebody saying '74 people confirmed dead.' I'm looking at my mate and thinking 'Did I hear that right?' We raced back to our own car, and then just sat there for three-quarters of an hour, listening to the radio.

Mike Lewis

We then went into the interview with the doctor, and Alan Green had an interview with a fan, who described what it was like to be in there, and how he'd got out. There was then a live report from Peter Jones, where he began by saying 'The biggest irony is that the sun is shining now.' It was a sensational piece. He just talked for a couple of minutes off the top of his head. He talked about images coming back to him from Heysel and he talked about how the gymnasium was being used as a mortuary. He described the ghastly scene in front of him and how he could see the hills. At the end he said 'And the sun is still shining.'

Mike Graham

Any thoughts about what had just happened at Villa Park were just completely forgotten, the overriding thought being 'It could have been us.' As everybody knows, the venues for semi-finals, given the distance that different teams have to travel, is all hit-and-miss, and you don't know whether you're going to be playing the tie at Hillsborough or Villa Park.

My mate couldn't drive and I couldn't drive. We had a walk around. Just unbelievable. When we did eventually get going, we turned the radio off and belted back along the motorway. The standard thing is to see scarves out of windows, but there were no scarves at all, just all these very sombre faces alongside you. The worst thing for me, as it was for a lot of people, was that you had people who you knew, and relatives, at Hillsborough, and it was just completely impossible to get near a telephone on the way back. In the service stations there were mile-long queues of fans, and people were very upset and distressed and not knowing. We decided to put our foot down and get back to Liverpool, and then make sure that everybody we knew was OK.

Colin Harvey, Everton manager

Bulletins started to appear on the radio on the coach on the way home. The mood went from being ecstatic to sombre. We couldn't put over how badly we felt. By the time we got back to Liverpool everyone's devastated because then you start to realise you've got friends at that game. I've got daughters, and a group of their friends, who live nearby, had gone to the game, and three or four of them couldn't be accounted for. Then you start to realise how important the news was, and how little your own joy was from that day. Basically you'd won a game of football, which was nothing then. For the first time in your life, the thing you'd thought most about, football, had just gone out of the window.

Mick Lyons, Everton coach

As it's gone on, we've heard more and more and more. On the way home there was no jubilation at all. It was like we'd just been beaten in the semi-final of the FA Cup. Our supporters were all down. We were down. It was like your own. I always say about Liverpool that, in the city, you don't give each other an inch. It's Everton, it's Liverpool and you don't give them an inch and you're arguing all the time in the pubs and all that. Outside the city, you don't let anyone else have a go at them. We'd won the semi-final of the Cup and it was really flat.

Sammy Lee, former Liverpool footballer, playing for Osasuna (Spain)

I was in Madrid. We were about to play Atlético Madrid the day after, on the Sunday, and we travelled down there on the coach. I got to the hotel and I knew something was wrong because there was a message left for me: 'Sammy Lee, please phone home.' Obviously I thought somebody in my family had died, whatever. As I'm going up to my room, to use the phone, I pass a room with a television on, and suddenly I see these pictures. They didn't know how many had died or whatever. I phoned home. I had relatives going to the game and I didn't know where they were and what-have-you. It was a terrible thing. It was one of those awful eerie feelings when you know something's wrong, when you get the message 'Please phone home.' You expect the worst and it was.

Steve Mungall, Tranmere Rovers footballer

That was one of the days I was suspended, believe it or not. We played at Hartlepool, and I was sat on the bench, and nothing really came through. It was only going off the pitch at half-time that we heard that the game at Hillsborough had been stopped. We didn't know why. The dressing-room at Hartlepool was a Portakabin at the time, so I was standing outside because it was a little poky place and I thought 'The less people in there, the better.' I was speaking to someone, and he said 'There's been a disaster at Hills-borough.' I said 'What do you mean?' He says 'There's been crowd trouble.' I said 'Is there a television handy?' He says 'There's a television room up there.' I went in there, and I couldn't believe it. I still didn't take in what was happening.

Obviously it had filtered through to the dressing-room then. Marty [Dave Martindale] said to me 'Find out what has happened at Hillsborough', because his brothers had gone to the game. I didn't know what to say because he still had to play the game. I said 'Something's happened, an overspill on to the pitch. People have been injured and whatever.' After the game, we just came out of the dressing-room and got straight on the bus. We were travelling back to Birkenhead and obviously we had the radio on. The toll kept mounting. A few of the boys were worried because they had family and friends at the game and they'd discovered that it had happened at the Liverpool end. It was probably the quietest bus ever, coming back from a game.

Alan Kennedy, former Liverpool footballer

I was playing non-League at the time for a team called Northwich Victoria. I came in after the game which we had won that afternoon. It was about twenty to five and somebody had switched the television on and was saying 'Oh, Liverpool fans again, they've been causing problems.' My mind immediately went back to the Heysel Disaster. I was in the Liverpool dressing room that night. I thought 'Oh, no, it can't be happening to the club again.' Then I started listening to what people were saying, that some fans had died, and you think 'What could have happened?' And someone said 'Well, you know what they're like these Liverpool supporters.' And my instinctive reaction was, of course, to defend the Liverpool fans. Some people were saying that thirty fans had died, fifty fans had died. It was beyond comprehension. I said 'Has a bomb gone off or the stadium collapsed, or what?' Those were my first reactions. I couldn't believe that so many people could die from something like 'overcrowding', but now as you look back, well, you know it is possible.

Glasgow Rangers supporter

During our own Cup semi-final at Parkhead [Rangers v St Johnstone] we began to get garbled accounts from men with trannies about 'the trouble' at the Liverpool v Nottingham Forest English Cup game. At first it seemed as though there had been a pitch invasion and fighting was taking place, then we heard two were dead, then four. By the end of the match we made our way back to the supporters' bus believing that 40 were seriously injured.

On the bus we sat listening to the radio about what had happened. Slowly everyone began to realise what had happened and just how serious the situation was. The usual banter and mucking about went by the board as Peter Jones gave a very graphic account of the events and their aftermath.

On other buses we passed the same air of sadness seemed to prevail as they too sat stunned. I have no doubt that the same quiet and sad reflection took place on buses of other clubs throughout the country. Helpless is the word which most sums up the way I felt. What can you do? The reports gave me the same unreal feeling I remember as a kid of seven, sitting watching the TV as news came in of the Ibrox Disaster [2 January 1971].

Mike Lewis

We took it up till six o'clock and had interviews with Kenny Dalglish, Peter Robinson [Liverpool chief executive], the Nottingham Forest chairman and Pat Nevin. Then 'News' took it over. The six o'clock news on Radio Four was completely dominated by that story. 'News' by that time had got reporters up there and in there. Peter Jones was used as one of the major planks for the bulletin, together with the interviews that Alan Green and Pat Murphy had done, but it started to become a world news story. Our job, the balancing act between 'News' and 'Sport', had finished. It was one of those days when you do your job and do the best you can, and then you feel a great sense of emptiness and depression at the end of it all. I guess it was the worst afternoon I've ever faced in a sports department.

Christina Surawy, Hostal Londres, Santiago, Chile

I learned about the football disaster from a Chilean newspaper on the Saturday. It was front-page news. I saw the horrible pictures of people pressed against the fence, close-ups of people's faces. Later that day someone told me that they'd heard it on the World Service. The Chileans thought it was another example of British soccer's bad record. The English people we were staying with were embarrassed. It was a mixture of feeling very sad and feeling embarrassed to be English.

Iain Taylor, Edmonton, Alberta, Canada

Edmonton is seven hours behind British time, so it was 10 o'clock on the Saturday morning when we heard the news. Half listening to CBC radio's light-hearted weekend banter, I caught the name Liverpool in the first story on the hourly newscast. (The name still catches the ear as well as the eye even after 15 years in Canada.) Something about a disaster at a 'soccer game' in Sheffield, many killed and injured. My heart went cold, not just for the abstraction of another one of the world's cruel twists of fate, but for my kid brother who was bound to be there, following our team to Wembley. I picked up the phone and his wife answered in a couple of rings. He had just phoned a few minutes before. He was fine. He had seen the whole thing but was in the stands nearby. A sad relief.

Ian Battey

Looking back, it was all over very, very quickly. By, say, ten to five or five o'clock, we had dealt with all the casualties that we were going to deal with. We had a call to say we weren't expecting any more casualties from the ground. We had something in the region of 98 people through the department in the first hour. Including all the walking wounded and so on, I think we topped a hundred. It was very difficult, I must admit, for us to make decisions at the triage point as to what were symptoms of a crush injury and what were symptoms of the hyperventilation that people had been going through because of the trauma, the anxiety, the fear, all those kind of things. We had people coming in who were extremely breathless, panting, weeping, people who couldn't get their breath. And we didn't know whether this was emotional or physical, and that was very difficult for us to make a decision on, and hopefully we always erred on the side of caution.

James Wardrope and colleagues

At the Royal Hallamshire Hospital the Accident and Emergency consultant and senior registrar arrived together at 15.37. The nursing staff had already begun to prepare the department to receive large numbers of casualties. When two police officers arrived and confirmed that a major disaster was taking place the hospital implemented the Major Disaster Plan.

The first two patients arrived at 15.40. One was dead and the other required intubation and was transferred to the Intensive Care Unit. Being further from the stadium, the hospital then had a quiet period, when the departmental plans could be organised. Between 16.00 and 17.00 the department received a further 69 patients, 24 of whom required admission. Forty-five were discharged after treatment.

Seventeen patients were admitted to Intensive Care at the Northern General Hospital and one at the Royal Hallamshire Hospital. Six of those initially admitted to the Northern General were subsequently transferred to the Royal Hallamshire for computed tomography and to relieve pressure on staff at the Northern General.

Ian Battey

There were people coming to the hospital in private cars and turning up in absolute emotional turmoil, because they were stood next to somebody who was taken away by ambulance, saying 'My son and daughter were in different parts of the ground', or whatever it may be. We were obviously trying not only to support them emotionally, but to get them to the right place for the support they needed. We had contact with the policemen who had travelled to hospital in ambulances with casualties, and I think they were going through very similar emotions that I'd gone through myself, whereby the emotional trauma doesn't hit you while you're actually doing something physically, and it maybe hit them as they were studying the situation, holding the bag of fluid above the head, when they'd got time to stop and think. I saw policemen in tears, I saw ambulance men in tears. That kind of emotion hit everybody and it didn't matter what you did for a living or what experience you'd got.

Dennis Cerrone

We were sent back to Woodseats Police Station. We walked from the ground to where the coach was, somewhere near Niagara, the police sports ground, which is just up the road. It looked like a funeral. People were stood at the side of the road while other people walked past. I saw coachloads of fans, and they were all sat staring and doing nothing. I expected them all to start shouting and jeering and get all het up. But they didn't. They were just as bad as we were. They were just subdued. They were obviously feeling it as well. The people in the shops didn't know what had happened, but they knew something horrendous had happened by the amount of people and bells and ambulances and Fire Brigade and all that. That was a long walk. It seemed ages to get back to the coach and then drive to Woodseats.

Steve Way

News is meant to travel fast, yet it does not over short distances. At 5.30 the long march hit Sheffield city centre and merged with Saturday shoppers. They knew nothing of nearby events and were clearly puzzled by two sets of dejected supporters en route to the railway station. Match-day inter-city trains are dry, and there was no booze from the buffet to drown sorrows. Fans sat quietly, scarves over shoulders, no one reading their official semi-final programme.

Andy Williamson

I'm not quite sure of the sequence of events afterwards. The ground was eventually cleared, after a considerable length of time. Obviously the Nottingham Forest fans departed, and there were no signs of any misconduct on the part of the supporters. The police actually announced that there would be a press conference subsequently at the police station in Sheffield. I would say it was probably about six o'clock. Before the press conference it was still the suggestion that the gates had been forced. That was certainly the impression that the people had in the area of the ground that I was in. It was only really when the chief constable gave his press conference that the true situation became apparent.

When the ground had been virtually cleared I did proceed down to the Leppings Lane end, walking round the pitch. At this stage it certainly wasn't apparent how desperate the situation was, but obviously the barrier close to the front of the central section had broken. I went round the back of the Leppings Lane end to look for myself if there was any evidence of gates being forced, and it was obvious that there hadn't been any gates forced. There was no evidence at all of that. They were metal gates which closed that tunnel and I think they had already been locked at that stage.

Alongside the river bank, which was a grassy area, screens had been erected. If I remember correctly, I think they were green canvas screens. I'm not sure whether they were some of the casualties. I don't think they were there then, but that's where they may have been taken initially. Everybody still around the ground was obviously completely devastated. I don't think people really knew how to react to the appalling situation that had occurred.

I can't actually remember phoning home. I mean it's something that one should have done, but I can't honestly recall ringing my wife to say that although I'd been there it had in no way affected myself. I did attend the press conference. I was given a lift to the police station by a journalist and, as I say, even then the suggestion was that the problem had been created by supporters rushing a gate, breaking a gate down and creating a crush. Even among the reporters, that was still the impression. In fairness to the police, at the press conference they immediately indicated that there had been no question of gates being broken down. Obviously one of the things that I've been involved with in football is dealing with the media, so I was particularly interested to know how the incident was being reflected by the media in terms of what sort of damage the incident would do to the game. But obviously at that particular stage we were still under the impression of two or three deaths and not ninety-odd. Even at the press conference the figure was nowhere near as high as ninety-odd. I would need to check but I think the figure given out by the police was fifty or sixty.

I think the scale of the tragedy really took over and dominated the initial media coverage. They were having trouble quantifying the scale of the problem. They weren't really at that stage beginning to question the emergency services and the way that they operated, or the Football Association or anybody else. Initially it was just the scale of the tragedy which they concentrated on, but as soon as the police press conference had been staged then the emphasis changed very much and the chief constable was put under enormous pressure at that press conference as soon as he admitted that there hadn't been gates broken down, and the build-up of supporters and so on had created that situation, it wasn't really a sudden surge of fans, and then was obviously put under a great deal of pressure about the response of the emergency services, in particular the police. As soon as the press conference had been held, the direction of the media coverage altered dramatically.

I went back to the ground, and actually spoke to a number of journalists. I remember Richard Faulkner was also there from the Football Trust. He actually rang Downing Street from a portable phone. I think this was actually before the press conference. I'm not saying he spoke to the Prime Minister but he obviously spoke to the Prime Minister's office to give them a first-hand account, if you like, of what had transpired. I'm sure that was before the police press conference, because most of the media were still there at that particular time.

After the police press conference I went back to the ground. By this time there were still plenty of people about but it was mainly the security forces and the other emergency services. The ground had been cleared of fans altogether. I can't recall how many Sheffield Wednesday and Liverpool and Forest and Football Association officials were still around at that time, but I eventually left Hillsborough at something like 7.30 or 7.45, but obviously, by then, the scale of the tragedy had begun to dawn on everybody, although, as I say, even then the numbers were nowhere near ninety.

I had a quiet word with Graham Kelly and also with Graham Mackrell, the secretary at Sheffield Wednesday, the host club, and offered my support and asked if there was anything I could do to help, whatever. To be perfectly honest, it was just very difficult to know what to do for the best. Obviously the tragedy had occurred, the scale of the problem had become apparent, but it was just a feeling of not knowing how to react. One felt very empty and very distressed but you didn't know what to do for the best. Being there and being very close to the tragedy and actually looking at the scene of it afterwards doesn't really bring it home. But you know then you have to come to terms with that ultimately and look at how the situation can be improved, how the game can progress.

Dennis Cerrone

I can't remember the drive back to the police station. I think I must have sat in the station for probably an hour before I went home. I don't know what time it was, but I do know I was back in my house about nine to half-past nine that evening, whereas some people worked all through the night. I don't know why our particular section had been told to go home, but we were.

Other people who weren't on duty were called in. I know they got some of the identification jobs. At the police station it was subdued. Everybody who'd been on 'days' had heard about it, obviously, and they'd not gone home, they'd just waited to see if they were needed and to see what had happened. The sergeant had gone in and told them what had happened and it was just deathly quiet. Everybody just sat there in the office saying nothing. Nobody was even asking questions. They just listened when information was volunteered. Nobody said 'What happened then?' like you would do in a normal incident: 'And then what happened?' They just sat there waiting for it to come out, and if it didn't come they didn't ask, at that point.

My wife was going frantic. She'd seen it on the TV and she'd been ringing up, like all the other wives, and all the lines were jammed. Nobody could get through to find out what had happened. I think a telly reporter had said that all these people had been killed and policemen were amongst them, and so obviously she thought . . . I never managed to find out whether that was right, whether anybody did say that or whether that was just my wife's imagination. Sometimes you do imagine things like that, don't you? I couldn't get through to her on the phone. I must have been half-an-hour trying to get through before I eventually got through and told her I was all right. It must have been even worse for people trying to get through to Liverpool.

A mate of mine was sat at home and he saw it on television and he was pacing around his house. He couldn't settle down. He felt really guilty that he wasn't there. He felt he should have been there to help. There was a lot like that afterwards, who felt really guilty, and all they'd done was decide not to work it.

Jenni Hicks

Then a police car pulled into the car-park. This Scottish couple whom I had passed, had flagged a police car down and said that there is a woman over there you have got to see. They had sent this police car. And the police just came over and said 'Get in.' They took me up to the police station [Hammerton Road] that then became the headquarters, and I was the first one there. In the police car, I just kept saying over and over again 'I can't find Sarah, Vicki and Trevor. I just can't find them.' They said 'They'll sort you out when you get there.' And they just dropped me off and left me outside the station. They didn't come in with me. They just said 'Go in there, give your names and descriptions and they will sort it out for you.'

I was thinking 'What am I doing here?' I felt as though I should have been at the ground. If Sarah, Vicki and Trevor were going to be anywhere, that is where they would be. If they weren't at the car-park, that is where they would be. I went into the station and there was nobody there. Obviously there was a desk sergeant. I gave names and descriptions and they just told me to sit over there. And the next thing I was joined by this other chap. I can remember looking at this other chap and it turned out that he was from Derbyshire and he said he was looking for his 18-year-old son. He had found all his mates, but nobody seemed to know where his son was. His son was a Liverpool supporter.

We were then taken into a small room and the two of us sat there. We were left on our own. I can remember the door opening, and a vicar put his head round the door. I shot up and I shouted at him 'My God, you are going to tell me they are dead!' And I think the vicar looked as frightened as I was. He was just lost in the police station. He hadn't come to tell either of us. And I can remember this chap from Derbyshire. When I stood up and shouted, he lost his colour. I thought I was in control and as soon as that vicar put his head round the door, I was so frightened. I thought that was it and we had been put in this side-room to be told, and it wasn't that at all. This vicar was as shocked as I was. He had been called to the police station for some reason, but he wasn't quite sure of the whys and wherefores.

We were left again for a while and then we were taken across a little road to the Boys' Club next door. And again we were the first there. It was a strange sensation. The Boys' Club was empty and neither the chap nor I wanted to admit just how frightened we were. And, would you believe, we were trying to make polite conversation. Because we were too frightened to mention what both of us were thinking, especially after me standing up and screaming at the vicar 'My God, you are going to tell me they are dead', because I had expressed in words what this guy was thinking.

People eventually started to come, and they were busy setting up tea-urns. There seemed to be more people there helping than survivors or relatives. I was just wandering about there. More and more people started to arrive and I lost track of the chap from Derbyshire. And then I was called back to the police station, where I was to give full descriptions. It took a very long time because I had to give full descriptions of three people, down to if they had moles. It started off with exactly what they were wearing. And did they have any marks on their bodies? Did they have any birth marks? Did they have any moles? Was Trevor carrying any credit cards in his wallet? Did he have any identification in his wallet? Were the girls carrying any identification? Were they carrying money? Were they carrying credit cards, cheque books? Everything was so detailed. It took an awful long time. And by the end of it, I don't know what I was thinking, to be honest. By this time I was emotionally drained, but still hoping. And then I was taken back to the Boys' Club where I wandered about again. It just seemed to be organised chaos, to be quite truthful. Looking back, I can't believe how I kept thinking it was all going to be OK. This seemed to be all going on around me, this just couldn't happen to my family. It wasn't going to happen to my family. This doesn't happen when you go for a family day out to a football match. What am I in the middle of here? I am in the middle of what turned out to be a major football disaster. It hadn't hit me and I was very, very frightened. It was a feeling of unreality.

I can't even remember who I saw as the place started to fill up. I can't remember going up to people. People were wandering around. Perhaps a lot of people were in this state, too frightened to face the reality of it, because this was for real. A lot of people, I think, were too frightened to even contemplate that it could be this. Shock, I suppose. I had never, never experienced anything like that in my life. This feeling of unreality, this dreamlike state. I was wandering around and I met a Catholic priest in the Boys' Club. I remember I couldn't sit down, I had to keep moving. Time just seemed to stand still. I hadn't got a clue about time. If I had to swear on oath about time, I couldn't. I am wandering around and this Catholic priest came up to me and asked me if I was all right. As soon as anybody asked me anything, I came out with the same thing: 'I've lost my two daughters and my husband, I can't find them anywhere.' If anybody said anything to me, that was all I could say. And this Catholic priest had a chap standing with him and he said that this gentleman has lost his wife. And I said 'Oh, I am sorry, I hope you find her soon.' And he said 'No, she is dead.' And this chap was standing holding his wife's handbag. The Catholic priest obviously thought that when I said that I had lost them that I had been told that Sarah, Vicki and Trevor were dead. And I can remember looking at him and I didn't know what to say. I just kept saying 'I am so sorry, I am so sorry.' And I thought 'My God, some people have died.' And that was my first real realisation that people were dead. Then I thought 'I have got to get out of here, I can't stand this.' And I walked towards the door to go out. I was going to leave. Another man came up to me. He turned out to be a social worker for Sheffield City Council. He again asked me if I was all right. And again, I gave this stock reply: 'I can't find Sarah, Vicki or Trevor.' And I said 'I have got to get out of this place because I can't stand it any more.' And he said 'Would you like me to take you to the hospital?' I thought 'That is the first sensible suggestion I have heard since this happened. Why didn't I think of that? Why hasn't anybody else thought of that? I have given all these descriptions and now I am wandering about and nobody's telling me anything.' There was no information given. There is an old saying that you are given the mushroom treatment. And it was true. You are kept in the dark and fed a load of shit. Sounds very rude, but unfortunately that is the best way I can describe it. I wasn't given any information. I was asked for lots of information, and I wasn't fed any back. There was no suggestion to contact the hospitals or anything until this social worker spoke to me.

Jill Thomas, at the gymnasium

The next thing I was told to do was to gather relatives that hadn't been reunited with their families and get them on the coach and take them round to the Boys' Club on Hammerton Road, where they were gathering all the family and friends. I did two or three trips and it took a lifetime because the traffic was so terrible. This must have been between five and six-thirty or seven. It was taking about 40 minutes to get from the ground to the Boys' Club and it was awful being on the coach. You can only say 'It'll be all right' so many times. We were stood up on the coach, talking to the families, telling them what we thought was going to happen when they got there.

We were trying to reassure people that a lot had been taken to hospital. A lot of the people on the coach were women in their forties and fifties and old people, people looking for teenage sons, families that you could organise, who wanted to do what they were told and needed to be shipped about. I remember being cross because they were asking me about their relatives and I hadn't got my bits of paper with all the details on. I thought 'Damn, I wish I'd still got that, then I could say to this lady, "It's all right, he's gone to the hospital".' But I had had to hand it over to the bureau when they set it up in an organised manner.

At the Boys' Club, all the social services and the Samaritans were there, and there was a reception desk for the families when they got there. I remember thinking 'This is well-organised.' I didn't know where they'd come from, whether they'd been at the match or what. They said afterwards that people were just ringing in, saying 'I'm a counsellor', or 'I'm a Samaritan, can I come and help?' We kept getting a coach full and then taking them to Hammerton Road and then going back. Then, the last one, I remember saying 'This is ridiculous, it's taking us longer to take them on the coach than it is to walk with them.' I remember walking with about two dozen people from the football ground through Hillsborough Park to Hammerton Road. I remember seeing fans. I did feel a bit threatened because I realised by then that we were getting some of the blame, but a lot of the fans were just wandering about in a daze. They were sat down. They were leant up against the trees, crying, sobbing. There was an eerie silence. It was just weird. But nobody ever threatened me or was aggressive towards me. Everybody was just in a state of shock.

Ray Lewis

I can't actually recall when I got changed. Probably about six o'clock. I know that it was probably about quarter to seven by the time I left the ground that night. I think at the time there was a certain amount of consoling that people had to do. Something that stands out in my mind was the work that the girls on the Sheffield Wednesday staff did. At 12 o'clock [noon] they were resplendent in their suits and button-holes and things like that, and by the time the afternoon had gone the mascara had run with all the tears and they were helping out. They were trying to bring water and tea and they were marvellous, as were the young apprentices at the club. They were carrying the advertising boards to make them stretchers and things like that, things that happened behind the scenes, things that people don't actually see and appreciate. Full credit to the club. The pressure on someone like

Graham Mackrell. The previous semi-final, between the same teams, had gone like a dream and all of a sudden he's in the middle of a nightmare.

I suppose that one could be of assistance in talking to the walking injured, just consoling them and helping out, and we were doing that type of thing and I suppose time flew really. At one stage I went up to the police-box, which is up on the Leppings Lane side, but to be quite honest I don't think one realised the severity of it until that evening and the next day. I hope that isn't dreadful to say, because we'd heard that one person had died, but one didn't realise at that time that it was the major disaster that it was. You do have deaths at football matches, heart attacks and things like that, but you couldn't comprehend the scale of it, to be quite honest.

You were picking up things like 'There was a rush on the gate and they let them in', but it was really only hearsay. You weren't picking it up from official people. I can remember late in the afternoon, when I still hadn't changed, and I walked through and there was Graham Kelly, just shell-shocked, basically, not knowing what to say or what to do. He was in shock himself. And in the bar was John Motson. Having gone there to commentate on a football match, he finds himself commentating on a disaster with absolutely no experience of doing that type of thing. Someone who had been in Biafra, or a World News man, would have seen that type of thing, but there he was. He'd seen the pictures of it actually happening, and was in a great deal of shock.

Trevor Hicks

We hadn't heard anything on the radio. I'd even forgotten I'd had my little radio with me. In fact I think I might have left it on the terrace—I've never seen it since. Nurses had all come into the hospital—they'd heard it on the radio—and at this time I was being looked after by a young psychiatric nurse, who'd come in off duty, and a young female padre, because obviously they knew I'd lost a daughter. I can't even remember the padre's name, it's awful to say. These people help you but you can't remember. I can remember them physically. But you're oblivious.

My immediate concern was to find Sarah. Something else I will never understand is that there was never any transport, even for people involved. You were relying on volunteers using their own car. Anyway, they took me in the padre's car to the Hallamshire Hospital. I didn't even know there was another big hospital but obviously we'd been told by this time that they were taking other casualties to the Hallamshire, so these two gave me a lift. The young padre stayed for a little while, the psychiatric nurse had to go off somewhere. I was handed over to the staff at the Hallamshire. There were also police there, and it was the same routine: give the descriptions, name and address, where I had left my car. I'd even asked if it was possible to get someone to go to my car, where I expected Jenni to have gone when we hadn't turned up at the rendezvous, because I was getting very concerned for her. I'd left a request at the Northern General Hospital that if she showed up there for them not to tell her about Victoria until I came back. I would try and find Sarah and then I'd come back to be there to look after Jenni when she was told, because I knew what she'd be like.

Again I went round the wards, looking at people, giving my name and address, and I was on auto-pilot. At this time there was talk of about 20 people dead. Now I didn't know whether there was nine at the Hallamshire and eleven at the Northern General or they doubled-counted the eleven, or whether it was twenty in addition to that eleven. The worst figure was about thirty in my comprehension at that time. But I'm still on auto-pilot, pursuing Sarah, wherever she is, looking for her so I can be there to look after her. In the main reception area at the Hallamshire an administrator of some kind came out. He stood up on the desk, shouted for attention and said 'Ladies and Gentlemen'. He started talking about some patients who had received attention at the Northern General and he started reading names out so that any relatives there could go over to the Northern General, the inference being that these people were alive and had received attention. As soon as he read Vicki's name out I just broke down. I think that was the point when I lost the auto-pilot bit. I had to be taken and sat down and nursed. From being the strong father doing his duty, I suddenly became a bit of a wimp, a weeping wretch, if you like. But I still had to find Sarah. As far as I'm aware, Sarah's still here and the communication was non-existent. People like myself were just left. Within the madness you are just trying to hang on to your sanity, you are trying to do your bit. I still had a job of work to do—I still had to find Sarah and make sure she got the best attention possible, because you couldn't rely on circumstances. But we were hearing by this time that there were people at hospitals as far away as Rotherham. Rumours were flying around. You didn't know whether it was true or not.

Lord Justice Taylor, interim report, paragraph 107
A police constable was detailed to attend and guard each of the dead [in the gymnasium] and a photograph of each was taken by a police photographer so that relatives coming to identify bodies could be spared the ordeal of searching amongst all who had died.

Jill Thomas

We went back to the ground at about 6.30 or seven and they were just in the process of deputing an officer to a body. One friend of mine was assigned to a person and she didn't get off duty until about two o'clock. I remember them saying to us 'There's nothing else for you to do here, you can stand down.' I think it was a relief, to be quite honest. I went to Niagara with the colleague I'd been working with in the morning. We had somehow found each other again. I remember at Niagara our sergeant going to get washed down because he was just covered in vomit. He was sat talking to us and saying that he'd been giving mouth-to-mouth to somebody and they'd retched and been sick all over him. I was sat with an officer who had been pulling them out of the gate. He was just dazed. He was out of it. I don't think he knew what had happened. It was just shock and not believing what had happened. Absolute total bewilderment that it could have happened, and that we'd all been there.

I remember worrying about the Gen 28, the arrest form, afterwards because it was still in my pocket. I thought 'Oh, my God, what's happened to those two lads that we arrested.' I found out of course that all the prisoners who had been arrested had just been released and let off the bus. And this Gen 28 seemed really important to me, the police force being what it is about paper-work and paper-work going with prisoners. I remember worrying about the Gen 28.

Jenni Hicks

I asked Alan, the social worker, to take me to the ground first, because I was sure they were going to be at the ground. They knew that is where I had to wait for them. I asked 'Do you pass the ground on the way to the hospitals?' (I didn't know where the hospitals were in Sheffield. I was a complete stranger to the city of Sheffield.) All of this time I thought 'Why aren't I back at the ground, because that is where I am supposed to be? They know that is where I am going to be. That was the rendezvous point.' So we went to the ground first. I said 'Just drive me round the streets to see if I can see . . .'

He drove me past the little shop. And then he took me to the Northern General Hospital. We arrived there, walked in. I went up to the reception desk and I said 'Have you got a Trevor Hicks, Sarah Hicks or a Victoria Hicks?' And they said that we have had a Victoria. And I assumed that she had been treated and gone. And then a nurse came over to me and said 'Would you come this way.' And I had a sneaky suspicion that it wasn't going to be good news, because they took me into a side-room and closed the door. It was a treatment room with just this long bed in it and a chair at the side and the equipment. I said to Alan, the social worker 'This is not good news, is it, Alan? I have got to get out of this little room, I don't want to stay in here.' I didn't want to hear what I had a suspicion they were going to tell me. I said 'Can you open the door please, I can't stand the door being closed. Would you please open the door?' I think he could hear my voice going. He said 'Jenni, just realise I am with you here. I am your friend here, I am on your side. If you want the door open you can have the door open. The door doesn't have to be closed.'

Just as he went to open the door, this young doctor appeared, in his white coat, with a nurse standing behind him in the doorway, because we were about to get out. I couldn't stand this little room. I knew they don't just take you into a side-room to tell you good news. The doctor didn't look at me. He had a clipboard. First of all he asked me to sit down. As he came in he said 'Would you like to sit down?' and I said 'No, I don't want to sit down.' He said 'Sit down.' And I said 'No.' I rcfuscd point-blank. I wanted to get out of this place. I didn't want to hear what I knew he was going to tell me. He said to me 'Are you the mother of Victoria Jane Hicks, long dark hair, blue eyes?' He started to go on about height, and a full description of her. And I looked up at him and said 'You are going to tell me she has died, aren't you?' And he said 'Yes.' He never looked at me once. He looked at the board. The clipboard stands out in my mind. With the patient record on it. He never actually told me. He didn't have the job of telling me. I told him: 'You are going to tell me she is dead, aren't you?' And he said 'Yes.' I shoved him out of the way, turned back and said 'Couldn't you have resuscitated her? Couldn't you have put her on a ventilator?' As if I was some kind of medical expert, which I am not.

They had brought the vicar with them as well. As I shoved the doctor out of the way to get out of this little room, the vicar was there, and as he went to give me some sympathy or compassion or whatever he was going to do, I told him he could shove his God up his arse. I am sorry about the language, but I pulled out language in that hospital that I thought I would never be capable of pulling out. Looking back on it, if you could have shot the scene, you would have thought it was something from a John Cleese sketch. It wasn't funny at the time, but you can imagine the scene. Remember we were in the middle of a casualty department. You have got people who go in there with their broken legs or their cut fingers or whatever they have gone to a casualty department with. They are all sitting in this row of chairs, as they do, back to back. I was running round with Alan Dunkley at my side because he is my friend and the one who is on my side, and I'm saying 'They let people die in this hospital, don't let them treat you', effing and blinding like a fishwife, and every so often turning back to these three in a line behind me—the doctor, the nurse and the vicar. And, every so often, when I was getting rid of this anger, I turned round to them and told the vicar what he could do with his God and said what they do at this hospital with their patients. I have gone from totally calm, keeping it in control, to this horrendous outburst. And I was throwing in all sorts of questions. As soon as I was told, I requested to see her. 'Where is she?' 'Well, you can't see her.' I asked 'Where's Trevor and where is Sarah?' And the doctor was trying to tell me that Trevor was there when Victoria died and eventually I did listen. Trevor had gone across to the other hospital to see if he could find Sarah. Don't forget that I didn't know that Trevor had gone onto the pitch and found the girls. I didn't know any of this. But now I knew that Trevor was alive. I didn't know if Sarah was. I assumed she was alive.

In the midst of all this, they are trying to tell me things, and then he said 'Is there anybody you would like to ring?' So I tried to ring my brother back in London, because I knew that if he had heard all of this, he would be terribly concerned. I couldn't get any reply. And in the meantime, they said 'We'll ring the Hallamshire Hospital and let Trevor know that you are here.' Apparently, he had left strict instructions that if I arrived at the hospital, I wasn't to be told until he was there, but they told me. He had said to them 'Look, if my wife, Jenni, finds her way here, please don't tell her about Vicki because I want to be here when you tell her. She is going to need somebody with her.' So we stayed at the Northern General and they telephoned from the Northern General to the Hallamshire Hospital. They said 'He is coming across to the hospital.' Then I am saying 'Has he got anybody with him?' And they said 'Yes, he has got a young girl with him.' And, another assumption, I thought it was Sarah. I couldn't wait in the hospital. I said to Alan, who was a smashing bloke, 'I have got to wait outside.'

Trevor Hicks

I then got this message that Jenni had arrived at the Northern General. This is about a quarter to eight at night, so we've gone from about three-thirty to nearly eight o'clock at night in this sheer chaos, absolute chaos. It's very difficult to describe the feelings. I think I was almost numb to them. I think you're protected by it all. Your body goes into some sort of 'hold' situation. I was collected by two people. One was a CRUSE counsellor, Hilary Taylor-Firth. There's still no transport available, even though it's about eight o'clock at night. Now Jenni had been told that I was across at the Hallamshire with a young girl, in other words with the padre, but no one said she was a padre. You can understand Jenni's thought-process. She thought I was with Sarah.

Jenni Hicks

I was standing outside, quite convinced that Trevor was going to come back with Sarah. And then my concern was not so much for Trevor as for Sarah, because I knew how close Vicki and Sarah were, and I thought 'Get yourself together for when Sarah comes because she is going to be devastated here. I am going to have to be OK here because when Sarah comes she is going to be really upset. I have got to be all right for Sarah.'

I stood watching the car-park at the front, and I thought 'This is where they are going to come', and I stood outside the hospital. When Trevor arrived, I saw him walking across and I yelled to him 'Where's Sarah?' Not 'Thank God, Trevor, you are OK', but 'Where's Sarah?' Strangely enough I always had a feeling that Trevor would be OK. And he was on his own, and as soon as Trevor saw me he shouted 'Oh, Jenni, Vicki's dead.' And I said 'I know.' He obviously knew they had told me. And he just broke down. And I said 'Where's Sarah?' I wasn't concerned. I wanted to know where Sarah was. And he said 'You are not going to like this, Jenni, but the last time I saw Sarah she looked in a worse state than Vicki.' This was the first time I realised that he had got onto the pitch. I said 'What do you mean? Have you seen them? Have you seen Sarah?' And he said 'Yes'. And it is all coming out and he is crying and he is trying to explain to me, and it is all coming out too fast and he is in a big emotional state. So am I. Horrendous really. And I said 'Well, where is Sarah now?' And he said 'I am trying to find out. That is where I have been. She was supposed to be coming here in the next ambulance.' He hadn't seen Sarah since he left her on the pitch. And that was something Trevor found very, very difficult, because there was no room for Sarah in the ambulance. When he got in the ambulance with Vicki, somebody was trying to resuscitate Sarah on the pitch. He assumed they were going to carry her into the ambulance and there was no room. So he didn't want the ambulance doors to close. But what could he do? He had two and they couldn't fit them both in. They assured him that they would come, that she would be brought in the next ambulance. But no more ambulances went onto the pitch.

He said to me 'Have you seen Vicki?' And I said 'No, I want to see her, I want to see Vicki, and they won't let me.' He said 'Well, she is in the Chapel of Rest here, so I can't see any reason why you can't see her.' So he called a nurse over and said 'My wife would like to see our daughter. She is in the Chapel of Rest.' And she said 'I am sorry, but you can't.' And Trevor said 'I am sorry, I have asked politely. I am not asking again, I am telling you, I am taking my wife to see our daughter.' And the nurse went off and brought a policeman. And this policeman came up to us.

Trevor Hicks

Jenni's frantic. She's running up and down in the reception. Not only have they told her that Vicki's dead, despite what I'd asked them, she's been refused access to her. Now I don't believe this. I am at my wits' end already. I go in and I have a very clear picture of a middle-aged woman with tears streaming down her face, still doing her job. I think she was the assistant matron or the duty matron, a beautiful woman, a lovely woman, and there was also this absolute swine, if I can call him that, of a police officer in the main reception. Now, they know who we are, they know we've lost a daughter, and they know we're still looking for another one. I went over and said to him 'I don't believe this: (a) you've told my wife and she's not supposed to be told until I come back; and (b) you're refusing to let her see our daughter. She's in the mortuary, there's no problem, what's up?' He replied 'She's nothing to do with you any more.' Believe me, the words are so emblazoned in our minds. We can recite them verbatim now, after all this time and through all of that. He said 'There has to be post-mortems, they are the property of the South Yorkshire coroner and they are nothing more to do with you.' So here's Jenni and I, in the foyer of the Northern General Hospital, something like quarter past eight at night, and Jenni's absolutely demented and for all good reason. She's lost a daughter, she doesn't know where the other one is, except she just thought she was with me and now she's found out she isn't. I almost hit the guy. 'You what!' And then we found that they were actually stalling, that Victoria's body had been taken out of the hospital, where she'd been laid to rest if you like, and taken back to the ground. To be put into the mortuary. Somebody had this bright administratively convenient idea—let's have all the bodies back here in one spot. Perhaps it's great for the disaster plan but what about the poor beggars who are involved?

Jenni Hicks

I said 'You have taken her back to the football ground from the Chapel of Rest in the hospital where she has died?' I didn't know there was a mortuary at the ground at this point. I just couldn't believe it. I thought 'This is unreal, I am going to wake up in a moment, this is crazy, I am having a turn here or something. Either this, or it is the night before the match and we haven't been there yet.' And he said 'Yes'. I said 'What right have you to remove my daughter from a hospital?' My daughter was fifteen. Nobody had any rights over her without our permission. And suddenly we have no rights. We were then told that she was moved under the instructions of the coroner of South Yorkshire: 'She is no longer your property. She is nothing at all to do with you.' Up until this point in time, nobody had any rights but us. If she had had to have major surgery, if she had had to have anything in her life, they would have to have parental permission. She was fifteen years old. And suddenly we are told she is not even our property, as if she had ever been property anyway. It was not what we wanted to hear. So I said 'Where is she?' 'She is at the football ground.' 'Well, what do we do?'

Trevor Hicks

Alan and Hilary, the two social workers, if you like, were just behind me. They said that if they hadn't have seen it with their own eyes, the callous way in which we were being treated, they just couldn't believe it. They've made complaints themselves over it. It isn't just me having a moan, if you like. This is life for real. I tell you, it's the closest I've ever got to thumping a guy in a police uniform . . . until a little bit later, because it gets worse, I'm sorry to say. Anyway, we're told that Victoria's body has been taken back to the football ground and we will have to go there, and we've no idea where Sarah is. She still has not been seen at the hospital. Now, as daft as it seems, I'm still of the opinion that she's injured somewhere and we just haven't found her. The thought that she's also dead hasn't even entered my mind. I think it's entered Jenni's from the discussions we've had afterwards. She thinks I think the same, but doesn't mention it. I'm genuinely thinking Sarah is only injured or we'd know about it by now. So we were sent down to the football ground, with no transport again.

Jenni Hicks

If we hadn't had Alan Dunkley with us, we'd have had no transport. We weren't offered transport. We weren't offered any compassion. We were just told 'She is in the gymnasium and she is not your property.' 'Why don't you just go home and leave it to us?' was the impression we were given. And that is the truth, incredible as it is. At the hospital they gave me a polythene bag, with Vicki's clothes in, and a big brown envelope with a hospital number, and her earrings were in this. That is something I don't very often go into great detail about. There were her earrings, and this ring that I am wearing now [on her middle finger]. It was a signet ring that was Sarah's when she was 11 and then when she outgrew it she gave it to Vicki. So it was something that they both wore. And I can't take it off because I am frightened of losing it. If it is on my fingers it can't ever be lost.

Pat Nicol, at home in Liverpool

So the next phone call was at eight o'clock from a social worker in a police station and she said 'We can't find your son.' She said 'I've got Austin with me, I'm worried. He and his friends won't go home until they've found their mate.' So I said 'Put him on.' I said 'Austin, you get on the train and come home, your Mum's worried about you.' And he said 'We're not going without my mate. We're here until we find him. I'm not leaving Lee, I can't find him, he must have ran out of the ambulance.' And then he stopped and he said 'He never ran out of the hospital Pat, he's dead.' So I said 'Austin, don't think like that.' He said 'If he was alive he'd be here with us now. They said he's not in the hospital, so he's got to be dead.' I said 'He isn't dead, Austin, get on the train and come home now. I'm on my way to Sheffield and I'll see you later on.' So he said 'No'. I said 'Austin, I'm telling you now, I'll fall out with you if you don't go and get on that train.' So they did. They went on the train and they went home. They gave me the numbers for the Hallamshire, the Northern General, the police station in Yorkshire and also a Liverpool police station (a 709 number that never answered right up to half past eight). I got through to the police in Sheffield, the hospitals answered, and every time I gave the description there was no one of that description there. I was saying 'A blond, 14-year-old boy in grey', but the clothes had all been ripped off him, he didn't look like that at all.

Then, at half past eight, a local number in Crosby flashed on the television screen. It was the Red Cross and they were the only people who gave me any help at all. A lady answered the phone and she said to me 'Do you have transport?' I said 'No, and I've got to get to Sheffield, I can't find my son.' She said 'We'll be with you as soon as possible. Don't worry.' Half an hour later, I'd heard nothing, so I rang her back, and she said 'Thank goodness for that, there was confusion and I couldn't find your number.' It must have been chaos there as well. I said 'It's all right.' She said 'We'll have someone there within 35 minutes.'

A man turned up in a car. He said his name was John, and he was with the Red Cross. He said 'Don't worry, I'll take you to Sheffield.' We picked up another couple from near the Cherry Tree on the East Lancashire Road and then John took us to the Hallamshire. It's hard to explain but I knew something awful had happened. I knew it. And I knew that Lee was unconscious. But something inside me said he wasn't dead. It all seemed to have happened in an hour but it wasn't—it was six hours.

We arrived at the Hallamshire. Social workers were based there, and they were absolutely marvellous. There were little groups of social workers sitting round and there was this man who was just an angel. This man came to me and he was a respectable looking man and I thought he was a social worker and he said 'What's your name?' and I said 'Pat'. He said 'My name's Michael and I'm going to be here. If you want me, look around and I'll be there.' And he was. He was Dr Michael West, a clinical psychologist from the university there, and he was so human. The man was an angel. He seemed to understand when you needed him. It was just one decision after another and every time I turned round and thought 'What am I going to do?' Michael was there. He was just there. He must have been there all of the time, but afterwards, when I spoke to him, he said 'No, I did go away for a while, I went back to my flat.' And I can't believe that he wasn't there 100 per cent because I could feel him at the back of me all the time. He seemed to know when he was needed and yet he didn't smother you. He was there.

When I got to the hospital there was a horrible atmosphere but you couldn't fault any of the staff. They'd laid on a buffet, there was tea and coffee. They just said 'Feel free, there's phones all along there, whoever you want to phone feel free to use the phones.' Then they allocated you people. Well, I had John, the Red Cross man, and Michael, my angel. I had Frances, who I think was in the local Social Services, and there was also a young girl who John had picked up to help him. And then it starts.

Peter Jackson

On the drive back [to Liverpool] everyone was obviously very subdued. There was very little talking going on. I remember suggesting stopping for a beer at one point but nobody was interested, perhaps understandably. We had Radio Merseyside on as soon as we could pick up the signal and they were playing subdued music, interspersed with news of the death count. It was like what I imagine a wartime catastrophe time to be like. There was not a lot more they could say, and the death count was getting bigger and bigger as we got back. We didn't have roadworks on the way back. I dropped everybody off and I was home for nine o'clock.

Ian Battey

From seven o'clock onwards I was trying to sort out who was going where, whether we had enough staff to run the department, those kind of things. Being a casualty department that is constantly running, we have to think about how we're going to deal with the whole night and the day after. We'd used our whole stocks of drugs and equipment on two hours' worth of patients. We actually had staff that came in and literally checked everything. They went through every drug-tray, every equipment-tray, and restocked everything to make sure that we'd got stocks of whatever we needed. They worked through the hours after we finished to put that together. I remember saying to somebody only hours after we'd stopped 'We've got to get everything right, because if Tinsley Viaduct falls down tonight, how are we gonna cope with it?' That kind of professionalism took over. We sent some people home at five o'clock, we sent some people home at eight o'clock or nine o'clock at night, and that staggered dispersal of staff meant that we staggered the next day and subsequent days to try and cover people who needed time and space to get their breath back and deal with the emotions of it.

One of the things that I hope we succeeded with to a reasonable degree was in the issue of providing support for staff. We had learned some lessons from previous incidents—the Kegworth plane crash, the Bradford fire, those kind of things—about how A & E staff had dealt with those situations. Before we'd finished dealing with casualties, we had people on the department who were there to offer counselling support to nursing staff. I saw it as my responsibility to make sure that before they went home they all spoke to somebody about what they'd just been through, either on a group basis or on an individual basis. Very easy to say, not as easy to do. A clinical psychologist came to me and said 'Look, Ian, can you just explain to me what's happened?' And I relayed—in hindsight almost without emotion—what we'd just gone through. I remember saying to this person 'Can you make sure that you speak to everybody before they go home?' And I then went off and started making notes to write my report.

I think it was probably ten o'clock before I left, having told people about what had gone off, but not spoken about it from my personal point of view. And in hindsight that was a major mistake. It took me a long time to realise that was a mistake, not talking to somebody about how I felt about it. I talked to them on a professional level, not on a personal level.

John Aldridge

I didn't take it in until that night, when we come home, me and the wife. We were just watching the telly and it come on the news, and we just broke down, the two of us, we just broke down. We couldn't believe it, what we'd seen, what had happened. We were crying all night, couldn't get to sleep.

Bruce Grobbelaar

I just go into my little world—my wife and myself. My wife knows me very, very well. In that situation she leaves me alone. I just go quietly by myself. I don't want to listen to the radio or see the TV. You think it's a dream, but the next day you read the papers and it's not a dream. It's all reality. It's true.

David Fairclough, in Belgium

News continued to filter through. I've met the lads at the stadium, and we had our pre-match meal and team-talk. One or two of the other players who were also keen on watching the BBC sport were saying 'Did you see the scenes at the Liverpool game? There's 20 dead.' Someone else was saying there was 24 dead, information obviously all jumbled up in the translation. But by the end of the afternoon . . .

We played the game and as normal were catching up on the sports news in the players' room, but the main news was the tragedy back in England. It must have been the same all over the world that night.

It is impossible to describe my real thoughts. With it being Liverpool, I was involved in the conversations much more than usual. The lads loved to talk about anything to do with English football, and particularly Liverpool FC, but on this occasion it was different, chilling, my mind was somewhere else and I couldn't fully understand what I wanted to do. Everyone wanted to do something, help in any way possible, and even in Belgium there was a genuine show of concern. Unfortunately, I was unable to contact the family back in Liverpool that evening. But on Sunday morning the phone rang early. It was my best pal from home, but this call was not a normal one. Usually such an amusing character, on this occasion he was in a dreadful state. I'd never heard him like that before or since. He was just struck—his former partner's son had died in the tragedy—and I was hearing things I'd never heard before. It was mind-blowing and devastating.

Dennis Cerrone

When I got home I was subdued. I wouldn't call it shocked because I knew what I was doing—I wasn't glassy-eyed—but I know there's different versions of shock. One of the inspectors phoned me up from work later that night, and he told me who he was and it just didn't register. I couldn't think who he was. He told me his name and I know him very well and I was talking to him, and I put the phone down and my wife said 'Who was it?' I said 'I don't know, I don't know who it was.' It was a few weeks later before I realised it was another bloke and not the bloke I'd thought I was talking to, even though he'd told me his name and I'd known him for years.

But I kept going over and over it with Eileen, my wife, telling her everything that had happened. I found that quite therapeutic. Afterwards I found out that one of the things is to keep talking about it. It's very good for you to talk to any of your mates at work who'll listen to you. But by that time all the people that were there were all telling their own stories and the conversation was going backwards and forwards and this natural reaction was starting to take place. I've spoken about and recalled these events dozens of times since but I still don't feel that I have ever managed to get my recollections into a smooth chronological order, or been able to make sense of the thoughts and feelings that went through my mind on that day.

Jill Thomas

I got home about nine or nine-thirty. My husband had been indoors, at an auction in Sheffield, when it was happening. The auction had started at two o'clock in the afternoon and finished at five. No radios on. I'm sure people must have been coming in and the news filtering through, but at the actual time it happened he was oblivious to it. They'd heard all the fire-engines and the ambulances going past and they thought there'd been a road accident or a fire somewhere. I watched it on the news when I got in. I had to watch it because I still had this dreamy feeling about me. I was in a state of shock. I couldn't believe it had happened. When the newsreader said it, that was the thing that made me believe it was true, because if it was on the national news it must have really happened. I was just sitting there, nursing my baby, watching the news.

Dr Colin Flenley

I got back home and I think the enormity of it didn't really strike home until I saw the news. You knew there were a few dozen dead people, and that was all you knew. Then the total started to go up and up on the news and I'd got no idea. Then this policeman came on the news—I can't remember his name—about the story that the gate had been knocked down, and that made me really annoyed. Then Graham Kelly came on the news and I can't remember exactly what it was, but that annoyed me.

Graham Kelly

The police had a press conference up in the city, at about seven o'clock I believe, and I was hanging on waiting to hear what came out of that press conference, and that was reported back to me. So I just take it from there. I only went across [to the Leppings Lane terrace] once and that was late in the evening when Colin Moynihan [then Minister for Sport] arrived. We'd heard that he was coming and it wasn't confirmed. I kept my eyes open for him and saw the party walking across the pitch. They didn't report to the board room area, they came in at the corner of the temporary morgue, I think, and walked across the pitch. You're walking across the pitch, it's in darkness, there's a light and you go and have a quick look at the back. You hear some of the stories but again it's not a scientific analysis of what happened. By that time you were convinced that there was something else to add to whatever element of that might be true. I just didn't know what was true. There had originally been one story. I think probably during the evening sufficient doubt had been cast upon it to put a very big question mark on it. But I had no way of knowing at that stage.

Jenni Hicks

When I came out of the hospital it was starting to get dark, and that is how I got to gauge the time. Alan Dunkley volunteered to take us back to the ground. How would we have got there? Presumably, something would have been organised or we might even have had to catch the bus. Who knows? Nobody seemed to be that concerned at this point.

Alan Dunkley drove us back to the temporary mortuary. Well, we didn't know it was the temporary mortuary. I keep forgetting what I know now and what I knew then. We went back to the football ground where we were greeted by a police inspector. We explained what we were looking for. We knew Victoria was there; we weren't sure whether Sarah was or not, because we had been told that those with serious head injuries had been taken to Rotherham Hospital, I think, rather than the two main hospitals because they had facilities there for them. We knew there was no hope for

Vicki, but we were still hoping for Sarah. We were told by the policeman on the gate 'Oh, no, we are not set up yet, we are not ready. Nobody's being allowed in yet. We haven't got it all sorted.' Trevor said 'Well, I am sorry, I don't care whether you have got it sorted or not, we are coming in.' 'No, you are not. They are no longer your property.' So, for the second time in half an hour, we were told the same thing: 'They are no longer your property. Don't forget they have got to have post-mortems.' Did he use 'they'? I can't quite remember. Yes, I think he did use the plural: 'They have got to have post-mortems.' And at this point I said 'I don't want them having a post-mortem.' And then I got the rights on post-mortems read to me: 'Everybody has to have a post-mortem in this position. You have got no rights on that.' And I started saying silly things like 'Well, they have never had an operation. They haven't got a scar.' Because I knew what a post-mortem involved. Well, vaguely. And I said 'Please'. And in my naivety, I suppose I thought that he meant that that is what they were doing then. Before I had even seen them. Because I didn't know. I had never been in this position before. I didn't know. I am relying on these people to look after me and to tell me things. He turned to me and said 'Well, you have got no rights, this is the law.' And I was read the rights on it. Not just me. Trevor and Alan Dunkley, too. The three of us got the rights read on it: 'You have got no rights here, they are now the property of the coroner.' I was told this all over again. I said 'We don't even know that Sarah is dead.' I think it was at this point that I thought that Trevor was going to take a swing at the policeman.

Trevor Hicks

It must be nearly nine o'clock at night by this time. We're back at the football ground and they won't let us in. This is the second incident with me and the police, which was photographed by a Swedish photographer. There's a big metal gate which is in fact the entrance off the Penistone Road which is the nearest point where you can get to what was the gymnasium. Now, we don't know yet that it's a mortuary. We just know that there are people down there and that Vicki's body's been taken there, and Sarah's there injured, I'm thinking, or, I should say, I'm hoping, by this time. We're refused access. There's this burly policeman plus a load of PCs: 'No you're not coming in.' I said 'I beg your pardon, do you know who we are?' Alan stood there. Even he tries explaining. Obviously I start being very calm and very polite. I start in my normal way: 'We're Mr and Mrs Hicks, we know we have one dead daughter, we're trying to find our other daughter, please let us in.' 'No, we're not ready for you yet.' I said 'There's no such thing as not ready for us yet, we want to find our daughter, we want to know.' 'Go away and come back in 20 minutes and we might let you in.' 'I'm going nowhere', I say 'We're coming in.' Anyway a big row starts then between me and this police inspector. I always remember because he's wearing one of these yellow traffic jackets with one of the big luminous things round. Now I don't know that these photographs are being taken. Later on, when I make a complaint about his attitude, I get a tip-off from one of the reporters that they've got photographs of this guy in Sweden. And that's how I tracked him down in the end.

Anyway, I'm at the entrance, and I am literally riled. I'm going to throttle this guy. I know it's wrong and he had a job of work to do but he was programmed: they will not pass. And it was the epitomy of the German SS Officer and I was just some Jewish person, if you like, who had to go in the chamber when it was his turn, and 'get in the queue, you.' I was so basically low-life that it didn't matter. Now, OK, the guy might have been operating on auto-pilot himself because it was the only way he could handle it but he was still a policeman, he was still part of what that uniform represented and he wasn't listening to reason. When I look back, I can't believe what I was prepared to do. I mean I would have driven a tank over him at the time but yet again I bit my tongue. I'll be honest, I almost thumped him.

Jenni Hicks
He said to Trevor 'Where is your car?' And he said 'It is in the car park. I am going to walk to the car park with Jenni, we were going to bring my car from the car park and we are bringing it back here and as soon as my car is parked outside here, we are coming in.'

Trevor Hicks
By this time it's 9.30 or so. Myself, Alan, Hilary and Jenni and a PC, sent, literally, on foot to go and get my car. I drive my car back round to the same gate and he still won't let us in. This is ten. I'm thinking 'Is he giving me a bit of breathing space to stop me doing something I'm going to regret, because I know you don't hit a police officer but I'm ready to do it.' We get back and we have an absolute re-run. Now I am at the point where I am about to explode. I'm probably ranting and raving. I'm probably swearing like a trooper. I don't remember. I'd just gone and that was it. And then fortunately there were two young CID officers, because I remember one had a leather jacket with a black badge that hangs on a little thing that they

tuck in their pocket, and they had the good sense to shove this guy out of the way and said 'Look, come on in.'

They took us through the police cordon. Myself and Jenni and Alan and Hilary, and I said 'Look, we're sorry about all that.' I'd got so close to attacking a police officer, something that I never thought I could ever do and when I look back it's so incredible. Anyway, a bit of faith is restored, I suppose, by these two young detectives. I think I found out later that they were sergeants. So they took us in. I can't remember whether it was a small ante-room or whether it was the end of the corridor that led into the gymnasium. I think it was a small ante-room, and we were there for perhaps four or five minutes. They came in and said 'We're terribly sorry but there are some seriously injured people here and we are having to sort this out.' They didn't tell us that everybody out there was dead, and we have no recollection of the numbers. I'm still thinking in terms of twenty, thirty top whack, and I think I'm pretty well informed because I've been to both hospitals. And Sarah's got to be injured. She isn't among them or we'd know by now.

Then they took us to a big notice-board. I don't know whether it was on trestles but it was up against the wall and there's these little three-inch square polaroid photographs pinned to it and it looked like a wall of photographs. You talk about visual images. And I remember Jenni's words to this day: 'Oh, my God, all them.' And the policeman who was still putting photographs on said 'There are still more to come yet, love.' Something like that. And so suddenly we were faced with a sea of polaroid photographs of badly kicked and battered and dead people, and we're asked to look at them. We have to look through 75 or 80 photographs.

Jenni Hicks

There was this big green board with all these little tiny photographs everywhere, and there was no compassion there. We were asked to walk up. He said 'Could you come and look at these pictures and see if your daughter is here?' They didn't refer to her as Sarah. I looked at this board and I said 'My God, are all these people dead?' And he said 'Oh, it is worse than that, love, we haven't even got all the photographs up yet.' Seriously. I think my knees went at this point.

We were made to look at every photograph, and I couldn't see Sarah and the relief was enormous. I can remember the relief when I first looked at the board. I looked at Trevor and said 'She is not here.' And to me that meant that there was still some hope. So the policeman said 'Look again, love.' So, obviously he knew she was there: 'Look again, love.' And when I looked the second time, I saw her. I saw a picture. Sarah was number 67. And I can still remember the second time I looked, spotting her picture. I didn't want to see it. I think that is probably why I didn't see it the first time, plus the fact that it wasn't a particularly good picture anyway. Obviously it was after she had died and her hair was back off her face and she didn't look very well at all. She didn't look the beautiful girl we had taken to the match that morning, the girl I had said goodbye to at quarter to two that afternoon. It didn't look like her at all. She looked about 40.

Trevor Hicks
Seven girls died, so if they'd used their loaves we could have only had to look at seven photographs, but, no, we had to look at eighty-plus photographs. Anyway we then see Sarah's photograph, so we've identified her and that's the moment when I know she's dead as well.

Jenni Hicks
Because Vicki had gone to the hospital first, she was 'number 89'. We spotted her quickly because she had been cleaned up at the hospital. The others hadn't. We looked at all the pictures, which I found a horrendous experience. These were pictures that had been taken of people after they had died, in the condition that they were as they were carried from the pitch. They were just on a big green baize. I will never forget that board. I will never forget having to look at ninety-odd dead faces. That board always stands out in my memory. That was the point when my knees went. I didn't want to look. I didn't want to see Sarah amongst the faces. And you had to look at every one quite closely because you wanted to see if that was your loved one. I had to look twice because the first time I didn't recognise my own daughter, somebody who I had left a few hours earlier. I even said 'She is not here.' The second time I saw her. I said 'There she is.' And then they said 'Would you like to see them?' I said 'Well, that is the whole point. Yes, I want to see them.' Then they said to me 'Would you like to see them together or separately?' I said 'Together.' So they said 'Just wait awhile and we will sort it out. We will call you in when we are ready.'

Trevor Hicks
Now this is the first chance Jenni has been offered to see them. Well, naturally we want to see them, we want to see them together as well, if we

can, so they took us into what is the main gymnasium and they've got these office partition things, these sort of half screens about four or five feet high, something like that, and they took us into a little area and we stood there and then they brought the two girls out on these low trolleys like you see going into the back of ambulances, sort of wheelable stretchers I suppose, and they were both in body bags and obviously we were devastated then. That was the moment we knew that it was all over. There was nothing that could be done.

Eddie Spearritt, Northern General Hospital

They put me on a ventilator. My two mates had obviously gone back to the car and there was no sign of Adam or me. They'd gone back to the ground, gone back to the car and then eventually they went to Hammerton Road police station about half six and reported Adam and myself missing. They were in the Boys' Club at twenty past seven when a bobby stood up on a table and read out a list of names of people who were alive and well. One of those names that was read out was Adam's, as being alive and well. So, consequently, from that, my mates got to a phone and rang Janet up to say that they hadn't found me but Adam was alive and well. He wasn't with them but he was alive and well.

William Derek McNiven and Anthony Curran, Liverpool supporters who travelled to the game with Eddie Spearritt

A policeman in uniform stood on a chair in the Boys' Club. He announced that the only list they had was one of people who had been reported missing at Hammerton Road police station and were known to be safe and well. There were about eight to ten names on the list and Adam Spearritt was included.

Eddie Spearritt

From there they were told to go to the gymnasium. And there were photographs of people that had died. They checked them, and Adam and myself weren't among them. Consequently all they were doing then was going to the gymnasium, having a look at more photographs, going to the Northern General, going to the Hallamshire, and they were just doing that.

Barry Devonside

There must have been a couple of hundred people there [waiting in the hospital] . . . people were very distressed, some were fainting, people were absolutely shellshocked . . . they were just sat there dumbfounded . . . The assistant hospital administrator came in and stood on a table and started reading descriptions out of people in the mortuary.

Social Worker

He started to reel off information. As he did, people were collapsing like dominoes.

Jenni Hicks, in the gymnasium

Sarah and Vicki were just on these very low trolleys in body bags. I didn't realise what they were. I had never seen a body bag in my life. They were just there and the relief, it seemed to me, that I had found them. The first sensation was that I had found Sarah and Vicki. I could take them home. I remember getting down on my knees, and Vicki was this side and Sarah was the other side. I picked Vicki up and lifted her up and really cuddled her and hugged her. And I can remember how cold she was. She had a little hospital gown on because obviously with dying in the hospital, the hospital had laid her out. She had their little white gown on. And then I went to give Sarah a hug and I remember the contrast in body temperature because Sarah was warm. Vicki was how I had imagined. It was like taking something out of the fridge. Sarah felt as if I had pulled her duvet back in bed and given her a cuddle. When I picked Sarah up, I looked up and said 'Are you sure she is dead, because she is warm?' These two CID officers went in with us, two typical officers, quite young, in their leather jackets and jeans, and they had tears running down their faces. These big husky, bulky guys. We were allowed what seemed like a couple of seconds.

Peter Jackson, at home in Liverpool

Pete Garrett and I decided that we really didn't want to be alone, if that's not too melodramatic, and Pete and his wife came round to our house. A substantial amount of Miller Lite was drunk, perhaps understandably, although it appeared impossible to get drunk in the sense of intoxicated. The phone never stopped ringing with well-wishers and enquirers, and, I suppose, busybodies, but I don't mean that. We had Radio Merseyside on and toyed with the idea of going to Radio Merseyside but we didn't as it happened. I think Roger Phillips had a phone-in. Pete and I phoned on that and were on for 45 minutes or whatever, which we taped and made notes from afterwards. For some reason we twigged that we would be involved in this at a later stage [with submissions to the Taylor Inquiry on behalf of the Football Supporters' Association].

Brian Barwick

I got in touch with Desmond Lynam and said 'Stay as long as you need to stay to feel you're in touch and on top of what's happening but then get yourself down the motorway because we're going to have to produce a ''Match of the Day'' that's not been produced before.' Throughout the evening we were getting a clearer picture all the time about the depth of the problem and the size of the tragedy, and Desmond and I and the producer sat down, and we worked out a running order. Strangely enough, although it was a major news story, and the news people could attack it from their experience of handling those sorts of things, we were almost in a stronger position because, firstly, Lynam's a good writer and, having been there, was able to be quite evocative. Secondly, I'm from Liverpool, and I had an absolutely inherent understanding of what it would mean and what we were looking at. I first saw Liverpool play in 1961 and this was 1989, and the very reason I'm where I am, and I do the job I do, is because I had a fantastically deep interest in football and a deep fond regard for Liverpool. (Mr Shankly adorns my wall, and Mr Dalglish's picture is over there.) I sensed that I knew the size and depth of what was going to follow it. And, thirdly, there was also Jimmy Hill. He's been widely castigated many times for being 'the wicked witch' but in fact he's a very experienced and sensible man, and he also recognised what he'd seen.

So we went on the air with a very different television programme from the one we had set out to do. We made an apology, but really we made no apology, for not showing Everton's 1–0 victory over Norwich City. I think we reduced the size of the 'Match of the Day' programme to about 30 minutes, and it was really a minute-by-minute eye-witness account from Desmond Lynam of what had happened. We built up a profile of the afternoon, and the balance of the programme was critical. It had to be accurately reported, given what we had to go on. Then we reported live from Hillsborough. Obviously there were still things going on at Hillsborough, people arriving, and the first sets of people with flowers. John Shrewsbury was still producing an outside broadcast at ten o'clock, having started one at two o'clock which he thought would be over by five o'clock. I was lucky in a way because in London I was divorced from the real horror of it. John Shrewsbury, a man of eminent experience, had to handle it at first-hand, and had to get out the scanner and walk into rows of dead people. It was something he didn't set out to do.

We were able to do a live two-way interview with Graham Kelly. I thought Graham was very good throughout. He was prepared to stand up and be counted, and he knew he had to do our piece live and he did it. I had spent most of the evening trying to get Colin Moynihan, who was then Minister for Sport, and I couldn't get him. Then Desmond and Jimmy swopped their feelings on the experience, and then we were able to say goodbye. It was the strangest programme I've ever had to do. In the whole history of the programme, it was the only 'Match of the Day' without any football in it.

I was sad that we had to do the programme at all, of course, but, as we had to, I'm pleased that I was the editor of it, because if somebody had to handle that programme, and handle the directional flow of it, and handle the emotion of it, at least I knew what we were talking about.

After the programme, it was a case of going out for a meal to almost purge yourself of the horror of it before going home and waking up to the horror of it. I've been critically hammered and critically applauded for programmes I've made and I treat both with just about the same pinch of salt but I've kept one critique that was written in the *Evening Standard* on the Monday after that 'Match of the Day'. I can't remember the exact words but it said it had got to the heart of the matter fairly quickly after the event had happened but had kept a level perspective. [Jaci Stephen's review described the programme as 'quite outstanding'. She wrote: 'Desmond Lynam presented the programme in a faultless manner that combined news (without attributing blame) with a real sense of the deeply personal tragedy of human loss and suffering.'] It's not something that you cherish because you wish it never had to be written but I thought 'That'll do', because we were trying to achieve something that none of us had set out to do and none of us had any true experience of doing. But in the end the journalist in you comes out, the balanced journalist, and I suppose what I brought to the fore was being a Liverpool person. Even to this day I can't go past the Hillsborough Memorial at Anfield without stopping. I find it impossible to do.

Graham Kelly

I was involved with the media all through the evening. I did live television interviews in 'The News' in the middle of the evening, and at eleven o'clock I did live 'Match of the Day' from the ground again. It may only have been on the radio driving home at midnight that the final horror of it started to become apparent. It doesn't even become apparent then. I think it takes a long, long time for the effects to come out. It takes a long, long time. I can't say exactly when during the intervening years.

I made a conscious resolve within the first few hours to make myself available and not hide. During the subsequent days I began to wonder whether that was a sensible decision. I think probably it was, but I had my doubts at certain stages during those few days because you get home at two o'clock in the morning, you leave messages to say you'll contact the media at 7am or whatever and you wake up at six o'clock anyway because of what's happened. You go to a studio, you go to another studio, you ring up somebody from your car phone, you have another press conference here and it's just unrelenting, and the media at the best of times is difficult to satisfy and at times like that it's relentless. I certainly hope I don't have to experience that media intensity in a similar way, but I can't conceive of anything that could compare with that in my professional career where the media interest would be so enormous. So I made that decision and immediately you make that decision you're into tackling issues: How did it happen? Why did it happen? And then, a few hours later, will this year's FA Cup carry on? And a few hours later, where will it carry on? How will it carry on? And then, the following day: How do you start preparing for the inquiry? How do you react to the statement in the House of Commons? And that just goes on and it only gradually diminishes over a number of weeks, and not until after the inquiry.

Ray Lewis

It fell on a weekend that we had a council meeting [of the Association of Football League Referees and Linesmen], so I had to go to Birmingham for the council meeting and stay overnight. I didn't get home until late on Sunday evening, which I think was quite beneficial to a certain extent because the phones were ringing quite a bit at home. The media was wanting to get my side of the story. My wife didn't say where I was going to be. To a certain extent, we have an unwritten rule in our house that depending on how well the game goes I don't answer the phone on Sunday. You do get media on and I've always attempted to be fairly low key as far as those types of things are concerned.

On my journey to Birmingham, I think there were news bulletins coming on every hour. I went to the hotel where we had the meeting. The rest of the council were there. They were eating, and they were quite surprised to see me, to be quite honest. Having spoken to my wife she felt it was probably best to go and do something like that, where I'd be concentrating my mind on something different. I think it was therapeutic, if you like, to get away and do that.

Jenni Hicks, in the gymnasium

The police and a vicar sat at one side of the table and Trevor and I sat at the other. Then it was statement time. At this point Trevor was quite angry, and I was in a state of disbelief. I had just been told this news. I had just seen my daughters. And we were supposed to be making these statements at this desk and I kept looking across the table and the vicar wanted to come and give us comfort.

This was a different vicar than at the hospital. I kept saying to him 'Just stay at the other side of the table, please don't get up and come round here, I don't want to hear how God loves me and how God loves my children and how they are OK now.' I didn't want to hear this. I wanted them to come home tonight. I wanted Liverpool to win that game that day and for us to go home. We had brought sandwiches for our tea on the way home. And Sarah was due to go back to university the next day and this was going to be our last night. She was going to go out with her boyfriend that night and we were going to have a nice evening. We were going to celebrate Liverpool's win. They were going to win, weren't they? It was going to be a great day. Like the year before had been. I kept saying to this vicar 'You just stay at the other side of the table, I don't want to know.'

Trevor Hicks

We were taken to a long canteen table, if I can call it that, and we're sat down. Another recollection I have is that Jenni was attacking anything in a dog-collar and I was attacking anything in a police uniform, and, yes, it must have been very difficult. We were sat down within five minutes of having identified both daughters, in the case of Vicki for about the fourth time, and I'm asked to give a statement. Now, with hindsight, I should have refused to give it. I should have given the basic bones and said nothing else, because it was later used a little bit against me, when I was giving my evidence to Lord Justice Taylor. And, under the cross-examination at the inquest, they tried, and to some extent succeeded, in confusing me a little bit on the times. As far as I'm concerned, I don't care what anybody else says, those problems started long before three o'clock. There was plenty of time for some people to be saved. It might not have saved Sarah and Vicki because, with hindsight, I think we now know they had their backs to the barrier and they would have been overwhelmed. Colin Flenley has told me that he is of the opinion that Sarah was dead when he got to her on the pitch, but he kept going just in case. Now, if a doctor's going to do that there's no way I'm going to do anything else. But when I put all this together and look back on it, I think 'Bloody hell, what did the police do for us that day?' They did less than nothing. They were against us. It was 'our fault'. We were 'drunken yobs' if you remember when we started.

Jenni Hicks

I was more interested in Vicki's things than in what the police were asking me. I wanted to open this bag and get Vicki's things out. I can remember holding Vicki's things and taking her earrings out and having a look at those. We were expected to sit there, then, after just identifying our daughters' bodies in these body-bags on these little trolleys. And we were expected to say what we had for breakfast, what time we left home, to describe the journey, what time we got in—all in such great detail. At this point in our lives. If they had asked if we wanted a cup of tea or coffee, we couldn't have told you.

We didn't know at the time, but we had a right not to make any kind of statement without a solicitor being present. But we didn't know our rights. Nobody told us our rights. Because we hadn't been involved with the police or legal matters before, we sat there and obeyed. And that is something in retrospect. I can't believe that we were so obliging even after this horren-dous treatment. We wanted to be helpful and, looking back, I think 'Why didn't I ask a few questions?' Like 'Why are my daughters lying there?' The only thing that separated us from them was these screens. On one side were all the bodies, and we were sitting at the other side of these screens. And we never asked 'Why are our daughters behind this screen?' We are sitting there trying to be good and behave ourselves because these are the police. We didn't ask questions. We were the ones being questioned. Did we have anything to drink? Did the girls have any alcohol? Did we call at a pub on the way? Did we have tickets? These are the important issues. We were the guilty ones. Our daughters weren't the victims, we were the guilty ones. The victims are the guilty ones here. And that was the attitude that came across. We were being questioned. We were under interrogation. They weren't compassionate questions. They weren't questions of 'How are you?' 'How are you feeling?' 'What can we do to help?'

I was still hugging these things of Vicki's. These were of interest to me, not what they wanted to know. I was hugging these things. And in the middle of all this we were asked what Sarah was wearing. And obviously she didn't have it on her, her leather jacket, which was quite an expensive leather jacket. It has got nothing to do with the cost of it, it didn't matter. If it cost £5 it would have been just as important. They eventually found it. So in the middle of all this, they bring this across. That is another one for me. I am then rocking backwards and forwards on the chair, with this leather jacket. I didn't want to know what they wanted to ask.

And then I had this terrible desire to go to the toilet. If I didn't get there then I think I would have done it there. I have got to go to the toilet. I am not allowed to go to the toilet on my own. I have to be escorted by a policewoman and I have also got to leave the toilet door open while she stands in front of the toilet door and watches me go to the toilet. This is all true. For some reason I just went along with it. I don't know why I went along with it. I don't know whether it was my conditioning that the police are in charge. I don't know. I went along with it. And all the policewoman told me was how she had been sick. Several of the police had been vomiting. It was still how *she* was feeling: 'Do you know I have been sick three times today?' I have just identified two dead children and she tells me how she has been sick three times: 'You know, it is not very nice for us'. And this is the conversation in the Ladies.

I go back and the statement somehow gets finished. These were formal statements that later on were going to be used against us in the inquest, the statements made at whatever time that evening after we had just identified our daughters, after Trevor had walked onto the pitch and seen them. We then have to get back to London. At this point the vicar was gradually working his way round the table. He said 'I know you don't want to talk to me, and I really do believe you have got to listen to what I have to say.' It turned out that he had had a tragedy. He had lost his only son at ten years old through a fatal accident. He had fallen and knocked his head on a Sunday afternoon walk. And he said 'I questioned my faith for two years.' That conversation went on and then it came to the point when I started shaking from head to foot. I couldn't control it. And they asked if we would like a doctor to come along and give me an injection. And I said 'No, I just want to go home.' I asked if I could take Sarah and Vicki with me. I was told 'No'. 'Could I see them again before I go?' 'No'. I said to Trevor 'I just want to go home.' They did offer to find accommodation for us in Sheffield that night. They even offered us a police driver to take us home.

Trevor Hicks

One thing I forgot to say was that earlier Jenni and I had left the hospital with Vicki's things in a white plastic bag, a little bin bag. We went to Sheffield with two lovely daughters, we came back with one leather jacket and a bin bag. The clergy offered us accommodation and the police offered to put us in a hotel, but we didn't want to stay in Sheffield. We just wanted to get out of the place. We were told we could not have access to our daughters. If I were you, listening to me now, I would have trouble accepting the story. I'd be thinking 'This can't all be right, he's exaggerating.' I think this is partly why I have had such great difficulty coming to terms with it. It might have been easier had I not been such a society man, such an establishment man. I'd respected these things and looked up to them, and they were rock solid to me, and now I've not only had to go through a fundamental change in my family life, all the practical things, but also in my whole theoretical appreciation. I'm not a young man, I'm in my forties, so I've had forty years of one thing and a few years of total opposite.

Detective Chief Superintendent Addis

It is normal procedure to ask for information concerning the medical history of the deceased. I instructed that this should be the case as pathologists need all of the relevant medical information and that concerning alcohol. Some of the people who died did not die from crush injuries. This had to be done immediately because the post-mortems started the next morning. If you allowed people to go home, how long would it take to gain the urgent evidence necessary? I must reinforce that at this stage I wasn't aware of any allegations concerning excess alcohol. I was trying to do a job to the best of my ability.

Lord Justice Taylor, interim report, paragraphs 109 and 110

By commendable hard work, a team of pathologists headed by Professor Usher completed post-mortem examinations on all the deceased within 48 hours. They found that 88 of the victims were male and seven female. [Ninety-five victims were pronounced dead in the immediate aftermath of the disaster and a ninety-sixth, Tony Bland, died in 1992, when a High Court action permitted his Life Support machine to be switched off.] Thirty-eight were under 20 years of age, 39 were between 20 and 29 years and only three were over 50. In virtually every case the cause of death was crush asphyxia due to compression of the chest wall against other bodies or fixed structures so as to prevent inhalation. In all but nine cases that was the sole cause. In one, pressure on the chest had been so great as to rupture the aorta; in six cases there were also injuries to the head, neck or chest; in the remaining two cases, natural disease was a contributory factor. In 18 cases bones were fractured. Thirteen of those were rib fractures. However, one was a fractured femur, one a fractured radius and the remaining three involved fractures of bones or cartilages around the voice box. These injuries suggest the victims may have been trodden while on the ground. Blood samples were taken from the dead. No alcohol was found in any of the females. Of the males, 51 had no more than 10 milligrams per cent in their blood which is negligible; 15 had over 80 milligrams per cent and six over 120 milligrams per cent.

Mrs Delaney, mother of 19-year-old James Philip

A social worker took us to the ground where our son was killed, and it was a terrible thing for my husband and I that we were taken where James was killed. As far as we're concerned, we feel they didn't give, not only our son, but the other poor people who were killed, they didn't give them any dignity. Surely they could have taken all those poor people, including our son, to a church or a school and covered them, even if it was only a white paper sheet.

When we got to the ground we had to look at these photographs to try and identify our son. We looked and looked, we couldn't recognise our son. Eventually we did see our son. So we were led into the sports hall and when we walked in our son was lying on a trolley, inside this green zipped-up bag, number 33, so his Dad and I bent down to kiss and to talk to James, and as we stood up, there was a policeman who came from behind me and was trying to usher myself and my husband out, straight out of the hall. The total attitude was: You've identified number 33, so go! So, unfortunately, I went hysterical, I'm afraid to say, I had to ask if I could take our son away from the public's eye, again there was poor people, unfortunate people like ourselves being ushered into the hall and our James was there, in the public's eye, people looking down at his poor face. I also had to scream at these police officers and ask them please to allow us privacy for the three of us to be together . . . thankfully the policeman pulled James over to another part of the hall. I started to examine my son's body. He had blood in his nostrils, blood in his teeth, his poor face was hardened with blood on the side of his cheek. His face was dirty, his hair was very dirty and dusty . . . My husband was ushered to a table to be asked questions. At which again I started to scream. I know these questions have got to be asked but as far as I was concerned there is a time and a place for everything . . . I thought it was only right that his Dad should be with him—we went together to look for our son James, and that was time that was owed to us, because at the end of the day, when you carry a child for nine months, and you bring them into the world, it is your right to be with your child. We asked if we could possibly—we wanted to stay with James—we were told 'No', that we couldn't. So I asked if we could be allowed to come back to see James—we were told 'No', it was for identification only.

Agency Worker
We had to stand for five hours and listen to the identification of sixty-odd people. The screams and crying could be heard everywhere. It was awful and will be with me for ever.

South Yorkshire Metropolitan Ambulance Service worker
One woman threw herself on the trolley and wouldn't be moved. Her screams echoed all around the gymnasium. The screams were more than a human could stand.

Ian Battey
I remember driving home and feeling very hyped up. It's often the same after a late shift; you've finished work at nine, ten or eleven o'clock at night, and you can't shut off, the body's going, the adrenalin's still pumping, the mind's still racing. This was like a very pronounced form of that. I drove home—I don't know to this day how I actually got home —- and I walked in the door and Caroline, my wife, just came and put her arm round me and said 'I've run you a bath.'

The bath was very nearly cold by then, but she poured me a stiff whisky and I went and laid in the bath. From previous things, one of my coping mechanisms is to go and lie in a bath, and I stayed there until I was like a prune. That was my way of getting my own space and gathering my thoughts. Caroline came in. I remember she sat on the toilet next to the bath and said 'Do you want to talk about it?' And I said 'No'. I stayed in the bath for about two hours. The water was absolutely stone cold. The kids were in bed. Sarah was asleep and I stood in the doorway and looked. I didn't go and wake her up. I couldn't sleep. I got up and I walked round the house.

Pat Nicol, at the Royal Hallamshire Hospital

I said 'Where is Lee? John, I don't want to stay here, I want to find Lee', not realising that the Hallamshire and the Northern General are like cities in themselves. You think our hospitals are big! They're two or three thousand bedders. It's amazing.

They convinced me that Lee wasn't in the Northern General, and they [the casualties] were only going to two hospitals. They said 'He's not in this hospital.' I said 'Where is he then? Is he roaming the streets? Has he lost his mind?' And they said 'No. You understand we've got to take you to the morgue.' This was at twelve o'clock and I said 'I'm not going to the morgue because he's not there.' I knew. 'I don't know, it's just an instinct', I said, 'He's not there, I'm not going.' So I said—I can laugh about it now—'I want to know all the people in this hospital, all their names and anyone not identified.' I mean they must have laughed when you think of the size of the hospital, ten floors, and they said 'No'.

I said 'Where's Michael?' Thinking he was a social worker, I said 'Michael, will you do me a favour—will you go and look in the wards?' and I can remember saying it now. 'And look for Lee. There's a photograph of him now that looks very like him. His hair's a bit long here and that, just go and look for him.' So he said 'Yes, I will do.' I mean obviously he didn't. When he came back he said 'Pat, there's only one boy who's fourteen, and it's not Lee.' Because Lee had severed a tendon on the day Fergie got married he had a very bad scar there, so I had told Michael that Lee had a scar on his knee from playing football. He said 'It's not Lee, he's a lot bigger than Lee.' And I said 'Michael, can I just go and have a look at him?' And he said 'He's in Intensive Care.' I said 'It doesn't matter, I'm not going to make a noise, I'll just creep in, have a look at him and come back out again.' But they didn't want me to, and I didn't know why they didn't. I mean, I understand now, because it was Intensive Care, and that was in the Hallamshire. But I wouldn't settle until I saw him anyway, so I went up. I was going to go and have a look in every bed until I found this boy you see. When I found him, it wasn't Lee. I came out and that was it. I said 'Well, he's not in this hospital, I'll go to the Northern General now. Where is it? I believe it's quite a distance.' They said, 'There's nobody there, everybody there has been identified.' I said 'Well, I'll go to the morgue then because you think he's there and I know he isn't.' I thought 'And when we're satisfied that he is not in those two places, I'll walk round Sheffield and find him.'

Eddie Spearritt

And then at half twelve my two mates went to the Northern General again, still believing Adam was alive and well, and they actually found me in the Intensive Care. I was on a ventilator. They said to the doctor that obviously they would ring Janet and say I was in Intensive Care, but would it be all right not to actually get her to come over? The doctor told them that she had to come because I mightn't get through the night and there again I'd probably have brain damage anyway. So she and our Robert came.

All the photographs in the gymnasium had been shown and they'd been told that there was nobody else. So they'd seen all the photographs so they were still convinced that Adam, wherever he was, could have been sitting in someone's house, with a few scratches or whatever. And Jan got over, and my brother, and there was still no sign, and the hospital then told Jan that I mightn't get through the night and I might have brain damage if I did. And she still believed that Adam was all right.

Anonymous Bereaved Mother

It was just waiting then. I just sat there with me head on me Mum's shoulder and we just sat and sat and then the phone rang about quarter to one in the morning and it was me brother–in-law and he said 'I found him, he's dead.' That was it.

Jenni Hicks

I can remember getting into the car in Sheffield and I can remember getting out of the car when we arrived home, but I don't remember the bit in between. I just assumed that I was asleep. I thought 'I must have gone to sleep.' It was months after when I said to Trevor 'I slept all the way, didn't I?' And he said 'No, you talked to me non-stop the whole of the way home.' And I don't remember. But I can remember arriving home and the first thing I did when I got into the house—it sounds unbelievable—I ran straight up the stairs to Sarah and Vicki's rooms to check if they were there.

Trevor Hicks

I don't remember the drive back. I was driving and I was back on auto-pilot again. We were numb. We stopped at one of the service stations and we tried to phone our friends to tell them what had happened and to try and have someone at the house when we got home. I can't even tell you which service-station it was. We parked the car, went in, found the change and rang the number. We actually spoke to their son and they'd gone away to a works dinner and they were staying away that night. In fact they came round very early the next morning because they'd got the message. They set off back at about five o'clock in the morning and came straight round to us and obviously were absolute pillars of support and we needed them.

We never went to bed. We couldn't. You're in this state of shock. I don't know what it is but we basically just wandered round. I remember when we got home we left all the curtains open and we put all the lights on. Jenni and I had just gone into their rooms and we'd looked at their things, and we wandered around like a couple of zombies. I remember Jenni cuddled Sarah's leather jacket, with all her belongings in, all the way home, presumably when we were on the telephone, back in the car, all the way down the motorway, and we'd gone in the house, and that's all we'd taken back, this bin bag with Vicki's personal stuff in it that we'd got from the hospital and Sarah's leather jacket which we'd collected at the mortuary.

Jenni Hicks

We had a path that went down some steps to get to the front door and the girls had planted red and yellow tulip bulbs in the garden because they were the Liverpool colours of the day. A red tulip, a yellow tulip—like the Liverpool strip—down both sides of the path. And they were all blooming. It must have been in the early hours of the morning, about two or three o'clock. I found a pair of scissors and went out and picked the tulips . . .

Anonymous Bereaved Mother

My son-in-law said he would look at the photos and for an hour or more we waited for him to be called. We waited with a social worker and a clergywoman who were doing their best under dreadful conditions. The whole area was one of absolute heartache and emotional turmoil. Those who were not sure if their relatives or friends were dead were subjected to the stress of witnessing the awful shock and grief of those who knew their loved ones were dead. It was in fact absolute chaos. My son-in-law finally came to me and said he had looked at the photographs and my son was among the dead. I ran to the door to run out. I fainted. The police did nothing to help, my husband went for the social worker and he and my son-in-law eventually found a doctor. After an hour or so I went to see his body. I could hardly recognise him, so I checked his teeth which I could identify and while doing so I noticed his body was warm as if he had only just died.

The time was about 2.30am. Spending time with the people who had died, we weren't allowed that, we truly weren't allowed.

Pat Nicol

We went to the morgue at about 2.00am. You went in there for a start. You couldn't fault the people. There was a little room of social workers and lovely Salvation Army people. They gave you a cup of tea, they asked you all the details. I know there were pretty important police there, flat-capped policemen, keeping an eye on you, up and down, and they gave you blankets and told you that all the bodies were in the Leisure Centre, next door to the football ground but within the ground. You had to queue up and there was a policeman keeping an eye on the queue and then they just opened the door and let a family in at a time. They took you along a corridor to a room. There were those double rubber doors on one side and on this side they had a board and easels stretching along the length of the room with coloured polaroid pictures. They'd all been taken with different cameras because some were green, some were orange, some were blue, and they were all numbered and they were all dead faces. The bags had just been opened and they were all horrific. Faces all along. I went along them and I said 'Lee isn't there.'

Eddie Spearritt

My brother and Derek and Tony then went to the gymnasium for the last time. When they got there a policeman said there was one other photograph, and there wasn't supposed to be any more. Derek was very angry and said 'You said there was no more.' And the policeman said 'This one was the other side of the room', because apparently they must have partitioned the gymnasium off. Unfortunately that photograph was of Adam. Robert identified him. That was at four o'clock in the morning, and my two mates had been searching for him from the word 'Go' really. Of course I didn't know because I was on a ventilator.

Then my brother had to go back to the hospital and tell Jan about Adam. I don't really know how she handled it really. I mean, she was told at first that he was alive. One of the sad things about it is that the police have never admitted that the list was read out. I've spoken since then to clergymen, doctors and social workers who were in that room and heard the list being read out. The police have said that no list was read out. Don't get me wrong, it was obviously a mistake. The policeman that read it out wasn't doing it on purpose. All we wanted really was for someone to own up and say 'I'm sorry, it was me that read it out.' But they've never ever done it. One of the problems we had was that they knew Adam's name but he didn't have any ID on him, so consequently we were left with the problem: Was he left on the pitch somewhere? Was he taken to hospital and the hospital staff thought he was all right, so he gave them his name, so they said 'OK, we'll put you in a cubicle' and then his heart gave in and he was on his own. We had all kind of things like that going through our minds because of his name. We've since found out that he wasn't on his own. He actually died at twenty to five. He was taken from the Leppings Lane end down to the Kop end by fans and there was a special bobby down there, a lad called David Pearson. He felt for Adam's pulse and couldn't find one, so he took his pants down and felt for a pulse in his groin and he found one. I think it's very crucial that he did that. I often wonder how many police officers there on that day had the presence of mind to actually do that, and I don't think there was many. And David Pearson felt a pulse and worked on Adam, and put him in an ambulance. He went with him. They got his heart beating again and went to Casualty. He was then taken up to Intensive Care. I've met David Pearson. I've met him basically to thank him, but there's no words in the English dictionary that can really express my feelings towards him, for what he did. And he told me that when Adam went to Intensive Care, they'd cracked it, he was all right, so he was just waiting then and unfortunately Adam's heart gave in. They tried but it was unsuccessful and he died at twenty to five [on Saturday afternoon].

Pat Nicol

My second visit to the morgue was at 5.00am. Most photos had gone and only eight were left. The inspector explained to me that when people are crushed to death their faces are very distorted, they can lose teeth, they can be bruised, their hair changes colour etc. So we had to go through again and study each photograph and eliminate each one. There were three I couldn't eliminate so they went in and checked each. I wrote a description of everything that Lee had on, all his birth marks, all his clothes. Even his vest had an American football thing on it. After half an hour they came out and the Inspector said 'Please believe me, your son is not in this morgue.' I said 'Well, I told you he wasn't here anyway.' We left there [the gymnasium] and I said 'If he's not there, he's in the Northern General. I don't know where this hospital is but I've got a feeling he is in there.' They said 'No'. Michael came then and I said 'Michael, I want to go to the Northern

General, I've got to see for myself.' Michael was everywhere. Michael was there on my shoulder. If I turned round Michael was there. It was uncanny. John was doing the driving, the other little girl was there and Frances, the social worker, but Michael's hand touched mine wherever I went. Then we went back and I said 'Michael, please help me because wherever Lee is I don't think he's dead but I've got to see him. He's unconscious. If he'd come round he would have said his phone number, I know he would have done. Just go and talk to somebody for me.' So he came back and said 'I've been on to the Northern, there's one little boy.' I said 'That's him.' He said 'Don't build your hopes up. There's one little boy and he's unidentified. He's only about nine or ten. He's a lovely little boy and they have him in Intensive Care.' I said 'Is it the Cerebral Unit?' and he said 'It is.' I said 'It's Lee.' Because I knew that Intensive Care is either heart or cerebral. He said 'Now, you're not to build your mind up.'

This was six o'clock in the morning. I said 'Just take me, Michael.' I only know that time because it was twenty past six when I found Lee. That's how I know it was six o'clock. Other than that it all seemed to happen in an hour. They took me to the Northern General, but they didn't want me to go in. Nobody believed that it was Lee. We went in the lift, we got out of the lift and I knew he was that way. There was ward 61A there and I knew he was through those doors, so I said 'It's this way.' Michael said 'Just hang on.' I said 'I'm going this way.' They followed me, and as we opened the door I looked along. The corridor looked the length of this street and there were doors off it. Right at the end a person was standing there. It was a girl and she had an enormous nurse's hat. As I walked towards her she was walking towards me and she said 'Please, please, we don't know if it's your son. My name's Cathy and I'm the sister on this ward. I've been looking after him.' I said 'It's all right, Cathy, I know it is Lee.' And I knew exactly the bed he was in.

As you turn into the ward there's a little reception and then there's two other rooms. There were three people on the left and one person on the right hand side of the ward. Lee was second on the left. As I walked in, I said 'Lee's over there. I know he's there now.' And when I went over it was him. Cathy was so delighted. 'Oh', she said 'We've had him down as "number two".' He was the second to be taken into that ward so they'd had him down as 'number two.' She said 'I couldn't call him by a name.' She sounded like Marti Caine. That's her voice. She was lovely. She went over and she was talking to him. When I saw him I knew he was dead, because the machine was on. I mean, I know everything about Life Support machines now but the machine was consistent. They were all on Life Support machines, except Eddie. He'd been on his for a few hours but he was in a private ward, although the door was open and you could see him. When I went over [to Lee], they were all very iffy, they were all watching me. I said to Michael 'I told you he was here, Michael.' And he said 'I'm awful.' I said 'No, don't apologise, I've found him now, that's it.' All I prayed was that he wouldn't be in that morgue. I mean, if you'd gone there . . . oh, it was awful.

This was twenty past six in the morning. Lee wasn't hurt in any way. He had no clothes on him. He had a little sheet across the middle of him. There was no marks. He wasn't dirty. His hair was dark. Obviously they'd cleaned him but he had been grubby, and he had a dressing on the back of his ear, there. I thought there was a tube going into it, and I thought they'd done it, but he'd caught it on the spikes as they were passing him over. And he had a little finger mark on the back of his heel and that was it. His chest had been crushed but he had this tube in and when I went over to him he wasn't breathing himself, the machine was doing it. And I said 'Is this a Life Support machine?' and Cathy said 'It is, don't you worry, you just talk to Lee.' And I said 'I know he's dead, Cathy, I can tell by looking at him.' Lee had tubes going in up his nose, in here, but his tongue was out. I said 'There's no way Lee could be alive and look like that. I know.' He was warm and that and so I knew there was something but Cathy said 'Don't think like that. Just talk to him and Mr Appleyard.'

Neil Appleyard was the brain surgeon in charge of the ward. She said 'He'll see you later.' I can't give you times because I'd no idea, but it must have been about nine or ten o'clock in the morning and I said 'I want to see him because I want to know.' And Cathy said 'He will see you in time.' And I said 'No, Cathy, I want to go and talk to him. I know Lee's dead and he's frightened to come and tell me. But that's OK, I want to explain to him that it's all right.' So they panicked again. Anyway, it must have been a couple of hours later, maybe, when Cathy took me in to see Neil Appleyard and he was terribly upset. I have never seen a doctor upset and I said 'I understand what's going on, I think you're keeping Lee. Is he damaged at all, his body?' He said 'No'. So I said 'Are you keeping him alive for his organs?' To be honest, he walked out of the room because I'd given him too much to think about, but I wanted to get it all out of the way so I knew what exactly was happening, you see. Anyway, he came back later and said that Lee's organs were in perfect condition and explained what had happened, that it was all a mistake, that he was dead. So anyway he said 'We'll discuss the organs', because Lee did have a donor card. He didn't have it on him, it was in his bedroom. So I said 'Lee carried a donor card anyway, Neil, so if there's no hope for him . . . but I've got to know that there's no hope.' I thought Lee would be just left on that machine for evermore, not doing anything. I didn't realise that when there is no flicker in the brain at all that they just turn the machine off. But I thought nobody's going to do that, only me. So they agreed to that and then came my ultimatum: 'I want the full team here to say goodbye to him, I want Princess Diana to come (because Lee thought she was beautiful) and I want Bon Jovi flown over from America.' Neil said he would do whatever he could.

Peter Jackson

I remember getting to bed at about 4 o'clock in the morning and finally breaking down crying. All I could see in my mind's eye was the sight we had seen on the terrace at 4.30 that afternoon: the spectacles, shoes, coats and newspapers that had been left behind.

Ian Battey

At four o'clock I decided to go back to work. There was no way I could have slept. I didn't get a wink of sleep, and I decided that it was time I went back to work and relieved some of the night staff that had been there in the afternoon. That was my excuse for going back. Really, I needed to be back there because I felt I could maybe do something. So I was back at work at four or half-past four in the morning, and it was a relatively normal shift. As far as the patients were concerned, it was very, very quiet. The people of Sheffield did not have accidents. The people of Sheffield did not need medical attention, because that whole night and the whole of the day after the numbers were almost zero. People just did not go. I don't know whether that was in response to the fact that they knew that the Casualty department had been busy, but it was so quiet that we were able to restock. We were able to prepare for it happening again.

I remember when I got home from work, just after lunch, something like that, my daughter Sarah came and gave me a big hug. The thing that really made me more emotional than anything was 15 April the year after, in 1990. Sarah came up to me on that morning and said 'Can I have a nice birthday this year, Daddy?' And that still makes me think. As a six-year-old, as she was in 1990, she understood to some degree the traumas that I'd gone through. But even 12 months afterwards I hadn't gone through the traumas that I was going to go through.

Pat Nicol

On the Sunday, at 11am, Mr Appleyard said 'The team are on their way, they'll be here by three o'clock.' Well, they arrived, and there must have been thirty of them. Kenny Dalglish gave me the football kit, and Bruce Grobbelaar was doing handstands for the patients. They all spoke to them. There were two there who knew Lee was 'dead'. One was behind me, he had his arms around me, and every time I turned he purposely turned. One player looked at Lee and just ran. My friend said 'That footballer is ill, he's in a terrible state.' I think he realised when he looked at Lee that he was gone. When you think, it must have been awful for them, but I was glad that they had come because it was what Lee would have dreamed of. Oh, he dreamed of meeting the players.

It was about 40 hours from me finding Lee to him actually dying, them switching the machine off. I was with him during that time. I washed him every half hour and gave him a bed bath and that. The only time I left him was when they had to do tests.

On the Monday afternoon Princess Diana came to see him. I didn't notice Charles until I had been speaking to her for at least five minutes. She was lovely, so caring, and she was talking to Lee and telling him how smart he looked in his kit and all the rest of it. She said 'He's still here, you know.' I said 'Do you think so?' She said 'I know so. He's still here. When you love somebody that much they don't go that quickly.' She seemed to understand the situation, so I said 'You do know he's dying?' She said 'Yes'. She was extremely strong. When she left she said she would keep in touch with the hospital and keep in touch with me.

The team at Harefield Hospital were getting everything together. They were getting people ready to take the organs, and a helicopter to fly them up. I wanted Lee baptised and Michael brought up an ecumenical assistant to the chaplain and she baptised Lee. When the helicopter landed I knew it was a matter of when they said. They put screens around the bed and left me with Lee, and the family were going in and out on their own to talk to Lee. They said goodbye to him. It was five to eleven when I walked out. Michael was waiting for me. He said 'The hands have gone together on the clock.'

Four people benefitted from Lee's organs. A small boy received Lee's liver. Two girls received his kidneys. A man received his heart valve. All are doing fine and leading new lives.

Late on Saturday evening, on the day of the Hillsborough Disaster, a small group of stunned fans assembled at Anfield and tied scarves to the Shankly Gates. The red and blue colours of the two local teams were soon inter-mingled. The city's collective mourning had begun, and those affected by 'Hillsborough' faced up to the long and complex process of healing their lives. May they never walk alone.

Those who died as a result of the Hillsborough Disaster

Jack Anderson *62 years*

Colin Mark Ashcroft *19 years*

James Gary Aspinall *18 years*

Kester Roger Marcus Ball
16 years

Gerard Baron (Snr) *67 years*

Simon Bell *17 years*

Barry Bennett *26 years*

David John Benson *22 years*

David William Birtle *22 years*

Tony Bland *22 years*

Paul David Brady *21 years*

Andrew Mark Brookes
26 years

Carl Brown *18 years*

Steven Brown *25 years*

Henry Thomas Burke *47 years*

Peter Andrew Burkett *24 years*

Paul William Carlile *19 years*

Raymond Thomas Chapman
50 years

Gary Christopher Church
19 years

Joseph Clark 'Oey' *29 years*

Paul Clark *18 years*

Gary Collins *22 years*

Stephen Paul Copoc *20 years*

Tracey Elizabeth Cox *23 years*

James Philip Delaney *19 years*

Christopher Barry Devonside
18 years

Chris Edwards *29 years*

Vincent Michael Fitzsimmons
34 years

Steve Fox *21 years*

Jon-Paul Gilhooley *10 years*

Barry Glover *27 years*

Ian Thomas Glover *20 years*

Derrick George Godwin
24 years

Roy Hamilton *34 years*

Philip Hammond *14 years*

Eric Hankin *33 years*

Peter Andrew Harrison
15 years

Gary Harrison *27 years*

Stephen Francis Harrison
31 years

Dave Hawley *39 years*

James Robert 'Jimmy' Hennessy
29 years

Paul Anthony Hewitson
26 years

Carl Hewitt   17 years

Nick Hewitt   16 years

Sarah Louise Hicks   19 years

Victoria Jane Hicks   15 years

Gordon Horn 'Goffer'   20 years

Arthur Horrocks   41 years

Thomas Howard   39 years

Tommy Anthony Howard
14 years

Eric George Hughes   42 years

Alan Johnston   29 years

Christine Anne Jones   27 years

Gary Philip Jones   18 years

Richard Jones B.Sc.   25 years

Nicholas Peter Joynes   27 years

Anthony P. Kelly   29 years

Michael Kelly   38 years

Carl David Lewis   18 years

David William Mather   19 years

Brian Christopher Matthews
38 years

Francis Joseph McAllister
27 years

John McBrien   18 years

Marian Hazel McCabe   21 years

Joe McCarthy   21 years

Peter McDonnell   21 years

Alan McGlone 'Gloney'
28 years

Keith McGrath   17 years

Paul Brian Murray   14 years

Lee Nicol   14 years

Stephen Francis O'Neill
17 years

Jonathon Owens   18 years

William Roy Pemberton
23 years

Carl Rimmer   21 years

Dave Rimmer   38 years

Graham John Roberts (HND)
24 years

Steven Robinson   17 years

Henry Charles Rogers   17 years

Andrew Sefton   23 years

Inger Shah   38 years

Paula Ann Smith   26 years

Adam Edward Spearritt
14 years

Philip John Steele   15 years

David Leonard Thomas
23 years

Pat Thompson   35 years

Peter Reuben Thompson
30 years

Stuart Thompson   *17 years*

Peter F. Tootle   *21 years*

Christopher James Traynor
      26 years

Martin Kevin Traynor   *16 years*

Kevin Tyrrell   *15 years*

Colin Wafer   *19 years*

Ian 'Ronnie' Whelan   *19 years*

Mr. Martin Kenneth Wild
      29 years

Kevin Daniel Williams   *15 years*

Graham John Wright   *17 years*

SOURCES

Detective Chief Superintendent Addis, quoted in Coleman, S., Jemphrey, A., Scraton, P. and Skidmore, P. (1990), *Hillsborough and After: The Liverpool Experience*, Edge Hill College of Higher Education, pp. 254–55.

Agency worker, quoted in *Hillsborough and After*, p. 256.

John Aldridge, interview by Tricia Longhorn quoted in *Hillsborough Interlink*, issue 7, and interview by Rogan Taylor.

Anonymous contributors, interviews by Tim Newburn and Social and Community Planning Research (SCPR), quoted in Tim Newburn (1993), *Disaster and After*, London, Jessica Kingsley, pp. 62–67.

Brian Barwick, interview by Andrew Ward.

Ian Battey, interview by Rogan Taylor and Andrew Ward.

Shirley Beer, letter in *Hillsborough Interlink*, issue 9.

Detective Constable Dennis Cerrone, interview by Rogan Taylor and Andrew Ward.

Mrs Delaney, discussion on 'After Dark', a Channel 4 television programme, quoted in *Hillsborough and After*, pp. 251–52.

Barry Devonside, quoted in *Hillsborough and After*, pp. 236–37 and p. 258.

Paul Edwards, quoted in *The Independent*, 2 May 1990.

Tony Ensor, interview by Rogan Taylor.

David Fairclough, interview by Rogan Taylor.

Dr Colin Flenley, interview by Rogan Taylor.

Glasgow Rangers supporter, anonymous column in *Follow, Follow*, issue 6, late April, early May 1989.

Mike Graham, interview by Rogan Taylor.

Bruce Grobbelaar, interview by Rogan Taylor.

Steve Hanley, letter in *Brian*, an unofficial magazine for Forest fans, issue 10.

Alan Hansen, interview by Rogan Taylor.

Colin Harvey, interview by Rogan Taylor.

Dr Tom Heller, 'Personal and Medical Memories from Hillsborough', *British Medical Journal*, Vol. 299, 23–30 December 1989, pp. 1596–98.

Stephen Hendry, letter published in *The Times*, 17 April 1989.

Jenni Hicks, interview by Rogan Taylor.

Trevor Hicks, interview by Rogan Taylor.

Peter Jackson, interview by Rogan Taylor.

Peter Johnson, interview by Rogan Taylor.

Graham Kelly, interview by Rogan Taylor.

Alan Kennedy, interview by Rogan Taylor.

R. A. Knowles, letter to Dr John Ashton, quoted in *Hillsborough and After*, p. 234.

Dr R. A. Lawson, letter published in *The Times*, 20 April 1989.

Sammy Lee, interview by Rogan Taylor.

Mike Lewis, interview by Rogan Taylor and Andrew Ward.

Ray Lewis, interview by Rogan Taylor.

Mick Lyons, interview by Rogan Taylor and Andrew Ward.

McMahon, S. with Harry Harris (1991), *'Macca Can!': The Steve McMahon Story*, Harmondsworth, Penguin, pp. 46–53.

William Derek McNiven and Anthony Curran, written statement, quoted in *Hillsborough and After*, p. 261.

Steve Mungall, interview by Rogan Taylor and Andrew Ward.

Pat Nevin, interview by Tricia Longhorn quoted in *Hillsborough Interlink*, issue 8.

Pat Nicol, interview by Rogan Taylor.

Simon Pinnington, letter in *Hillsborough Interlink*, issue 7.

Jeff Rex, letter in *Hillsborough Interlink*, issue 8.

Peter Robinson, interview by Rogan Taylor.

Social Worker, quoted in *Hillsborough and After*, p. 258.

South Yorkshire Metropolitan Ambulance Service worker, quoted in *Hillsborough and After*, p. 251.

Eddie Spearritt, interview by Rogan Taylor.

Christina Surawy, personal travel diary and interview with Andrew Ward.

Iain Taylor, interview by Rogan Taylor.

Lord Justice Taylor, from *The Hillsborough Stadium Disaster: 15 April 1989: Inquiry by The Rt Hon Lord Justice Taylor, Interim Report*, Cm 765, London, HMSO.

Woman Police Constable Jill Thomas, interview by Rogan Taylor and Andrew Ward.

James Wardrope, Frank Ryan, George Clark, Graham Venables, Λ. Courtney Crosby, Paul Redgrave, 'The Hillsborough Tragedy', *British Medical Journal*, Vol. 303, 30 November 1991, pp. 1381–85.

Steve Way, 'Spion Kop—Standing', *The Spectator*, 22 April 1989.

Peter Wells, quoted in *The Independent*, 17 April 1989, and *The Times*, 17 April 1989.

Rob White, *Hillsborough, 15th April, 1989: A Personal Account of the Tragedy*, previously unpublished, May 1989.

John Williams, 'C'mon, la'! We'll get in', *New Statesman and Society*, 21 April 1989.

Andy Williamson, interview by Rogan Taylor.